RETHINKING PEER REVIEW: CRITICAL REFLECTIONS ON A PEDAGOGICAL PRACTICE

PERSPECTIVES ON WRITING
Series Editors: Rich Rice, Heather MacNeill Falconer, and J. Michael Rifenburg
Consulting Editor: Susan H. McLeod | Associate Editor: Olivia Johnson

The Perspectives on Writing series addresses writing studies in a broad sense. Consistent with the wide ranging approaches characteristic of teaching and scholarship in writing across the curriculum, the series presents works that take divergent perspectives on working as a writer, teaching writing, administering writing programs, and studying writing in its various forms.

The WAC Clearinghouse and University Press of Colorado are collaborating so that these books will be widely available through free digital distribution and low-cost print editions. The publishers and the series editors are committed to the principle that knowledge should freely circulate and have embraced the use of technology to support open access to scholarly work.

Recent Books in the Series

Megan J. Kelly, Heather M. Falconer, Caleb L. González, and Jill Dahlman (Eds.), *Adapting the Past to Reimagine Possible Futures: Celebrating and Critiquing WAC at 50* (2023)

William J. Macauley, Jr. et al. (Eds.), *Threshold Conscripts: Rhetoric and Composition Teaching Assistantships* (2023)

Jennifer Grouling, *Adapting VALUEs: Tracing the Life of a Rubric through Institutional Ethnography* (2022)

Chris M. Anson and Pamela Flash (Eds.), *Writing-Enriched Curricula: Models of Faculty-Driven and Departmental Transformation* (2021)

Asao B. Inoue, *Above the Well: An Antiracist Argument From a Boy of Color* (2021)

Alexandria L. Lockett, Iris D. Ruiz, James Chase Sanchez, and Christopher Carter (Eds.), *Race, Rhetoric, and Research Methods* (2021)

Kristopher M. Lotier, *Postprocess Postmortem* (2021)

Ryan J. Dippre and Talinn Phillips (Eds.), *Approaches to Lifespan Writing Research: Generating an Actionable Coherence* (2020)

Lesley Erin Bartlett, Sandra L. Tarabochia, Andrea R. Olinger, and Margaret J. Marshall (Eds.), *Diverse Approaches to Teaching, Learning, and Writing Across the Curriculum: IWAC at 25* (2020)

Hannah J. Rule, *Situating Writing Processes* (2019)

Asao B. Inoue, *Labor-Based Grading Contracts: Building Equity and Inclusion in the Compassionate Writing Classroom* (2019)

Mark Sutton and Sally Chandler (Eds.), *The Writing Studio Sampler: Stories About Change* (2018)

RETHINKING PEER REVIEW: CRITICAL REFLECTIONS ON A PEDAGOGICAL PRACTICE

Edited by Phoebe Jackson and Christopher Weaver

The WAC Clearinghouse
wac.colostate.edu
Fort Collins, Colorado

University Press of Colorado
upcolorado.com
Denver, Colorado

The WAC Clearinghouse, Fort Collins, Colorado 80523

University Press of Colorado, Denver, Colorado 80202

© 2023 by Phoebe Jackson and Christopher Weaver. This work is licensed under a Creative Commons Attribution-NonCommercial-NoDerivatives 4.0 International license.

ISBN 978-1-64215-196-1 (PDF) | 978-1-64215-197-8 (ePub) | 978-1-64642-503-7 (pbk.)

DOI 10.37514/PER-B.2023.1961

Library of Congress Cataloging-in-Publication Data

Names: Jackson, Phoebe, editor. | Weaver, Christopher C., 1962– editor.
Title: Rethinking peer review : critical reflections on a pedagogical practice / Edited by Phoebe Jackson and Christopher Weaver.
Description: Fort Collins, Colorado : The WAC Clearinghouse; University Press of Colorado, 2023. | Series: Perspectives on writing | Includes bibliographical references and index.
Identifiers: LCCN 2023029001 (print) | LCCN 2023029002 (ebook) | ISBN 9781646425037 (paperback) | ISBN 9781642151961 (adobe pdf) | ISBN 9781642151978 (epub)
Subjects: LCSH: Peer review. | Writing—Study and teaching (Higher) | English language—Rhetoric—Study and teaching (Higher) | Critical pedagogy. | English language—Study and teaching (Higher)—Foreign speakers.
Classification: LCC LB1031.5 .R48 2023 (print) | LCC LB1031.5 (ebook) | DDC 371.39/4—dc23/eng/20230713
LC record available at https://lccn.loc.gov/2023029001
LC ebook record available at https://lccn.loc.gov/2023029002

Copyeditor: Caitlin Kahihikolo
Designer: Mike Palmquist
Cover Photo: "College Students Studying Together in a Library," by Monkey Business Images (Shutterstock 15590890). Licensed.
Series Editors: Rich Rice, Heather MacNeill Falconer, and J. Michael Rifenburg
Consulting Editor: Susan H. McLeod
Associate Editor: Olivia Johnson

The WAC Clearinghouse supports teachers of writing across the disciplines. Hosted by Colorado State University, it brings together scholarly journals and book series as well as resources for teachers who use writing in their courses. This book is available in digital formats for free download at wac.colostate.edu.

Founded in 1965, the University Press of Colorado is a nonprofit cooperative publishing enterprise supported, in part, by Adams State University, Colorado State University, Fort Lewis College, Metropolitan State University of Denver, University of Alaska Fairbanks, University of Colorado, University of Denver, University of Northern Colorado, University of Wyoming, Utah State University, and Western Colorado University. For more information, visit upcolorado.com.

Land Acknowledgment. The Colorado State University Land Acknowledgment can be found at landacknowledgment.colostate.edu.

CONTENTS

Introduction. Rethinking and Reframing Peer Review 3
    Phoebe Jackson and Christopher Weaver

Part One. Peer Review: Evaluating the Challenges

Chapter 1. Teachers' Beliefs about the Language of Peer Review: Survey-Based Evidence 17
    Ian G. Anson, Chris M. Anson, and Kendra L. Andrews

Chapter 2. Resisting Theory: The Wisdom of the Creative Writing Workshop. 41
    Bob Mayberry

Chapter 3. A Troubled Practice: Three Models of Peer Review and the Problems Underlying Them 59
    Christopher Weaver

Part Two. Peer Review: Rhetorically Situated

Chapter 4. Interrogating Peer Review as "Proxy:" Reframing Peer Response within Connective Practice 75
    Kay Halasek

Chapter 5. Peer Persuasion: An Ethos-Based Theory of Identification and Audience Awareness. 99
    Courtney Stanton

Chapter 6. Positioning Peer Review for Transfer: Authentic Audiences for Career Readiness and Workplace Communication 119
    Nora McCook

Part Three. Peer Review: Cultivating Inclusiveness

Chapter 7. Peer Review and the Benefits of Anxiety in the Academic Writing Classroom. 147
    Ellen Turner

Chapter 8. Multimodal Peer Review: Fostering Inclusion in Mixed Level College Classrooms with ELL Learners 169
    Beth Kramer

Contents

PART FOUR. PEER REVIEW: THE PROMISE OF TECHNOLOGY

Chapter 9. Leveling the Playing Field for ELL Students: The Case for Moving Peer Review to an Online Environment 187
    Vicki Pallo

Chapter 10. Learning from Peer Review Online: Changing the Pedagogical Emphasis. 205
    Phoebe Jackson

Chapter 11. The Potential of Peer Review Software that Focuses on the Review, Not the Draft. 229
    Nick Carbone

Afterword. Accepting, Sharing, and Surrendering Control: Combining the Best of Old and New in Peer Review and Response. 245
    Steven J. Corbett

Contributors 257

Index 261

RETHINKING PEER REVIEW: CRITICAL REFLECTIONS ON A PEDAGOGICAL PRACTICE

INTRODUCTION.
RETHINKING AND REFRAMING PEER REVIEW

Phoebe Jackson and Christopher Weaver
William Paterson University

This edited collection re-examines peer review as an established practice in writing and writing-intensive courses. The chapters interrogate both the theory behind peer review and the ways in which peer review has evolved in the decades since the practice has become foundational to composition as a discipline. With the emergence of the writing process movement in the 1960s and 1970s, the introduction of peer review in the writing classroom ushered in a major paradigm shift in writing studies. To date, no single activity is more central to the writing classroom than peer review. The decades since the emergence of peer review have seen a host of different theoretical approaches to teaching writing. They include social constructivism, critical pedagogy, rhetorical, multi-modal, writing about writing, and teaching for transfer, just to name a few. Yet peer review has remained a permanent feature of each of these diverse models. It has now been so thoroughly integrated into writing classrooms not only in colleges, but to a certain extent, secondary schools, that it is difficult to imagine a writing class that does not regularly "break into groups" in order for students to share drafts of their writing and get feedback from each other.

While most instructors embrace the theory behind peer review as well as its goals, some skepticism exists about its efficacy as a practice. These reservations include a litany of complaints that all of us who teach writing and/or writing-intensive classes would recognize. From the teacher's perspective: (1) workshop groups tend to fall apart quickly into socializing groups; (2) students don't know how to write an effective peer review; (3) their peer reviews too often focus on lower order concerns of the essay like grammar at the expense of higher-order concerns like ideas. From the student's perspective: (1) students don't feel qualified to give advice to other students; (2) better writers feel resentful about getting advice from students whom they perceive as poor writers; (3) students don't feel the comments that they get are helpful. This litany of complaints from both professors and students alike has led to skepticism about the practice with some compositionists questioning its continued importance. Others have advanced the idea that peer review be reserved for upper level university students, who, they argue, are better able to write an effective peer review (Flynn; Jesnek). Faced with these ongoing difficulties, both students and teachers often become frustrated that the comments and conversations generated by peer review do not help them either to revise their writing or to become better writers. For the instructor, assigning peer review becomes a rote exercise; one performed out of a sense of necessity or obligation or as a way to lessen the labor of paper grading.

And yet there is still a hunger for new perspectives on this established practice. At conferences, panels on peer review consistently draw large audiences, testifying to teachers' desire for more conversation. Meanwhile, as the field of writing studies moves further into the 21st century, we grapple with new approaches to teaching writing with new technologies. Moreover, demographic shifts among college students and the nation as a whole call to us with more urgency than ever to address students with diverse educational and language backgrounds. In light of these changes to the discipline, the time is ripe for a collection of essays that assesses where peer review stands a half-century after its emergence, and that challenges us to rethink and reframe the practice going forward.

The goal of this book is to reevaluate peer review and to provoke renewed discussion from both theoretical and practical perspectives. Among the issues the chapters grapple with are: How do students' perceptions, goals, and values around peer review differ from those of their instructors? How are our peer review practices informed by theories of collaborative learning? How do rhetorical approaches enlarge and complicate our understanding of peer review? What are the practical and theoretical implications of a shift in emphasis from instruction in writing to instruction in peer review? How do emerging technologies change peer review? How do these technologies allow us to gather information about peer review, and what can that information allow us to do? How do increasing numbers of English Language Learners (ELL) challenge our models of peer review, and how should we respond to those challenges? These questions have led us to this collection.

THE HISTORY OF PEER REVIEW AS COLLABORATIVE PRACTICE

It is helpful to see writing studies' engagement with peer review in terms of its history—a history that links an examination of peer review's goals to its effectiveness as a practice. From its inception, a key goal of peer review has been to have students engage in writing as a collaborative practice. Just what collaboration means, however, has been the subject of extended discussion. Over the history of peer review, collaboration has been an unstable principle, an idea that has evolved as it has been questioned.

Early advocates of peer review promoted it as a transformative practice, and collaboration was a key component of this transformation. Its advocates have not merely asserted that it results in better learning outcomes; they have argued that it changes the role of students from passive recipients of knowledge to active collaborators in its creation. The seeds for a more interactive approach to the teaching of writing generally and to peer response specifically can be traced to earlier pedagogical practices in writing from the 1960s and 1970s with the beginnings of the process movement. For process scholars, collaboration involved creating a dialog between writers and readers. Peter Elbow's 1973 book, *Writing Without Teachers,* describes a teacherless writing class where writers use each other to work out meaning and gain control over their own words. Elbow provides techniques that writers can use in order to identify and develop the important elements in a piece of writing. The key to this practice is an active collaboration between writers and readers: "The conversation with [others] helps you see the whole [draft] in better perspective, gives you new ideas, and helps you make up your own mind about what you think" (140). Elbow stresses the need to be able "to see your words through the eyes of others" (145). Proponents of the process movement like Elbow's called on students to take control of their own learning—a move towards student autonomy—and in doing so, they put writing groups at the service of the author. In their view, the goal of peer review is to help writers test out their words on readers. The role of readers is to help writers clarify their meaning and to find their voices.

However, this idea of peer review as conversation soon took on a larger social dimension. In "Collaborative Learning and the 'Conversation of Mankind'" (1984), Kenneth Bruffee suggests that teachers may struggle with peer review because they fail to understand the role that conversation plays in learning. Bruffee extends his model of collaboration beyond a writer working out meaning in dialog with readers. Instead, conversation is the means through which students enter a new discourse community by learning and practicing the normal discourse of that community. In order to make peer review more effective, teachers need to shift the emphasis from editing to conversing, but they also need to shape the nature of that conversation in ways that help students enter a new community because "[t]he way they talk with each other determines the way they will think and the way they will write" (642).

Bruffee warns that peer review "requires more than throwing students together with their peers with little or no guidance or preparation" (652). This theme that students must be guided by teachers through the peer review process has been echoed by countless scholars, and indeed, all of us are familiar with the plethora of handouts and guided response sheets that are associated with peer review. However, Bruffee's caution offers an important insight—*how* we guide students through the process is determined by *what* our goals are. After Bruffee, those goals, particularly the nature of collaboration, would continue to be questioned.

Anne Ruggles Gere, another social constructivist frequently mentioned in tandem with Kenneth Bruffee, interrogates the nature of collaboration in her book, *Writing Groups: History, Theory and Implications* (1987). Like Bruffee, Gere insists writing be seen in terms of its "social dimension" rather than a "solo performance" (3) and that the process of collaboration "enables writers to use language as a means of becoming competent in the discourse of a given community" (75). However, Gere acknowledges the tension between the autonomy of the writer and the authority of the community. In her book, she analyzes how writing groups function in the classroom, defining them in terms of "semi-autonomous or non-autonomous" (101).

This distinction is important because it describes the way that teachers involve themselves in peer writing groups. In a "non-autonomous" group, the instructor runs the writing groups without ceding authority to students. In a semi-autonomous writing group, students, through the guidance of the instructor, can assume more authority. Gere acknowledges writing groups at the university can never be completely autonomous because of the structure of the university and the fact that they receive a grade. But writing groups can play a semi-autonomous role.

This distinction between non-autonomous and semi-autonomous groups is crucial to the evolving understanding of collaboration and its role in peer review. Like Bruffee, Gere emphasizes the need for preparation and training in creating effective peer review groups, moving the scholarly conversation about peer review towards instructor guidance and away from its early emphasis on student autonomy. As she explains, writing groups "are more likely to succeed when groups are sufficiently prepared and committed, when appropriate tasks are clear and/or agreed upon by all participants, and when debriefing or evaluation is built into the life of the group" (112). Gere's observation that the success of peer review depends upon whether tasks are clear and agreed to by students is an important but problematic one: What is it that students are agreeing to? Whose tasks and goals are accepted by the groups?

While Gere was problematizing autonomy, writing classes continued the widespread use of peer review groups. Karen Spear's *Sharing Writing: Peer Response Groups in English Classes* (1988) is a good example of where the discipline's thinking on peer response stood in the late 1980s. Like Gere, Spear is aware of the importance of autonomy and the danger that student writing groups will try to replicate the teacher's authority rather than engage in true collaboration. Yet she remains optimistic that authentic collaboration can be achieved if teachers "accept the responsibility of teaching students how to communicate in a group setting" (8). Spear's call for teachers to devote significant time and energy to training students in peer review continues to resonate even today, with many compositionists suggesting that instructing students how to do peer review should become a more central (if not *the central*) focus in the writing classroom (Parfitt; Zhu; Reid). However, her emphasis on making meaning with the writer rather than appropriating the writer's text reflects a model of peer review that is clearly rooted in process pedagogy. This model of collaboration would be debated and problematized by later scholars.

COLLABORATION: A RECONSIDERATION

One of the more recent composition scholars to consider the state of peer review is Elizabeth Flynn. In an article written in 1984, "Students as Readers of Their Classmates' Writing: Some Implications for Peer Critiquing," Flynn discussed the problems with peer review, arguing that students' ability to give good feedback was hampered by the fact that they were not particularly good readers of each other's work. The critique ended with the familiar refrain that students require more training to help them become better readers of each other's texts—to be able to learn how "to point out gaps, inconsistencies, and irrelevancies" (127).

Twenty-seven years later, Flynn wrote a follow-up article, "Re-viewing Peer Review" (2011), that focused on research of peer review in the ensuing years. With this new project, Flynn noticed a dramatic decline in the number of articles published about peer review—a trend that began in the 1990s. Recent research, Flynn discovered, has moved into a new direction, primarily concerned with peer review for L2 learners and the use of computer-assisted peer review.

It's interesting to speculate on the reason for this quiet period between the early 1990s and the present decade in the literature of peer review. One possibility is that as peer review became accepted practice, many teachers simply stopped questioning the theory behind it. Another possibility is that composition scholars were simply unable to find answers to the tension between student autonomy and teacher authority that was central to questions about collaboration. Yet another possibility is that as standardized testing and the call for greater accountability began to trickle down to writing programs, teachers shifted their attention towards outcomes and away from the collaborative process.

Whatever the reason, compositionists have begun to revisit earlier work in peer review to suggest possible solutions to the problems it poses. In an article entitled "Peer Response in the Composition Classroom: An Alternative Genealogy" (2007), Kory Lawson Ching revisits Gere's 1987 book on writing groups, searching for a way to resolve the central tension of collaboration between student autonomy and teacher authority. As Ching argues, Gere's narrative "provides a valuable window onto the way peer response was conceptualized and promoted in the 1980s" (304). In Gere's genealogy, according to Ching, peer response is a way to authorize students putting teacher authority on the back burner. Refusing to think in binary terms, Ching suggests a third alternative: "student/ teacher collaboration" (314). "Students," as Ching states, "do not learn from teachers or from peers, but rather by engaging in the practices of writing and reading alongside both" (315).

By encouraging a type of "co-participation" between students and teachers, Ching sketches out the multiple benefits that can accrue with this model: namely that the student writer gets feedback from the instructor and student reviewers and that by working alongside the instructor, students learn how to give valuable feedback. Ching's article offers a provocative and thoughtful discussion of the dichotomy between student autonomy and teacher authority—a topic that continues to be debated and informs the way that instructors think about and practice peer review.

In a recent collection on peer review, *Peer Pressure, Peer Power: Theory and Practice in Peer Review and Response for the Writing Classroom* (2014), editors Steven J. Corbett, Michelle LaFrance, and Teagan E. Decker assure readers in their introduction that the rewards of peer review "can be significant even transformative" even though they may be "difficult to reap in practice" (6). As their starting point, they frame the practice of peer review in terms of what they collectively call "collaborative peer review and response" or CPRR—an approach that places a greater value and emphasis on the collaborative aspects of peer review whereby students and instructors contribute to each other's learning (1).

For many in the collection, this act of collaboration in peer review underscores the importance of instructor involvement. In the chapter "The Instructor-Led Peer Conference: Teachers as Participants in Peer Response," Kory Lawson Ching expands the discussion of his 2007 article to explain how instructors can participate effectively in peer response groups by using a "small-group conference" or "group tutorial" (21). Such models, Ching argues, enlarge the audience for peer review. Students give each other feedback in this triad of reviewer, writer, and instructor, but equally important, with the instructor's participation, students learn how to give effective feedback.

Moreover, the authors in this collection also place a greater emphasis on the instructor's involvement with peer review, a move away from past practices that focused on student autonomy and teacher authority. Rather than an add-on activity to essay writing, they consider peer review to be a central component of a writing course, one that is taught and developed throughout the course term. As E. Shelley Reid contends in her chapter "Peer Review for Peer Review's

Sake: Resituating Peer Review Pedagogy," for peer review to be more successful, instructors "need to spend proportionately more time teaching it" (218): in other words, to think of peer review as a genre that can be taught.

The Corbett collection ultimately advances two primary assertions: the importance placed on the value of peer review as a collaborative venture between instructors and students and on the centrality of peer review to the writing process. In their reconsideration of peer review, the authors maintain that collaborative learning forms the basis of the practice for both instructors and students. With its focus as "both a theoretical and practical sourcebook," the Corbett collection of essays provides writing instructors, writing centers, and writing tutors with a valuable guide for understanding and for teaching peer review (2).

Rethinking Peer Review: Critical Reflections on a Pedagogical Practice extends the conversation initiated in Corbett's collection. As the discipline of writing studies changes, so do our ideas about how we conceptualize and reconceptualize practices like peer review. Such moments offer teacher/scholars an opportunity to reflect on the purpose and goals of this foundational practice and its interplay with new theoretical approaches. While collaborative learning has always been at the heart of peer review, new approaches and theories of writing have increasingly complicated this idea. Collaboration no longer means the simple give and take between writer and readers that it did in peer review's earliest iterations. Contemporary scholars emphasize collaboration as a more complex practice embedded in a particular rhetorical context and complicating issues of agency and autonomy. In the eyes of many scholars, it also requires devoting significant time to training students to understand how peer review is situated within the dynamics of a classroom, an institution, and even, in some cases, the larger culture.

This collection, then, attempts to situate peer review in a new era for writing studies. While peer review undeniably has its roots in process pedagogy, contemporary scholarship grapples with the assumptions and practices of that early history. As Nora McCook writes in this collection, "even with many of [process pedagogy's] instructional practices still in place, there are new vantage points through which to utilize peer review" (130). As the field of writing studies has become more rhetorically focused, the question of how writer, reviewer, and instructor are embedded in a specific rhetorical situation has become one of those vantage points, as exemplified by several of our chapters.

The cultural and academic environment in which we teach has changed as much as our theories and our pedagogies. Despite the call from some scholars to value peer review as a process that teaches students critical thinking rather than as a tool that results in better papers, educators today also face demands for accountability that can explain how writing skills will transfer to other college courses as well as to future employers. These competing demands force us to repurpose peer review in ways that demonstrate relevance to both students and administrators. (See, for example, Nora McCook's focus on peer review as a method of teaching "soft skills" needed in the workplace.) Additionally, demographic trends of the past decade challenge and force us to rethink how well past approaches and assumptions currently work with today's students. And finally, technology, accelerated by changes during the covid years, continues to shape our field in ways that greatly impact how students practice peer review. All of these are issues tackled by the writers in this book.

Peer review, we want to suggest, has moved into a new era. In addressing this new era, we have found it useful to divide our collection into four parts. The first addresses the fundamental challenges of peer review and urges us to reconsider and re-address some basic premises. The next three parts consider theoretical and practical changes in writing instruction that have reframed our thinking about peer review: the ways in which rhetorical approaches enlarge and complicate our understanding of peer review, the ways in which diverse language communities necessitate educational change and help to reshape former peer review practices, and the ways in which technology informs different aspects of the peer review process—all of which make peer review both an exciting and challenging part of the writing classroom.

PEER REVIEW: EVALUATING THE CHALLENGES

The chapters in this part evaluate some of the challenges of peer review and the ways in which it has been put into practice. In their chapter, "Teachers' Beliefs about the Language of Peer Review: Survey-Based Evidence," researchers Anson, Anson, and Andrews explore why "faculty either gravitate toward or shy away from using peer review." For their study, they surveyed close to 500 instructors to examine their perceptions about the practice of peer review. Their research points out that the language we use to describe peer feedback reveals an underlying disjunction about what teachers value and concludes that peer feedback means different things in different types of institutions. Though the results of their study demonstrate that the practice of peer review varies widely throughout colleges and universities depending on numerous variables, the authors nonetheless agree that peer review needs to remain an important part of the writing curriculum.

In his chapter, "Resisting Theory: The Wisdom of the Creative Writing Workshop," Bob Mayberry analyzes the difference between the creative writing workshop model versus the peer review model typically used in first-year composition courses. Mayberry maps out the changes in composition studies that moved away from the discipline's earlier expressionist roots to one that became "more a professional, research-based discipline" (47). In his chapter, Mayberry urges instructors to reconsider the creative writing workshop model with its focus on "learning about writing" (56). He argues persuasively that the instructor's job is to "facilitate *their* conversation" allowing students to cast themselves as engaged "writers" working in concert with other writers (58).

Christopher Weaver's chapter, "A Troubled Practice: Three Models of Peer Review and The Problems Underlying Them," argues that teachers' dissatisfaction with peer review stems largely from the problematic nature of the goals underlying the practice. He examines three different models of peer review: the collaborative model, the proxy model, and the disciplinary/professional model. Despite their differences, each model holds out the same promise of peer review as a transformative practice. However, this promise runs up against a hard truth: that students, at best, struggle to understand the transformation being asked of them, and at worst, they resist it. Weaver argues that freeing peer review from the expectation of transformation allows us to make space in the writing class for its more attainable benefits.

PEER REVIEW: RHETORICALLY SITUATED

In this part, the chapters examine the complex relationship between the student whose writing is being reviewed, the peer reviewer, and the classroom teacher. Coming from a variety of different perspectives, the authors argue that the success of peer review depends on how the practice is rhetorically situated. Kay Halasek, in her chapter, "Interrogating Peer Review as 'Proxy': Reframing Peer Response as Connected Practice," views the failure of peer review as a result of positioning the reviewer as proxy for teacher feedback, where students mimic what the teacher expects to hear. Making a distinction between peer review and peer response, Halasek argues for the more expansive approach of peer response. Situated within the framework of "connective practice," peer response is repositioned as a genre, one that becomes an integral part of the writing course.

Courtney Stanton's chapter, "Peer Persuasion: An Ethos-Based Theory of Identification and Audience Awareness," shifts the focus from the writer deciding how to respond to a review to the reviewer understanding the review as an act of persuasion. In a provocative move, Stanton argues that the instructor should not be displaced from a central role in the peer review process. Rather, the instructor needs to become an active contributor along with the other students. Doing so sets up the "concept of reviewer-instructor identification." Through this identification, peer reviewers can be empowered by borrowing some of the "ethos" of the instructor. Ultimately, such a move on behalf of the instructor enables students to grasp the sense of audience in its broadest sense, creating an implicit trust between student reviewers and the instructor, all of whom are working together.

In "Positioning Peer Review for Transfer: Authentic Audiences for Career Readiness and Workplace Communication," Nora McCook argues that the model of peer review that emerged out of student-centered pedagogy has been ineffective precisely because it has failed to position itself as a rhetorically valuable tool beyond the classroom setting. To replace that model, McCook looks to transfer pedagogy, using backward and forward reflection in order to reframe peer review as a workplace practice. As she explains, this type of reflection helps students "to develop precisely the types of useful, collaborative workplace skills that they will encounter with their colleagues after college."

PEER REVIEW: CULTIVATING INCLUSIVENESS

This next part looks at the experiences that both native and non-native students face when they feel unsure about their writing abilities. Ellen Turner, in "Peer Review and the Benefits of Anxiety in the Academic Writing Classroom," examines how anxiety about peer review can be a significant obstacle for non-native speakers of English. In a counterintuitive move, Turner challenges the premise that anxiety must necessarily "always [be] negative," explaining that it can also have a "positive effect, particularly amongst non-native speakers of English" (162, 165). To overcome individual student anxiety, Turner assigns a "reflective learning journal," where students write about their experience of peer review "before, during, and after feedback sessions" (169, 171). Turner's research notes a decrease in anxiety through the use of the learning journal with an attendant increase of student interest in peer review.

In the chapter "Multimodal Peer Review: Fostering Inclusion in Mixed Level College Classrooms with ELL Learners," researcher Beth Kramer gives voice to the unique "challenges of mixed level composition classrooms." Like the students that Turner discusses, ELL students also experience "anxiety about their performance and skill levels." The question becomes how to work with a mixed group of students that include ELL students and native speakers who are at different levels while simultaneously challenging both groups when doing peer review. For Kramer, the answer has been to assign more frequent lower-stakes assignments of peer review to decrease anxiety while increasing social collaboration and to introduce the use of podcasts as a means to increase "oral reflection."

PEER REVIEW: THE PROMISE OF TECHNOLOGY

This last part looks at the role that technology plays in the practice of peer review. The discussion begins with demonstrating the effectiveness of putting peer review online. In "Leveling the Playing Field for ELL Students: The Case for Moving Peer Review to an Online Environment," Vicki Pallo, like Turner and Kramer, acknowledges the anxiety that ELL students confront when taking a writing course, which is especially true when students are called upon to do peer review. To overcome their unease, Pallo advocates moving peer review online asynchronously. While instructors might be reluctant to put their students in such a position, Pallo rigorously challenges that notion explaining that the asynchronous online environment affords students opportunities, including more time to read and write than is otherwise available to them in a face-to-face course. This ultimately leads to greater student participation.

Phoebe Jackson's chapter, "Learning from Peer Review Online: Changing the Pedagogical Emphasis," examines research on peer review from the field of education. Unlike compositionists, education scholars start with the premise that peer review is a beneficial practice and that student writers can learn from *providing* a peer review. This change in pedagogical emphasis shifts the focus from a concern about outcomes (the student's comments) to one that zeroes in on what students can learn when *doing* peer review. Jackson further argues that the online environment can better enhance and reinforce the learning that takes place for students when doing peer review, helping to build their own spontaneous discourse communities.

This part ends with Nick Carbone's "The Potential of Peer Review Software That Focuses on the Review, not the Draft," taking us into wholly new territory: the promise of peer review software. As Carbone explains, because peer review software aggregates all student comments, it makes them visible to both students and the instructor. This visibility works on multiple levels, allowing, for example, students to "see how their feedback is used and how it compares to feedback given by other reviewers." The aggregation of student comments, moreover, gives instructors detailed material to better advise students and discuss different aspects of the actual peer review. At its best, this software helps to showcase the importance of peer review as an integral part of the writing process.

Today, almost half a century removed from its origins, peer review remains a mainstay in most writing courses from high school to college. We hope this collection provokes new thinking about this foundational practice for those teachers who already use peer review successfully, those who use peer review but might harbor misgivings or frustrations with it, and for graduate students about to embark on a teaching career. Taken together, the chapters in this collection offer all practitioners involved in composition studies and the teaching of writing an opportunity to reconsider and possibly reconceptualize peer review. The authors begin with the premise that peer review is an integral and essential component of any writing course and then go on to provide multiple ways to re-envision and rethink it from a various perspectives. They include such topics as the intersections of rhetoric, student inclusiveness, and technology with peer review, bringing new considerations to a long-standing practice. In so doing, the chapters provoke a renewed discussion of peer review, one that is long overdue, from both theoretical and practical perspectives. All of this, we hope, will lead to further enhancement and development of an essential practice and a continuing dialogue about the importance of peer review as a pedagogical practice in all writing courses.

WORKS CITED

Bruffee, Kenneth A. "Collaborative Learning and the 'Conversation of Mankind.'" *College English*, vol. 46, no. 7, Nov. 1984, pp. 635–52.

Ching, Kory Lawson. "Peer Response in the Composition Classroom: An Alternative Genealogy." *Rhetoric Review*, vol. 26, no. 3, June 2007, pp. 303–19.

———. "The Instructor-Led Peer Conference: Teachers as Participants in Peer Response." *Peer Pressure, Peer Power: Theory and Practice in Peer Review and Response for the Writing Classroom.* Fountain Head Press, 2014, pp.15–28.

Corbett, Steven J., Michelle LaFrance, and Teagan E. Decker. *Peer Pressure, Peer Power: Theory and Practice in Peer Review and Response for the Writing Classroom.* Fountain Head Press, 2014.

Elbow, Peter. *Writing Without Teachers*. Oxford UP, 1998.

Flynn, Elizabeth A. "Re-viewing Peer Review." *The Writing Instructor*, Dec. 2011, *ERIC*. Accessed 6 May 2023, https://files.eric.ed.gov/fulltext/EJ959705.pdf.

———. "Students as Readers of Their Classmates' Writing: Some Implications for Peer Critiquing." *The Writing Instructor,* Spring 1984, pp.126–28.

Gere, Ann Ruggles. *Writing Groups History, Theory, and Implications*. Southern Illinois UP, 1987.

Jesnek, Lindsey M. "Peer Editing in the 21st Century College Classroom: Do Beginning Composition Students Truly Reap the Benefits?" *Journal of College Teaching and Learning,* vol.8, no. 5, 2011, pp. 17–24.

Parfitt, Elizabeth. "Establishing the Genre of Peer Review to Create New Rhetorical Knowledge." *Compendium2*, vol.5, no.1, 2012, pp. 1–8.

Reid, E. Shelley. "Peer Review for Peer Review's Sake: Resituating Peer Review Pedagogy." *Peer Pressure, Peer Power: Theory and Practice in Peer Review and Response for the Writing Classroom*. Fountain Head Press, 2014, pp. 217–31.

Spear, Karen. *Sharing Writing: Peer Response Groups in English Classes*. Boynton/Cook, 1988.

Zhu, Wei. "Effects of Training for Peer Response on Students' Comments and Interaction." *Written Communication*, vol. 12, no. 4, 1995, pp. 492–528.

PART ONE. PEER REVIEW: EVALUATING THE CHALLENGES

CHAPTER 1.

TEACHERS' BELIEFS ABOUT THE LANGUAGE OF PEER REVIEW: SURVEY-BASED EVIDENCE

Ian G. Anson
University of Maryland Baltimore County

Chris M. Anson
North Carolina State University

Kendra L. Andrews
Wake Forest University

Despite concerns about the lack of research on peer review (e.g., Haswell, 2005), studies of the method have recently been accumulating, especially to test assumptions about the effectiveness of peer review in promoting revision and strengthening students' writing abilities. Recent scholarship, for example, includes studies examining what kinds of comments promote revision (e.g., Leijen; Nelson and Schunn); comparing student and teacher ratings of essays (Moxley and Eubanks; Falchikov and Goldfinch; Cho, Shunn, and Charney); considering peer review from the student's perspective (Brammer and Rees); and tracking what students focus on as they read vs. what they point to when asked to comment (Paulson, Alexander, and Armstrong).

This and other research follows in the wake of decades of instructional advocacy for peer review that links the method with improved writing ability and the development of skills for collaboration (Bean; Spear; Elbow and Belanoff). But it is also clear that peer review involves highly complex cognitive, linguistic, and social-psychological processes that are not always easily employed by novice student writers or taught effectively as part of the writing process. Reflected in the challenges of making peer review work well, these complexities may account for the relatively poor uptake of peer review in higher education, as demonstrated in Braine's survey showing that peer review was the least implemented of the recommended teaching practices for supporting writing. The reasons faculty either gravitate toward or shy away from using peer review are not well known, nor whether specific demographic or teaching-related factors affect these dispositions.

DOI: https://doi.org/10.37514/PER-B.2023.1961.2.01

To explore these questions, we conducted a non-probability, voluntary survey of nearly 500 professional writing scholars and educators about peer review. While one goal of the survey was to compare the key terms preferred by teachers to those expressed by students in actual peer review assignments (see Anson and Anson), in our contribution to this collection, we leverage the survey data to more closely examine the dynamics of teacher expectations for peer review. Our goals were first to study the effect of several variables on instructors' attitudes toward peer review, such as workload, institution type, grading load, and academic rank. We questioned if any of these factors related to teachers' attitudes toward peer review and the likelihood that they will employ it in their teaching. Second, we wanted to examine the relationship between teachers' attitudes toward peer review and the key terms, or "quasi-threshold concepts" (Anson, Chen, and Anson) that teachers privilege in response to student writing contrasted with the key terms they think students use in peer review, asking if teachers' attitudes toward peer review related to their faith in students' abilities to use appropriate language reflecting important writing-related concepts. In particular, we were interested in whether the language and concepts teachers privilege in response could provide us with guideposts for how we can encourage the development and use of effective practices for peer review, including the teaching of threshold writing concepts (Adler-Kassner and Wardle).

POSSIBLE SOURCES OF ATTITUDES TOWARD PEER REVIEW

Although the practice of peer review has been popular since the late nineteenth century within academic literary societies and writing clubs, it was not until the 1980s that it appeared in the composition classroom (Gere 304). The process movement brought an intense focus on and interest in revision, with peer review serving as a central activity to promote the improvement of drafts and the learning of rhetorical strategies (see Anson, "Process"). With the subsequent social turn came the introduction of collaborative learning (Bruffee) and the "teacherless writing class" (Elbow, *Writing*), both of which supported in-class activities in which students responded to each other as interested readers and co-creators of meaning. Peer review (also known as peer response, peer editing, or peer feedback) has been a staple in composition classrooms since then, but it has not always been employed in the same way. Some instructors use guided peer-review questions, some have students read their papers to each other, some do a roundtable review, some match students in pairs, some keep readers anonymous and some do not, some use word clouds to facilitate response (Illich), and some have students provide their responses using digital peer review systems (Breuch).

Although there is no preferred method for implementing peer review in writing courses, certain principles appear to be consistently valued in the pedagogical literature. Many of these, such as emphasizing constructive criticism and comments that can lead to revisions that focus on global over local concerns while providing a friendly tone, are aligned with similar standards in teacher response (Anson, *Writing*; Elbow, "Closing My Eyes"; Knoblauch and Brannon; Sommers, "Revision"; Sommers, *Responding;* Straub, "Responding"; Straub, *Practice*). Yet the generally positive orientation of the pedagogical literature is not reflected in faculty attitudes toward peer review. The reasons for these disparities are not entirely clear. For example, there may be a reciprocal relationship between the care with which faculty prepare students for and orchestrate peer review, the success they see as a result, and their subsequent attitudes. Weak implementation from a lack of exposure to best practices can lead to poor results, which can, in turn, further diminish faith in the method. In a study designed to gauge the effectiveness of peer review, Charlotte Brammer and Mary Rees administered an end-of-semester survey to students and faculty. The results revealed that "most students find peer review 'not very helpful'" despite how commonly it is used in composition classrooms, pointing to preparation as the key variable for successful peer review (see also George; Graff). Without believing that peer review can realize learning goals, instructors may not invest time in orienting students to the method and helping them succeed (Brammer and Rees 81). The seeming lack of effective revision among peers (and their dislike of the method) convinces the instructors that the time could be better spent doing other things.

In "Peer Editing in the 21st Century College Classroom," Lindsey M. Jesnek uses Brammer and Rees' study as evidence that methods of peer review have not responded to its complexities. While conceding that peer review is an accepted practice supported by research on collaborative learning (Roskelly; Bruffee; Howard; Stewart and McClure), Jesnek points to the challenges facing students when they engage in the practice, which pushes them toward "peer editing" rather than "peer response." The disappointments instructors experience with the method may be predictable in the context of the conceptual and social requirements of successful peer review, such as navigating uncomfortable positions of ego, authority, and agency, and the cognitive requirements of knowing writing-related perspectives that translate into the kind of rhetorical, linguistic, and structural language used in effective response. In many ways, the complexities of peer review parallel those of teacher response, about which Nancy Sommers writes that "although commenting on student writing is the most widely used method for responding to student writing, it is the least understood" (*Responding* 148).

Research on teachers' own response practices is also relevant to their potential uptake of peer review (see Li and Barnard; Nicol). Across a variety of studies with different methodological approaches, findings indicate that instructors view the provision of "appropriate" feedback as important, echoing Sommers' conclusion from a major longitudinal study of undergraduate writing at Harvard that "feedback, more than any other form of instruction, shapes the way a student learns to write" (Sommers "Across"). Yet some teachers' "chicken scratch" style commentary, necessitated by their workloads and/or lack of training, is ineffective. In a sample of 48 instructors at one university, most felt that feedback practices were remarkably lacking in quality because of instructors' heavy grading loads. When instructors provided feedback to students, these time constraints led them to write terse snippets of commentary on final drafts—summative, "end-loaded" comments rather than more formative types of feedback (Bailey and Garner). Jackie Tuck shows that instructors are aware of their inability to provide quality feedback stemming from both institutional and personal pressures. Faculty are motivated to provide good feedback, but as institutions demand high-quality teaching while simultaneously increasing their workloads, they are generally unhappy with the results—to say nothing of the dissatisfaction of their students (see Sommers "Beyond"). These results suggest a gap between practices advocated in the field, which emphasize ongoing, formative interactions between instructors and students about their writing, and those the instructors used, which focused on summative comments on final texts.

In the context of this problem, peer review would seem to offer at least a partial solution (Nicol; Thomson; and Breslin). In the absence of formative responses from teachers (which may double the teacher's workload), peer review is positioned as a viable way to generate thoughtful commentary that can precipitate productive revision and improvement. We might predict, then, that instructors with high grading loads, especially those early in their careers and/or on the tenure track, will be among those likely to view peer feedback favorably, as a way to overcome the problems noted by Tuck, Bailey and Garner, and others. At the same time, the attractiveness of peer review may be entirely mitigated if teachers don't have confidence that their students can provide useful peer response to their peers' writing in progress. That confidence is reflected in the kinds of language students use to provide feedback. We would expect faculty with confidence in peer review to include richer content in their description of the terms and concepts used by students, more closely matching the terms and concepts used by instructors when they respond to student writing. In contrast, we would expect those less optimistic about peer review to predict students' use of terms and concepts that less closely match the terms and concepts used by instructors. Our study sought to examine these expectations and relate them to the demographic factors described earlier.

WHAT TEACHERS VALUE IN PEER REVIEW: A SURVEY

To conduct our study, we developed, advertised, and distributed a survey designed to assess writing teachers' perceptions of contemporary response practices, as well as conventional assumptions about the content of peer and instructor feedback to writing. The survey was administered on two large e-mail listservs: WPA-L (recently replaced by writingstudies-L but populated at the time by over 3,500 writing teachers and writing program administrators), and the listserv of the European Association for the Teaching of Academic Writing (EATAW), populated primarily by teachers who support and/or study writing in European higher education, especially in English. After two weeks of deployment, the overall N of responses collected across these two listservs totaled 475: 410 from WPA-L, and 65 from the EATAW listserv. Given the size of these listservs' membership, our rate of response was somewhere between 10 and 15 percent. This nonprobability survey allowed us a first glimpse at the perceptions of writing teachers across institutions, nations, academic appointments, and workloads.

The first part of the survey was designed to measure basic demographic information of our sample. As there are no accurate estimates of the population demographics of individuals in the writing studies community, we collected this information as an exploratory exercise. Some demographic information, including measures of racial diversity, educational attainment and background, and marital status, were not collected due to the preliminary nature of the study (and the need for brevity because of the likelihood of drop-out among our respondents, who were not compensated in any way for their efforts). We focused our demographic measurements on three main categories: basic personal attributes such as age, gender, and country of residence; and institutional information such as academic appointment and workload.

Our principal measures of interest focused on respondents' perceptions of the quality of both peer and instructor feedback at the college level, using closed-ended, five-point question batteries asking for overall appraisals of quality. These questions asked respondents if they found peer feedback to be "extremely," "fairly," "moderately," "only a little," or "not at all" helpful to students, and if college and university instructors across the disciplines provide "very high-quality," "high-quality," "moderate-quality," "low-quality," or "very low-quality" feedback on written assignments.

The survey also asked respondents to provide open-ended content describing the terms they expected to find in the feedback of teachers and novice student writers. Instructors' terms, we theorized, represent underlying "threshold concepts" important to the development of effective writing (see Adler-Kassner and Wardle). As a result, the terms respondents believe that students use when providing peer review would then show the "distance" from the teachers' terms and potentially reflect respondents' experiences using peer review and their perceptions of what students typically know and bring to the peer review process. We first asked respondents to think about concepts that are important for high-quality responses to writing, providing them with ten open-ended text boxes. Next, we asked respondents for terms that might be likely to appear in novice students' responses to writing, providing them with ten additional open-ended text boxes. This data-collection strategy allowed teachers to input their expectations about the type of key lexical content encapsulated in writing-related terms that might appear across a variety of writing assignments among both students and teachers. While this strategy affords a greater degree of generalizability in the lexicons leveraged by our respondents when compared to responses to specific writing prompts, it also potentially widens the range of psychological referents used by respondents, rendering our lexicon quite diverse. Our approach nevertheless resulted in several terms appearing regularly across respondents, meaning that we have likely captured a baseline set of concepts that teachers perceive as important regardless of context. Future studies could use this latter approach to examine teacher response lexicons for more targeted comparisons.

WHO RESPONDED?

Before examining differences across respondents' portrayals of feedback, it is important to first consider the demographics of the sample. Table 1.1 presents basic descriptive information that allows us to assess the nature of our sample of teachers.

An important insight to emerge from Table 1.1 is that our sample of teachers, though predominantly based in the United States, is highly diverse in terms of academic position, workload, and demographics. For example, while roughly 72% of the sample is female, ages range from 25 to 77, with a standard deviation of almost 12 years. We have captured a cross-section of the field that includes members of the composition community at many points in the academic lifecycle—7% of the sample identifies as graduate students, while 11% are untenured tenure-track faculty, 20% are tenured associate professors, and 17% are full professors. Other members of the sample identify their academic position as full- or part-time instructors, administrators, or other appointments; no one type of academic position predominates.

In addition, while the majority of respondents (82%) are responsible for teaching composition as part of their responsibilities, the respondents are spread across four-year public institutions (64%), four-year private institutions (24%), and other institution types (13%).

Table 1.1. Demographic Characteristics of Teacher Survey Sample

Variable	Mean/ Proportion	SD	Min.	Max.	N
U.S. (1) vs. Int'l (0)	0.86		0	1	475
Age	50.04	11.65	25	77	337
Female	0.72		0	1	343
Assistant Prof.	0.11		0	1	345
Associate Prof.	0.20		0	1	345
Full Prof.	0.17		0	1	345
Full-time Non-TT	0.12		0	1	345
Administrator	0.07		0	1	345
Graduate Student	0.07		0	1	345
Other Position/NA	0.26		0	1	345
4-Year Public Institution	0.63		0	1	344
4-Year Private Institution	0.24		0	1	344
Other Institution	0.13		0	1	344
Teaches Composition	0.82		0	1	345
# of Students Graded per Sem.	3.33	1.12	1	8	344

Teachers also report substantially different grading workloads: the mean value of the categorical workload variable is 3.33 on a scale from 1–8, while the mode is 3 (a category that reflects a grading load of between 25 and 49 students per semester). As reflected in Figure 1.1, this distribution is skewed and has a high variance.

A significant number of respondents report direct grading responsibility for between 25 and 50 students per year. However, one non-negligible group of respondents reports having no grading responsibilities at all (perhaps because they have administrative roles that release them from teaching) while another group reports grading responsibilities that exceed 100 students per semester. Given that our survey has achieved substantial variation on this potentially important predictor of perceptions of peer feedback, we next proceed to developing and analyzing models that predict these attitudes.

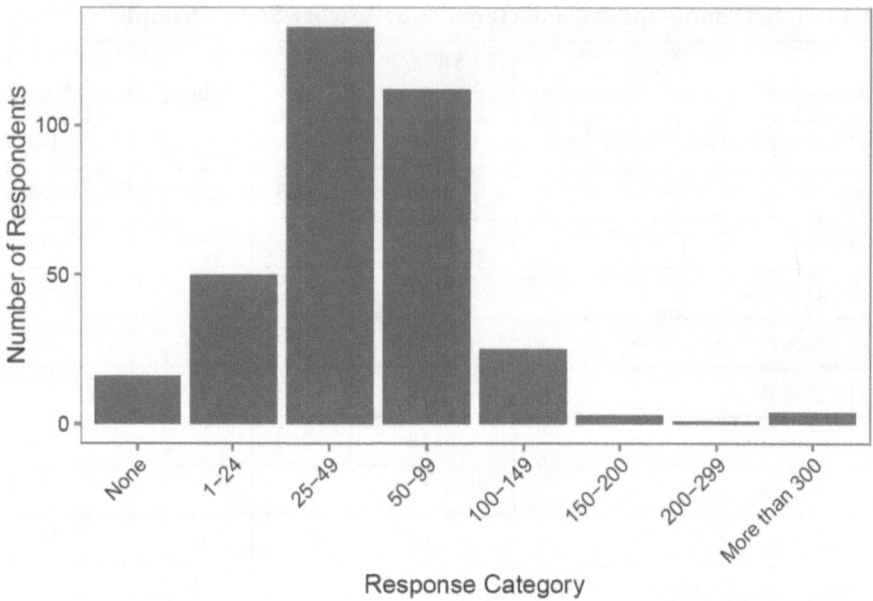

Figure 1.1. Distribution of respondents, grading load per semester (self-report).

RESULTS: PERCEPTIONS OF PEER FEEDBACK PRACTICES

First we examine the overall distribution of our sample's perceptions of instructor and peer feedback, as seen in Table 1.2. The results show that while few respondents perceive instructor or peer feedback to be of low overall helpfulness (3.2% and 0.3%, respectively), respondents are far less confident about instructor feedback than peer feedback. Only 12.8% of respondents perceive instructors to provide feedback of very high or high quality, compared to 25.8% stating that instructor feedback is likely to be of low or very low quality.

Table 1.2. Expert Perceptions of Instructor and Peer Feedback

Instructors Provide Feedback of . . .	Very High Quality	High Quality	Moderate Quality	Low Quality	Very Low Quality
Percent of Sample	0.9	11.5	61.8	22.6	3.2
Peer Feedback Is . . .	Extremely Helpful	Fairly Helpful	Moderately Helpful	Only a Little Helpful	Not at all Helpful
Percent of Sample	29.4	34.7	22	14.4	0.3

Note: Percentages may not sum to 100 due to rounding.

However, peer feedback is seen as "helpful" or "extremely helpful" by a narrow majority of respondents (64.1%), indicating teachers' optimism about the potential for this mode of feedback to improve the experience of novice writers. We can't probe the reasons why some respondents identify peer feedback as being "moderately," "only a little," or "not at all" helpful (36.7%), but this proportion of respondents is large enough to indicate that enthusiasm about peer feedback is by no means universal among writing teachers. What might predispose some teachers to view this feedback as helpful or unhelpful to students?

DETERMINANTS OF PEER FEEDBACK PERCEPTIONS

Earlier, we suggested that support for peer feedback may depend on considerations like grading load and faculty rank and age. In a linear regression model, we regress demographics and perceptions of instructor feedback on support for peer feedback practices. The results are presented in Table 1.3.

The results of Table 1.3 provide evidence that, as expected, demographics like gender and nationality have little impact on support for peer review practices, but institutional type, academic rank, and grading load each exert substantial effects on these perceptions. Notably, we find that respondents with academic appointments at private 4-year institutions are substantially less likely to support peer review (a decline of nearly 0.5 points on the 5-point scale; $p = 0.002$). This finding is interesting in light of assumptions that private institutions, especially smaller liberal arts colleges, emphasize the undergraduate learning experience, leading to more frequent use of experiential learning techniques. While the reason for the finding is not clear, it's possible that faculty at such institutions successfully use a greater number of other evidence-based techniques for writing instruction and therefore rate peer review as less useful relative to these strategies. For example, the lower student-teacher ratios at smaller liberal arts colleges may allow teachers to provide their own response on drafts instead of using peer review. Our data bear out this assumption: among respondents at private 4-year colleges, the mean on the teaching load variable is 3.125; among those at public 4-year colleges, the mean is 3.390 (p(t) = 0.023). Or it could be that these faculty are more likely to have experimented with peer review relative to other groups and found these experiences to be unsatisfactory. An alternative possibility is that faculty at these institutions are less likely than those at larger public four-year universities to have invested time to fully examine the current research on peer review or to have been introduced to the method and prepared to use it. Further studies could examine the less robust relationship between private college/university settings and support for peer review.

Table 1.3. Linear Regression Model Predicting Support for Peer Feedback Practices

Age	0.003
	(0.005)
Female	-0.069
	(0.127)
United States	-0.146
	(0.167)
Private 4-Year Inst.	-0.444‡
	(0.142)
2-Year Inst.	-0.076
	(0.257)
Full Professor	-0.230
	(0.176)
Associate Prof.	0.310†
	(0.155)
Assistant Prof.	0.388†
	(0.180)
Administrator	0.142
	(0.240)
Teaches Composition	0.002
	(0.151)
Grading Load	-0.141‡
	(0.052)
College-Level Feedback is High Qual.	-0.080
	(0.081)
Constant	4.586‡
	(0.429)
Observations	328
R^2	0.084
Adjusted R^2	0.049
Residual Std. Error	1.003 (df = 315)
F Statistic	2.405‡ (df = 12; 315)

Note: *$p < 0.05$ †$p < 0.01$ ‡$p < 0.001$

While other findings from Table 1.3 provide evidence to support our expectations, one result runs counter to conventional wisdom. Assistant professors (around 0.3 points, $p = 0.047$) and associate professors (around 0.4 points, $p = 0.032$) have higher average perceptions of peer review than other groups, all else equal, which accords with the assumption that recently-minted and mid-career professors in the field have been exposed to current literature or teacher-development efforts supporting the use of peer feedback in the classroom. However, the unexpected finding to emerge from Table 1.3 is that a one-unit *increase* in grading load leads to a *decrease* in support for peer review of roughly 0.15 points ($p = 0.007$). Although this finding deserves more study, two possible reasons arise. First, because of their higher teaching loads, these individuals may be less likely to have been exposed to literature on peer feedback or have engaged in local faculty development efforts in the context of the time they must spend on their teaching. If the above expectation were to find support in future studies, it would point to the importance of lower class sizes and a stronger provision of workshops, training sessions, and the dissemination of best practices to faculty who are underexposed to state-of-the-art research because of pressures and responsibilities related to teaching, grading, and administration. Second, the additional time and effort required to manage and account for peer review (tracking exchanged papers, ensuring adequate response or evaluating its quality, comparing drafts and revisions, etc.) could be a disincentive for heavily burdened teachers who would rather use an "assign/collect/grade" approach to writing instruction.

FACULTY CHARACTERIZATION OF FEEDBACK

Our second research question was designed to explore teachers' conceptions of response quality based on the kind of language they expect to be used in high-quality responses and the kind of language they believe students use in peer review. In part, we wanted to see whether skepticism for peer review arises from a concern that students don't know how to provide high-quality responses based on the focus of their comments. If teachers believe that students provide responses similar to that provided by teachers, then skepticism must come from some other factor(s) than student ability.

To analyze the data we collected, we constructed document-term matrices that tabulate the presence of terms in each lexicon by respondent and term. These matrices create corpora of terms representing feedback to writing likely to be given by teachers and by students. In Figure 1.2, we manipulate these matrices to produce frequency histograms of the most common terms to appear in the dataset. This figure shows all terms that were mentioned by at least 10% of the respondents in the sample.

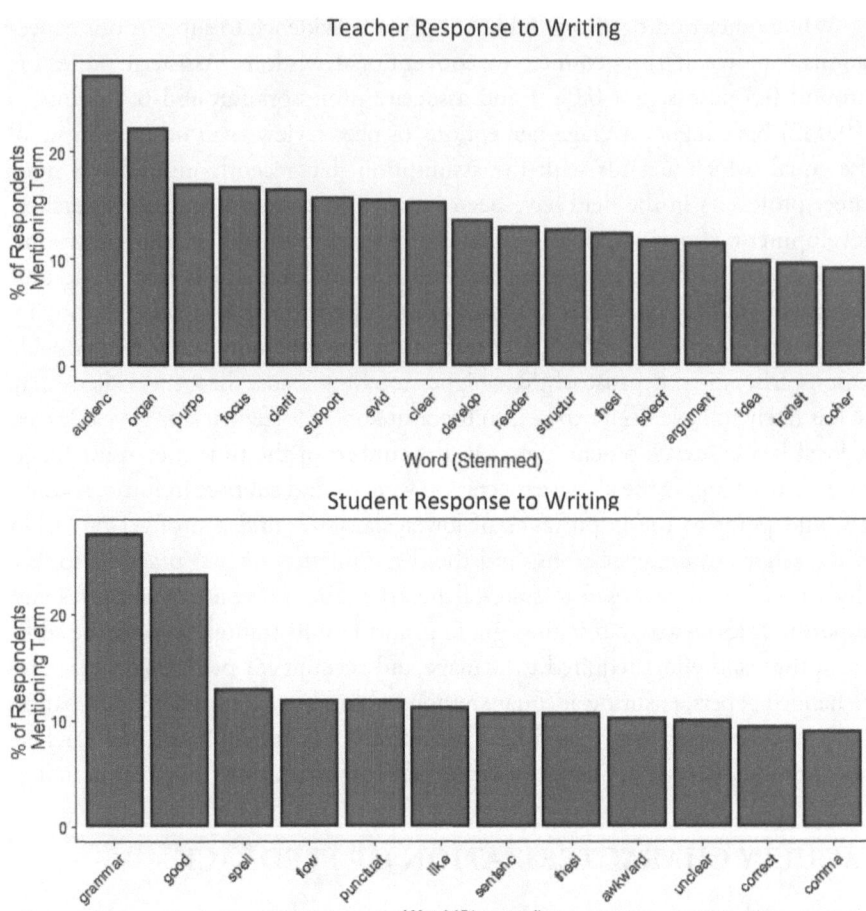

Figure 1.2. Histograms of most frequent terms, teachers' descriptions of teacher and student response to writing.

Figure 1.2 shows that the teacher and student feedback lexicons differ substantially in several ways. First is the observation that teacher feedback contains more global, rhetorical, and conceptual-level terms like *audience, purpose, focus,* and *reader*. In comparison to these broad conceptual terms, teachers' expectations of student feedback include affective generalities (*good, like, awkward*) and sentence-level minutiae (*grammar, spelling, sentence*).

The teacher dataset also incorporates a greater overall number of terms related to evidence and support for arguments, indicating that this may be a primary concern among teachers with experience responding to developing writers. Interestingly, teachers are also more often in agreement about the key terms: a greater number of terms are *shared* by at least 10% of the respondents in the expert lexicon. When it comes to student response, fewer teachers could agree on the most relevant keywords—there is less consensus about what kinds of concepts are likely to emerge in student response to writing. Perhaps this heterogeneity is related to respondents' different grading loads, meaning that some respondents have had fewer opportunities to gain a working understanding of how student writers approach revision. Whatever the reason, this pattern holds despite a greater diversity of teacher-oriented terms mentioned across all respondents in the dataset (after data cleaning, 964 unique teacher-oriented terms were collected, compared to 749 student-oriented terms).

SOURCES OF VARIATION IN TEACHER LEXICONS

While the above description shows some meaningful variation in the way that teachers characterize student and teacher feedback, we also examined how the demographic characteristics and perceptions of the respondents influenced the patterns of keyword mentions. That is, did the response lexicons vary as a function of workload, academic position, and/or other variables? Our first glimpse at these relationships comes from Table 1.4, in which we present binary logistic regression models predicting the likelihood of term occurrence. Each column in Table 1.4 represents a separate regression model, in which predictors of the most prevalent teacher-associated feedback terms include age, gender, nationality, type of institution, academic rank, grading load, and perceptions about feedback.

The results of Table 1.4 show that while some variables like institution type, composition instructor, and administrator role exert minimal influence on the incidence of terms across the dataset, other variables, most notably institution, have more meaningful effects. Across the terms in question, respondents from outside the United States (likely those who responded from the EATAW listserv) provide very different types of feedback. This may reflect some differences in translation, despite the survey being conducted in English; it may also be rooted in cultural and educational differences in feedback practices and the "language of response" in different countries, which is a subject deserving further study.

It also appears that for terms such as *audience* and *purpose*, which reflect knowledge of contemporary rhetorical approaches to writing, one of the most influential variables is instructor feedback perceptions. On average, a teacher who becomes one unit more positive in their perceptions of instructor feedback in higher education is expected to be around 1.7 times more likely to mention "audience," for example ($p < 0.01$). This substantial difference contrasts many nonsignificant predictors of these key terms: it appears that teachers who are optimistic about the quality of instructor feedback, regardless of academic position or demographics, are more likely to associate these key concepts with high-quality response.

Table 1.4. Binary Logistic Regression Predicting Likelihood of Use of "Principled" Terms (Part 1)

	Dependent variable:				
	Audience	Organization	Purpose	Focus	Clarity
Age	-0.020*	-0.002	0.018	0.008	-0.0004
	(0.012)	(0.012)	(0.013)	(0.013)	(0.013)
Female	0.496*	0.152	-0.029	-0.359	1.032‡
	(0.283)	(0.284)	(0.302)	(0.296)	(0.374)
United States Institution	1.904‡	1.963‡	2.057‡	2.618†	-0.108
	(0.518)	(0.558)	(0.756)	(1.034)	(0.386)
Private 4-Year Inst.	-0.364	-0.215	-0.300	0.222	0.059
	(0.311)	(0.320)	(0.355)	(0.331)	(0.348)
2-Year Inst.	-0.438	0.766	0.276	0.116	-0.109
	(0.588)	(0.543)	(0.591)	(0.598)	(0.693)
Full Professor	0.228	-0.938†	-0.011	0.160	-0.419
	(0.390)	(0.416)	(0.423)	(0.434)	(0.448)
Associate Prof.	0.703†	-0.164	0.432	0.870†	-0.156
	(0.339)	(0.336)	(0.368)	(0.370)	(0.368)
Assistant Prof.	0.210	-0.341	0.150	0.434	-0.994*
	(0.400)	(0.412)	(0.464)	(0.462)	(0.529)
Administrator	0.047	-0.118	-0.110	0.662	0.053
	(0.516)	(0.503)	(0.592)	(0.543)	(0.546)
Teaches Composition	-0.138	-0.056	-0.510	0.114	0.206
	(0.350)	(0.363)	(0.438)	(0.387)	(0.353)
Grading Load	-0.122	-0.037	-0.202	0.023	0.090
	(0.122)	(0.125)	(0.150)	(0.144)	(0.120)
Perception of Feedback Quality	0.534‡	0.007	0.421†	0.087	-0.239
	(0.187)	(0.185)	(0.207)	(0.209)	(0.197)
Constant	-3.282‡	-2.244†	-3.844‡	-4.586‡	-1.544
	(1.064)	(1.087)	(1.318)	(1.496)	(1.040)
Observations	329	329	329	329	329
Log Likelihood	-192.410	-187.448	-161.038	-161.127	-165.817
Akaike Inf. Crit.	410.821	400.897	348.075	348.255	357.635

Note: *$p<0.1$; †$p<0.05$; ‡$p<0.01$

Table 1.4. Binary Logistic Regression Predicting Likelihood of Use of "Principled" Terms (Part 2)

	Dependent variable:				
	Support	Evidence	Clear	Develop	Reader
Age	0.002	-0.001	-0.011	0.003	0.033†
	(0.013)	(0.013)	(0.013)	(0.015)	(0.016)
Female	-0.012	0.583*	-0.117	0.146	0.240
	(0.308)	(0.342)	(0.318)	(0.341)	(0.389)
United States Institution	1.348†	1.350†	0.150	1.568†	0.379
	(0.632)	(0.570)	(0.428)	(0.762)	(0.522)
Private 4-Year Inst.	0.229	-0.061	0.085	0.050	-0.644
	(0.336)	(0.349)	(0.355)	(0.386)	(0.454)
2-Year Inst.	0.225	-0.732	0.541	0.116	-0.834
	(0.590)	(0.797)	(0.629)	(0.633)	(1.085)
Full Professor	0.458	0.288	-0.196	0.388	-0.683
	(0.421)	(0.425)	(0.436)	(0.467)	(0.553)
Associate Prof.	0.310	0.101	-0.603	0.277	0.533
	(0.385)	(0.383)	(0.421)	(0.417)	(0.416)
Assistant Prof.	0.093	-0.209	-0.293	0.138	-0.511
	(0.476)	(0.488)	(0.460)	(0.508)	(0.665)
Administrator	0.696	-0.727	-0.154	0.342	-0.378
	(0.539)	(0.679)	(0.579)	(0.642)	(0.711)
Teaches Composition	-0.148	0.349	0.682*	-1.101*	0.330
	(0.393)	(0.372)	(0.350)	(0.566)	(0.439)
Grading Load	0.031	-0.057	-0.173	0.077	-0.223
	(0.140)	(0.142)	(0.135)	(0.156)	(0.160)
Perception of Feedback Quality	-0.165	0.063	-0.033	0.325	0.164
	(0.212)	(0.209)	(0.204)	(0.231)	(0.231)
Constant	-2.315*	-3.385‡	-1.090	-3.521†	-3.432‡
	(1.220)	(1.202)	(1.048)	(1.473)	(1.305)
Observations	329	329	329	329	329
Log Likelihood	-161.921	-157.705	-160.238	-138.611	-123.312
Akaike Inf. Crit.	349.841	341.409	346.476	303.222	272.624

Note: *$p<0.1$; †$p<0.05$; ‡$p<0.01$

Table 1.5 shows differences in teachers' mention of student terms across key demographic and perceptual measures. Many respondents seemed to have fewer things to say overall about student feedback, perhaps reflecting some respondents' lack of experience seeing what students write to each other. However, several patterns emerged. While the country of origin of the institution again plays a major role in predicting the lexicon used to describe student response, another variable of interest is that of institutional type. Respondents who identified as instructors at 2-year colleges were more likely than average to mention terms corresponding to affective considerations, such as "like" ($p < 0.01$) and "unclear" ($p < 0.05$), but less likely to mention "grammar," perhaps reflecting a belief (or experience) that their students more often identify surface problems experientially ("I'm confused") than concerning explicit rules ("this comma splice obscures the meaning of your sentence"). However, across the survey, respondents actively teaching composition were less likely than average to mention the affective term "good," perhaps because they more systematically direct their students toward specifics. These and other patterns relating to the student lexicon reflect the heterogeneity that characterizes teachers' determination or understanding of student feedback.

A CLOSER LOOK AT PEER FEEDBACK PERCEPTIONS

In the preceding analyses, we examined differences in the teacher lexicons on the basis of demographics and perceptions of overall feedback quality. Now we take a closer look at perceptions of *peer feedback* as a critical determinant of the type of content used by respondents. This analysis allows us to examine, consistent with the findings above, whether skeptics of student peer review think about feedback differently than their more supportive counterparts.

To perform the analysis, we divided the sample into those expressing positive views of peer feedback (it is "extremely helpful" or "helpful") and those expressing neutral or pessimistic views. The distribution of the resulting binary variable leaves us with a tally of 36.4% skeptics and 63.6% proponents in the sample. Figure 1.3 provides a depiction of *differences* in the likelihood that these two groups mention the most prevalent keywords in the "high-quality" (teacher) corpus. The left-hand side of the figure shows terms that skeptics were substantially more likely to mention than supporters of peer feedback (black bars denote statistical significance on the basis of Welch two-sample t-tests at the $p < 0.05$ level). On the right-hand side of the figure, we see the opposite: these are terms that *proponents* of peer feedback mentioned substantially more than skeptics. Terms in the middle were mentioned by both proponents of peer feedback and skeptics at roughly equivalent rates.

Table 1.5. Binary Logistic Regression Predicting Likelihood of Mention of Student Terms (Part 1)

	Dependent variable:				
	Grammar	Good	Spell	Flow	Punctuation
	(1)	(2)	(3)	(4)	(5)
Age	0.002	-0.017	0.016	-0.004	0.041‡
	(0.011)	(0.012)	(0.014)	(0.015)	(0.015)
Female	-0.081	0.115	0.214	0.517	0.163
	(0.267)	(0.283)	(0.340)	(0.380)	(0.349)
United States Institution	0.693*	0.589	0.235	1.784†	0.436
	(0.392)	(0.404)	(0.456)	(0.781)	(0.510)
Private 4-Year Inst.	0.220	-0.200	-0.598	0.044	-0.294
	(0.294)	(0.326)	(0.403)	(0.395)	(0.392)
2-Year Inst.	-1.146*	0.165	-0.254	0.477	-0.692
	(0.678)	(0.534)	(0.692)	(0.713)	(0.816)
Full Professor	-0.055	0.071	-0.231	-0.403	-0.227
	(0.375)	(0.394)	(0.496)	(0.524)	(0.506)
Associate Prof.	0.695†	0.017	0.610	0.110	0.832†
	(0.323)	(0.341)	(0.390)	(0.416)	(0.405)
Assistant Prof.	-0.169	-0.125	0.546	0.038	0.703
	(0.395)	(0.398)	(0.461)	(0.505)	(0.496)
Administrator	-0.141	-0.561	0.443	-1.075	0.578
	(0.511)	(0.607)	(0.590)	(0.829)	(0.605)
Teaches Composition	-0.537	-0.822†	-0.070	-0.896	-0.217
	(0.340)	(0.401)	(0.419)	(0.571)	(0.443)
Grading Load	-0.196*	0.095	0.024	-0.423†	0.037
	(0.119)	(0.119)	(0.133)	(0.187)	(0.143)
Feedback Qual. Percep.	-0.074	0.124	0.019	0.152	0.106
	(0.174)	(0.181)	(0.209)	(0.239)	(0.219)
Constant	0.242	-0.637	-2.545†	-1.706	-3.907‡
	(0.943)	(1.013)	(1.173)	(1.446)	(1.290)
Observations	329	329	329	329	329
Log Likelihood	-204.539	-191.237	-150.745	-128.048	-140.132
Akaike Inf. Crit.	435.078	408.474	327.489	282.095	306.265

Note: *p<0.1; † p<0.05; ‡ p<0.01

Table 1.5. Binary Logistic Regression Predicting Likelihood of Mention of Student Terms (Part 2)

	Dependent variable				
	Like	Sentence	Thesis	Awkward	Unclear
	(6)	(7)	(8)	(9)	(10)
Age	0.025	0.018	0.014	-0.012	-0.018
	(0.016)	(0.015)	(0.015)	(0.015)	(0.016)
Female	0.033	-0.104	-0.240	0.047	0.988†
	(0.361)	(0.363)	(0.346)	(0.367)	(0.472)
United States Institution	1.572†	0.298	1.416*	0.350	-0.549
	(0.770)	(0.538)	(0.765)	(0.509)	(0.439)
Private 4-Year Inst.	-0.795	0.343	-0.196	-0.203	-0.411
	(0.493)	(0.391)	(0.423)	(0.422)	(0.471)
2-Year Inst.	1.619‡	-0.436	-0.159	-0.996	1.108*
	(0.581)	(0.815)	(0.698)	(1.071)	(0.672)
Full Professor	-0.300	-0.077	-0.030	-0.044	-0.570
	(0.513)	(0.508)	(0.500)	(0.511)	(0.644)
Associate Prof.	0.410	0.514	0.155	-0.537	0.320
	(0.432)	(0.415)	(0.437)	(0.487)	(0.447)
Assistant Prof.	0.555	-0.070	0.295	-0.004	0.165
	(0.516)	(0.560)	(0.513)	(0.492)	(0.506)
Administrator	-1.320	-1.169	0.026	0.129	0.142
	(1.090)	(1.075)	(0.715)	(0.636)	(0.707)
Teaches Composition	-0.806	-0.402	-1.585†	-0.219	0.106
	(0.648)	(0.490)	(0.755)	(0.457)	(0.451)
Grading Load	-0.207	0.064	0.017	-0.115	-0.110
	(0.185)	(0.160)	(0.169)	(0.152)	(0.146)
Feedback Qual. Percep.	0.407*	0.025	0.171	0.333	0.151
	(0.243)	(0.236)	(0.240)	(0.232)	(0.233)
Constant	-3.816†	-2.580*	-2.245	-2.012	-1.905
	(1.586)	(1.358)	(1.585)	(1.239)	(1.243)
Observations	329	329	329	329	329
Log Likelihood	-120.323	-126.683	-126.551	-130.979	-123.105
Akaike Inf. Crit.	266.647	279.365	279.102	287.959	272.210

Note: *$p<0.1$; †$p<0.05$; ‡$p<0.01$

Teachers' Beliefs about the Language of Peer Review

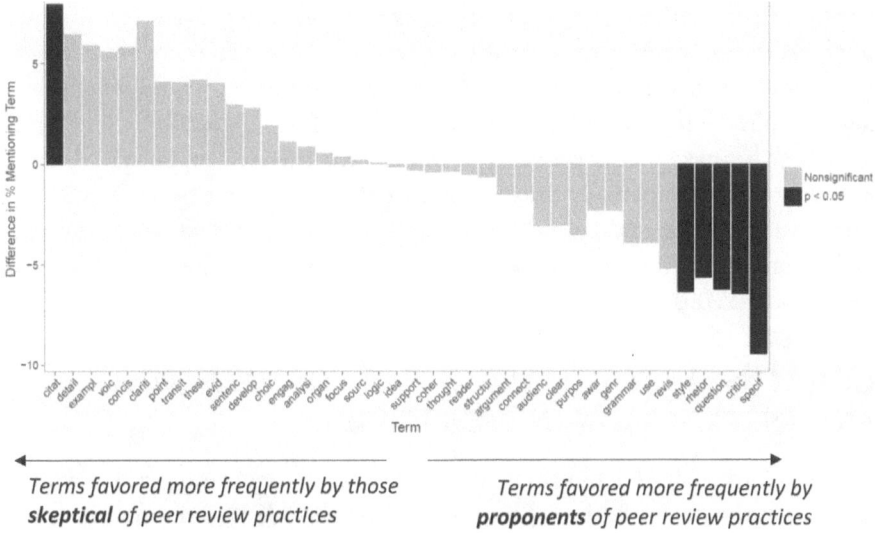

Figure 1.3. Comparison of high-quality term mention rate,
peer review skeptics vs. proponents of peer review

The results presented in Figure 1.3 demonstrate interesting patterns among proponents and skeptics of peer review. The leftmost bars show that many key terms are mentioned substantially more often by skeptics, despite the fact that only "citation" attains statistical significance at the $p < 0.05$ level. However, these terms, like "detail," "example," "concision," and "point," suggest that skeptics of peer review devote more attention to sentence-level concerns than do proponents. In fact, we see that peer feedback skeptics are around 35% more likely than proponents of peer review to mention the word "sentence" (a difference in the rate of mention of roughly 3%), though this difference is not statistically differentiable from 0 ($t = 0.87, p = 0.39$).

The rightmost bars of Figure 1.3, however, reveal more statistically significant differences when considering terms that skeptics used *less* often than proponents of peer review. Here, many broader concepts like "question," "criticism/critique," "style," and "revision" are used more frequently by proponents of peer review than by skeptics. To a lesser (nonsignificant) extent, we also see that rhetorical terms common in contemporary approaches to writing, such as "audience," "purpose," and "genre," are used more frequently by peer feedback proponents.

Taken together, these results point to differences in the way that skeptics and proponents of peer review think about high-quality feedback. It may be that this relationship occurs because those with a greater focus on specifics and mechanics in writing find peer review to be a dubious method to help students improve their writing: if the purpose of peer review is to provide broad structural, rhetorical, and informational responses, there may be more trust in students' abilities than if the purpose is for students to find errors, for which they may not have appropriate skills (Anson, "Talking"). Or it could be the reverse: teachers who have had negative experiences with peer review practices might find themselves increasingly prioritizing surface-level matters (such as error) in their own responses, as they find them to be critically overlooked across students' evaluations of writing. Regardless, future studies should further investigate the causal roots of this relationship.

CONCLUSION: THE ROAD AHEAD FOR RESEARCH AND INSTRUCTION IN PEER REVIEW

Results of our analysis demonstrate that while overall, teachers of writing appear fairly receptive to the idea of peer review, considerable variation exists across public and private university settings, as well as across academic ranks (though age does not play a role). Interestingly, we also observe decreasing support for peer review practices among instructors tasked with heavier grading loads. Analyses of key term usage also show differences across national context and perceptions of peer feedback effectiveness. We also find that instructors who are pessimistic about the implementation of peer review identify different concepts as important components of teacher-provided response compared to the response provided by students.

Taken together, these results suggest that the field has asymmetrically incorporated peer review in writing instruction. We must continue to advocate for the practice of peer review, which the pedagogical literature as well as newer research supports on the basis not only of improved final texts but practice of revision and the learning of useful collaborative communicative skills often expected in the workforce (Bruffee). Advocates of peer review argue that it is most effective when instructors fully orient students to the process and coach them in how to provide insightful feedback. These orientations include working through a sample draft together with the class, showing videos of successful response sessions and ones that get derailed for different reasons, providing peer-response guides that help students to focus on specific issues of importance to the development of their drafts, and asking for meta-commentaries of the peer-review sessions after they're done. Others focus their advice on ways to incorporate good peer review practices within the context of a well-supported and integrated approach to writing at the department or institutional level (Anson, Gonyea, and Paine). These approaches might involve leveraging new technologies adapted to such a task, such as digitally-mediated peer review systems (Moxley) or calibrated peer review programs (Reynolds and Moskovitz). These and other approaches may involve providing greater support for faculty hoping to incorporate peer review.

Further research is also needed to study the relationship between teachers' and students' attitudes toward peer review (for the latter, see Mulder, Pearce, and Baik), because this relationship may also influence how effectively students use the process. Deeper and more robust information is needed about teachers' opinions of peer review based on their experiences; variations in the use of peer review as these relate to its success; the experiences of students as they engage in peer review; and peer review as a function of assignments, genres, learning contexts, developmental stages of students as writers, instructor variables such as ideologies of teaching and learning, and student variables such as measures of self-efficacy, writing anxiety, and prior experience.

Finally, and perhaps most importantly, scholarship on threshold concepts is increasingly pointing to the relationship between the language of writing instruction and the underlying concepts and understandings associated with the production and use of written text and the ability of writers to "transfer" their understandings to other contexts and genres (Adler-Kassner and Wardle; Anson and Moore; Yancey, Robertson, and Taczak). Downs and Robertson, for example, suggest four domains of threshold concepts to emphasize in foundational writing courses: human interaction (rhetoric); textuality; epistemology (ways of knowing); and process. Comparing skilled and novice writers, they point to differences directly relevant to peer review:

> Seasoned writers usually treat writing as a rhetorical human interaction in which readers and writers interact to shape writing and meaning. Novice writers are much less likely to recognize the interactional nature of writing. To them, writing is strictly about getting sentences right rather than interacting with or being responsible to readers. Building an understanding of writing as a rhetorical activity, as human interaction, seems an essential threshold concepts for FYC [first-year composition]. 107

Because an understanding of such threshold concepts is revealed in the language and terminology writers use to talk about their own and others' writing, peer review will succeed or fail in proportion to this understanding. Reciprocally moving between the experience and practice of peer review and discussion of the meta-level threshold concepts at the heart of successful writing may strengthen students' abilities to respond to each other's writing and subsequently build confidence in teachers that the time spent in peer review will help students to grow as writers.

WORKS CITED

Adler-Kassner, Linda, and Elizabeth Wardle, eds. *Naming What We Know: Threshold Concepts of Writing Studies*. Utah State UP, 2015.

Anderson, Paul, et al. "The Contributions of Writing to Learning and Development: Results from a Large-Scale Multi-institutional Study." *Research in the Teaching of English*, vol. 50, no. 2, 2015, pp. 199–235.

Anson, Chris M. *Talking About Mistakes: Mining Students' Oral Peer Reviews for Constructs and Practices in Error Detection*. Paper delivered at the European Association for Research on Language and Instruction (EARLI) SIG Writing conference, Liverpool, England, July 6, 2016.

———. "Process Pedagogy and Its Legacy." *A Guide to Composition Pedagogies* (2nd ed.), edited by Amy Rupiper Taggart et al., Oxford UP, 2013, pp. 212–30.

———. "Response and the Social Construction of Error." *Assessing Writing*, vol. 7, no. 1, 2000, pp. 5–21.

Anson, Chris, ed. *Writing and Response: Theory, Practice, Research*. National Council of Teachers of English, 1989.

Anson, Chris M., and Jessie L. Moore, editors. *Critical Transitions: Writing and the Question of Transfer*. The WAC Clearinghouse and UP of Colorado, 2016.

Anson, Ian G., and Chris M. Anson. "Assessing Peer and Instructor Response to Writing: A Corpus Analysis from an Expert Survey." *Assessing Writing*, Vol. 33, 2017, pp. 12–24.

Anson, Chris M., et al. "Considering What They Say: An Analysis of Key Terms Used by Faculty Across the Curriculum." *Considering What We Know: Threshold Concepts for Writing Studies*, edited by Linda Adler-Kassner and Elizabeth Wardle, Utah State UP, 2019, pp. 314–27.

Bailey, Richard, and Mark Garner. "Is the Feedback in Higher Education Assessment Worth the Paper it is Written On? Teachers' Reflections on their Practices." *Teaching in Higher Education*, vol. 15, no. 2, 2010, pp. 187–98.

Bean, John C. *Engaging Ideas: The Professor's Guide to Integrating Writing, Critical Thinking, and Active Learning in the Classroom*. 2nd ed., Jossey-Bass, 2011.

Braine, George. *Writing Across the Curriculum: A Case Study of Faculty Practices at a Research University*. National Center for Research on Teacher Learning, 1990. (*ERIC* Document Reproduction Service ED 324 680)

Brammer, Charlotte, and Mary Rees. "Peer Review from the Students' Perspective: Invaluable or Invalid?" *Composition Studies*, vol. 35, no. 2, 2007, pp. 71–85.

Breuch, Lee-Ann Kassman. *Virtual Peer Review: Teaching and Learning About Writing in Online Environments*. SUNY Press, 2012.

Bruffee, Kenneth A. "Learning and the 'Conversations of Mankind.'" *College English*, vol. 46, no. 7, 1984, pp. 635–52.

Cho, Kwangsu, et al. "Commenting on Writing: Typology and Perceived Helpfulness of Comments from Novice Peer Reviewers and Subject Matter Experts." *Written Communication*, vol. 23, no. 3, 2006, pp. 260–94.

Downs, Doug, and Liane Robertson. "Threshold Concepts in First-Year Composition. *Naming What We Know: Threshold Concepts for Writing Studies*, edited by Linda Adler-Kassner and Elizabeth Wardle, Utah State UP, 2015, pp. 105–21.

Elbow, Peter. "Closing My Eyes as I Speak: An Argument for Ignoring Audience." *College English*, vol. 49, no. 1, 1987, pp. 50–69.

Elbow, Peter. *Writing Without Teachers*. Oxford UP, 1973.

Elbow, Peter, and Pat Belanoff. *Sharing and Responding*. Random House, 1989.

Falchikov, Nancy, and Judy Goldfinch. "Student Peer Assessment in Higher Education: A Meta-analysis Comparing Peer and Teacher Marks. *Review of Educational Research*, vol. 70, 2000, pp. 287–322.

George, Diana. "Writing with Peer Groups in the Composition Classroom." *College Composition and Communication*, vol. 35, no. 3, 1984, pp. 320–26.

Gere, Anne Ruggles. *Writing Groups: History, Theory, and Implications*. Southern Illinois UP, 1987.

Graff, Nelson. "Approaching Authentic Peer Review." *The English Journal*, vol. 98, no. 5, 2009, pp. 81–87.

Haswell, Richard. "NCTE/CCCC's Recent War on Scholarship." *Written Communication*, vol. 22, no. 2, 2005, pp. 198–223.

Howard, Rebecca Moore. "Collaborative Pedagogy." *Composition Pedagogies: A Bibliographic Guide*, edited by Gary Tate, Amy Rupiper, and Kurt Schick. Oxford UP, 2001, pp. 54–70.

Illich, Lindsay. "How to See a Text: The Word Cloud Peer Review." *Journal of Teaching Writing*, vol. 28, no. 2, 2013, pp. 1–18.

Knoblauch, Cy H., and Lil Brannon. "Teacher Commentary on Student Writing: The State of the Art." *Freshman English News*, vol. 10, 1981, pp. 1–4. Rpt. in Richard Graves, ed., *Rhetoric and Composition: A Sourcebook for Teachers and Writers*. Boynton/Cook, 1984.

Jesnek, Lindsey M. "Peer Editing in the 21st Century College Classroom: Do Beginning Composition Students Truly Reap the Benefits?" *Journal of College Teaching and Learning*, vol. 8, no. 5, 2011, pp. 17–24.

Leijen, Djuddah. "Applying Machine Learning Techniques to Investigate the Influence of Peer Feedback on the Writing Process." *Methods in Writing Process Research*, edited by D. Knorr et al. Peter Lang Verlag, 2014, pp. 167–83.

Li, Jinrui, and Roger Barnard. "Academic Tutors' Beliefs about and Practices of Giving Feedback on Students' Written Assignments: A New Zealand Case Study." *Assessing Writing*, vol. 16, no. 2, 2011, pp. 137–48.

Moxley, Joseph. "Datagogies, Writing Spaces, and the Age of Peer Production." *Computers and Composition*, vol. 25, no. 2, 2008, pp. 182–202.

Moxley, Joseph M., and David Eubanks. "On Keeping Score: Instructors' vs. Students' Rubric Ratings of 46,689 Essays." *WPA: Writing Program Administration*, vol. 39, no. 2, 2016, pp. 53–80.

Mulder, Raoul A., et al. "Peer Review in Higher Education: Student Perceptions Before and After Participation." *Active Learning in Higher Education*, vol. 15, no. 2, 2014, pp. 157–70.

Nelson, Melissa M., and Christian D. Schunn. "The Nature of Feedback: How Different Types of Peer Feedback Affect Writing Performance." *Instructional Science*, vol. 37, no. 4, 2009, pp. 375–401.

Nicol, David. "From Monologue to Dialogue: Improving Written Feedback Processes in Mass Higher Education." *Assessment & Evaluation in Higher Education*, vol. 35, no. 5, 2010, pp. 501–17.

Nicol, David, et al. "Rethinking Feedback Practices in Higher Education: A Peer Review Perspective." *Assessment & Evaluation in Higher Education*, vol. 39, no. 1, 2014, pp. 102–22.

Paulson, Eric J., et al. "Peer Review Re-Viewed: Investigating the Juxtaposition of Composition Students' Eye Movements and Peer Review Processes." *Research in the Teaching of English*, Vol. 41, No. 3, 2007, pp. 304–35.

Reynolds, J., and Cary Moskovitz, "Calibrated Peer Review Assignments in Science Courses: Are They Designed to Promote Critical Thinking and Writing Skills?" *Journal of College Science Teaching*, vol. 38, no. 2, 2008, pp. 60–66.

Roskelly, Hephzibah. "The Risky Business of Group Work." *ATAC Forum 4*, Spring, 1992. Reprinted in *The Writing Teacher's Sourcebook*, edited by Gary Tate et al., 3rd ed., Oxford UP, 1994, pp. 141–48.

Sommers, Nancy. "Across the Drafts." *College Composition and Communication*, vol. 58, no. 2, 2006, pp. 248–56.

Sommers, Nancy. *Beyond the Red* Ink (video). St. Martins, 2012. Available at https://www.youtube.com/watch?v=PKfLRz7h7gs.

Sommers, Nancy. *Responding to Student Writing*. Bedford/St. Martin's, 2013.

Sommers, Nancy. "Revision Strategies of Student Writers and Experienced Adult Writers." *College Composition and Communication*, vol. 31, no. 4, 1980, pp. 378–88.

Spear, Karen. *Shared Writing: Peer Response Groups in English Classes*. Boynton/Cook, 1988.

Stewart, Trevor Thomas, and Greg McClure. "Freire, Bakhtin, and Collaborative Pedagogy: A Dialogue with Students and Mentors." *International Journal of Dialogic Science*, vol. 7, no. 1, 2013, pp. 91–108.

Straub, Richard. *The Practice of Response: Strategies for Commenting on Student Writing*. Hampton Press, 2000.

Straub, Richard. "Responding—Really Responding—to Other Students' Writing." *The Subject is Writing*, edited by Wendy Bishop. Boynton/Cook, 1999, pp. 136–46.

Tuck, Jackie. "Feedback-Giving as Social Practice: Teachers' Perspectives on Feedback as Institutional Requirement, Work and Dialogue." *Teaching in Higher Education*, vol. 17, no. 2, 2012, pp. 209–22.

Yancey, Kathleen Blake, Liane Robertson, and Kara Taczak. *Writing Across Contexts: Transfer, Composition, and Site of Writing*. Utah State UP, 2015.

CHAPTER 2.

RESISTING THEORY: THE WISDOM OF THE CREATIVE WRITING WORKSHOP

Bob Mayberry
California State University Channel Island

Creative writing classes and composition courses share a commitment to peer review practices, which historically grew out of the workshop models developed in the early part of the twentieth century. But the two have followed very different lines of development since then: the workshop model prevalent in creative writing classes remains relatively unstructured, while peer review activities in composition classes have become quite varied and deliberately structured. Part of the answer lies in the very different ways the two disciplines have theorized their own teaching practices. And part of the answer lies in the history of those disciplines. Understanding how and why that happened may lead teachers in both disciplines to reconsider their current practices and, if there's something to be learned from the other discipline's approach, to discover better ways of doing what we all do.

So, the questions I'm exploring include the following: When did peer review activities in composition classes veer so far away from the workshop model still used in creative writing classes? What caused the two kinds of writing classes to evolve different methods of providing peer commentary on works in progress? And why is it that, for the most part, creative writing workshop pedagogy has resisted the movement towards theory that dominates other English studies?

To begin with, let's explore just how different those practices are. Join me in a thought experiment.

Imagine a composition class near the middle of the semester, students busy revising an essay for a midterm evaluation of some sort. The comp teacher announces that Monday's class will be a peer review session. What do we imagine will happen during that class time?

Will the teacher conduct a practice round of feedback, where the students make comments and then discuss what and why they responded the way they did? Will the teacher identify the more useful types of response or encourage students to discuss their previous experiences with peer review? Will the teacher use Google docs, inviting the students to comment on each other's essays, or provide an extensive set of questions to guide responses? Will the teacher determine who responds to whom, perhaps pairing the strongest writers with each other or each of the weakest writers with one of the strongest? Will responses focus on ideas, organization, supporting evidence, sentence fluency, mechanics, or all of the above?

Will the class refer to course grading criteria when responding? Will students read their drafts aloud, will someone else read them aloud, or will respondents read the drafts silently and by themselves? Will they mark each other's papers or write comments on a separate sheet of paper or make their comments orally to the writer? Will students be required to submit a completed draft for peer review, or will incomplete drafts or outlines be welcome? Will the students praise each other's work, identify what confuses them, or correct what they perceive to be errors? Will students be required to respond to their peers' comments or make the suggested changes?

Whew! The range of possible approaches and techniques is staggering, yet all are part of what composition faculty call "peer review." Such a wide range of activities suggests how thoroughly peer review activities have become part of the typical college composition classroom since the 70s. My first composition director assigned me two sections in 1972 and advised me to "remember to teach revision." Having students revise essays was still a new practice in freshman comp classes. Process pedagogy had no name yet; the idea just whispered between sessions Conference on College Composition and Communication (CCCC). Peter Elbow's *Writing Without Teachers* hadn't been published. Peer review activities were unheard of.

A lifetime later—46 years to be exact—peer review has become common practice. It's hard to imagine a composition classroom without some sort of peer review activities. The practice has been thoroughly assimilated and repeatedly theorized.

The same can't be said for the creative writing workshop.

Imagine a graduate creative writing class in the middle of a semester. The instructor announces that next week the class will spend an hour or so engaged in peer review activities—no, I can't imagine it. Why would a creative writing teacher announce peer review activities when the vast majority of creative writing classes follow the workshop model, which is built *entirely* upon peer review? Teachers don't need to plan a specific time for classmates to respond to each other's drafts because that is all, or nearly all, that a workshop class does.

So is the creative writing workshop just composition's peer review writ large and extended to fill the entire semester? Hardly. In composition, as you can tell from my list above or from the extensive discussions in the literature, peer review has many faces and plays many roles. But the workshop model that dominates creative writing classes seems monolithic—at least, we creative writing teachers speak of it as though we were all speaking of the same thing. I asked the composition faculty in my department to email me a brief description of their peer review activities, and from their notes I constructed the two paragraphs above listing the variety of techniques employed by one small (12 faculty) composition program.

Reading their many varied descriptions of something they each called "peer review," I felt like I had stepped into the fable of the blind men and the elephant. But when I spoke with my creative writing colleagues about how they organized their creative writing workshops, I wondered if we'd all earned our MFA's from the same school. During the week I made my inquiries, my playwriting class was workshopping one act plays, a colleague teaching a fiction section said his class had just begun workshopping stories, another colleague teaching a multi-genre introduction to creative writing said her students were preparing to workshop their stories next week, and the poet in the department described how her students posted their poems online and then how they read and discussed the poems in small groups. Workshopping, every one of us.

While the poet organized her class into small groups to workshop, I had my students move their desks into something vaguely resembling a square so we could face each other during discussion. One of the fiction teachers was fortunate enough to teach in a classroom with a huge library table everyone could sit around while they talked about their work. But whether they were in desks or at a table, in a square, rectangle or circle, the students were workshopping their writing, that is, they were talking with each other about their writing. There were none of the more elaborate kinds of structured feedback activities that typified what my composition colleagues were doing for peer review. In the creative writing classes, student work was discussed in a relatively unstructured and often unpredictable way.

Reading academic articles about creative writing workshop practices reinforced my sense of an undefined but shared practice called "workshopping." In the introduction to the ground-breaking book he co-authored with Wendy Bishop, *Colors of a Different Horse: Rethinking Creative Writing Theory and Pedagogy*, Hans Ostrom describes the creative writing workshop "in its simplest form: 'going over' poems and stories in a big circle" (xiv)—an ambiguous description at best. What constitutes "going over"? Graeme Harper, in his foreword to *Does the Writing Workshop Still Work?*, insinuates that a workshop can't be described except loosely as "an exchange of human experiences" (xix). Philip Gross reiterates the same point, calling the workshop "a very human situation" (52), refusing to define it as more than "communication between people" (58).

In essence, the workshop method is a conversation, not a series of exercises. While it may produce some of the same kinds of feedback that the structured exercises commonly used in composition classes do, that is neither the goal nor the intention. The purpose of the creative writing workshop is to have writers, plural, talk about their writing. What form that conversation takes, what kinds of ideas it generates for the writer whose work is being discussed, and what use the writer makes of any such ideas depends entirely on the participants. Ideally, the creative writing teacher facilitates that conversation rather than shaping or directing it to predetermined ends. In practice, of course, all of us who teach creative writing betray our own biases and preferences in comments we make about the writing being workshopped. That's inevitable, unavoidable, and utterly human. But it's not our goal to generate a specific kind of feedback for the writer. That's what makes the workshop so different from the kinds of feedback assignments and exercises common in composition classes.

The very openness of the creative writing workshop model makes it adaptable to a multitude of classes and students, but it has also left workshop pedagogy largely untheorized. While creative writing programs have flourished in terms of enrollment, they continue to struggle for legitimacy among academics because of their lack of theories that might guide pedagogy. In her article "Teaching Creative Writing if the Shoe Fits," Katharine Haake points out that while most creative writing workshops have little or no theory shaping them, the workshop has dominated creative writing pedagogy. How has that happened?

The writing workshop model established by the University of Iowa Writers Workshop in the early 20th century has been imitated by nearly every MFA program in the country since then. First Iowa, and then an increasing number of creative writing programs, graduated their students, who took with them to whatever jobs they landed a workshop model they internalized while in grad school. The result was the dissemination of a single, dominant, nearly exclusive pedagogy in creative writing programs. While variations exist, a clear set of conventional behaviors are shared by most creative writing workshops: a practicing writer leading student writers in oral commentary in response to something written by one of the members of the community, with an emphasis on the potential in each writing and an exploration of choices the writer might make in subsequent drafts—plus, a deliberate deferral of academic evaluation, i.e., grading.

Workshop pedagogy flourished for a time in both creative writing and composition. The work of Peter Elbow, Janet Emig, Donald Murray, Ken Macrorie, Kenneth Bruffee, et al., put student writers at the center of the composition classroom. Peer feedback became central to the process of developing a piece of writing through several drafts, with peers providing largely unstructured, oral responses to drafts either read aloud or made available through ditto or xerox copies. Bruffee's ideas about collaborative learning in the classroom spawned numerous workshop-like conversations. Macrorie's validation of student writers' voices seemed a perfect fit with Murray's nondirective conversations with student writers as well as with Elbow's freewriting exercises. A convergence of ideas and approaches gave rise to the student-centered expressivist movement in composition, and for a while (a brief Camelot-like moment?), composition and creative writing pedagogies seemed to merge around the workshop.

What happened to distinguish them? Composition veered away from the workshop model as it became a more professional, research-based discipline; teachers adopted more structured and more accountable teaching methods. When I graduated from the Iowa Playwrights Workshop in 1985, I was committed to the workshop method in all my writing classes, creative and composition. In fact, my experiences at Iowa in a theatre workshop reinforced my earlier doctoral work in composition pedagogy, so it was natural to organize and conduct workshops in all my writing classes. I continued to do so well into the 90s, but with an increasing sense of being out of step with the profession—the composition profession, that is, which was paying my salary. Though I persisted in writing plays, my teaching assignments were predominantly in composition, and my academic position included directing or assisting the director of various composition programs. But listening to presentations at CCCC and reading articles in the growing number of composition journals made it clear that while the workshop was still central to my pedagogy, it no longer was for most of my composition colleagues. A shift was taking place in pedagogy that paralleled the development of composition as a legitimate academic discipline, and one of the places that shift was visible was in peer feedback.

Perhaps because of the pervasive academic pressure to theorize—to justify and expand disciplines through the development and application of theory—or perhaps because of a desire to distinguish composition from creative writing, composition teachers moved away from expressivist models and adopted more accountable teaching practices. By "accountable" I mean researchable, providing data that can be measured and analyzed. It's nearly impossible to measure the outcomes of a writing workshop conversation. Both "accountability" and "student learning outcomes" became the lingua franca of academe in the 90s.

At roughly the same time, graduate schools across the country began offering Ph.D. degrees in rhetoric and comp, and these newly minted scholars examined classroom practices through the lenses of the theories they had learned. The result was a slow shift in the teaching of composition over two decades away from Romantic and expressivist pedagogies and toward more research-based and theoretically grounded approaches—away from student-centered workshop dialog to teacher-monitored feedback activities. Still, in spite of their differences, both practices depend on students providing feedback to other students. What separates composition from creative writing today is *who* is doing the teaching, whose voice takes precedence.

In the creative writing workshop, students are teaching students. The teacher's role is to facilitate a conversation among peers, the primary channels of discourse being students-to-students rather than students-to-teacher. In fact, many creative writing teachers complain that their experience and knowledge are marginalized in the traditional workshop. Typical of the criticisms leveled against the workshop model by creative writing teachers is Joseph Michael Moxley's assertion that the workshop approach assumes students already know how to write and are able to tell if a written piece "works" (xiv). Suggestions for improving the workshop model, from Moxley and others, include instruction in prewriting strategies and the writing process, plus a central role for the teacher's feedback. All of which sounds very much like the changes that evolved in composition.

The assumption that novice writers might provide useful feedback to their peers strikes many writing teachers, both compositionists and creative writing instructors, as naive and specious. While Colin Irvine has adapted the workshop to his composition classes, he nonetheless points out that the workshop method asks students to read *developing* drafts and respond meaningfully to what the writer *intended* to achieve. That, he says, is "folly" (138).

Irvine isn't the only teacher to question the wisdom of letting novice writers teach other novice writers. Composition faculty responded by designing exercises to train students in giving feedback, shape and focus their responses, and replace the open-ended conversations typical of the workshop with more limited and directed kinds of feedback, thereby instituting more accountable and more measurable types of peer responses. To do that necessitated more structure and more teacher control, the very things creative writing workshops eschew.

While the various modes of peer review common in composition classrooms rely on peer relationships and peer assistance, the classroom instructor typically remains the central authority, guiding students in the use of whatever rubric or heuristic the activity relies on to generate useful and measurable feedback. While the writer still hears the advice of a peer, that advice is typically structured by the assignment the teacher creates.

In the creative writing workshop, on the other hand, no central authority presides, no single entity shapes responses to the work being discussed; rather, it is the collective and often divergent voices of the many writers in the room that compete for attention. The moment the instructor sets herself or himself up as the model of how to respond to a story or poem or play, the workshop ceases to be a workshop and becomes a class in which students are trying to emulate and please their teacher. A writing workshop is at its liveliest and most useful when no one voice is privileged. The writer hears a cacophony of responses to his or her piece and has to decide which are useful. As Anna Leahy points out in her article "Teaching as a Creative Act: Why the Workshop Works in Creative Writing," the teacher's first responsibility is to create a space in which writers can discover for themselves what works and what doesn't work in their writing. The workshop, in Leahy's words, "allows collective wisdom to flourish" (66). The workshop relies on the collective, while composition classes typically turn to the teacher for the final word of approval.

Perhaps at this point we can articulate a clear and succinct distinction between the creative writing workshop and feedback exercises in composition classes as follows: the goal in the composition class is *generation of useful feedback*, to which end teachers design the exercises and model the kinds of feedback they want. In the creative writing workshop, the goal is creation of *a space in which novice writers may talk about their writing* the way professional writers do. Any feedback the conversation generates is incidental and unpredictable. The conversation has a life of its own, and the workshop teacher's principal—if not exclusive—responsibility is to keep that dialog alive. We don't direct it, we nurture it in whatever direction it goes.

This is not to say that any and all workshop conversations are valuable. Creative writing teachers regularly bemoan the lousy workshop days we all experience, days when all we want is to tell students what is and is not working in their drafts. But to do so destroys the workshop's dynamic, which depends on maintaining the writer's authority. Do it just once, and your students will return the following class period *expecting* you to weigh in again with your judgments. You will have undermined the authority of every writer in the room, except yourself, and disempowered the very voices you wanted to empower.

While composition teachers often spend time training their students in giving useful, pertinent feedback, creative writing teachers risk losing the whole enterprise if they do so. No doubt, training can improve the quality of feedback, but it does so by creating a model of "good" feedback that students strive to achieve. That model inevitably embodies the values of the teacher who assigns it. One result of such instruction is that student writers try to win the teacher's approval by conforming to the teacher's expectations. That seems to work well in first year composition, where one of the goals is competence in a certain kind of academic writing, a genre perceived to have a discernible set of expectations and conventions that shape the discourse. But creative writing faculty hope to nurture the talents of non-academic writers, who work in genres where expectations are ambiguous, conventions fluid, and the demand for "originality" much greater.

Conforming to prescribed expectations, whether by imitating the style of latest PEN/Faulkner Award winner or writing to please the teacher, subverts the workshop's intention of nurturing individuality in style, voice, and subject. A former colleague of mine describes writers who write to please any audience but themselves as "workshop hacks." And it's true that one of the criticisms leveled against creative writing programs that slavishly follow the Iowa model is that the writing produced by students in the program can become quite predictable, so much so that such writing is often characterized as having a definite "workshop style."

So creative writing faculty try to set a course that avoids both Scylla and Charybdis by orchestrating or facilitating a workshop that provides useful feedback to their student writers without imposing on them any expectations, criteria, or guidelines that would subvert their autonomy or authority over their own writing. The workshop model is repeatedly reconsidered, revised, and reinvented by teachers of creative writing, but still, we hang on to it despite our own doubts or the criticisms of our colleagues. One reason for our reluctance to abandon the model is that we are products of writing workshops ourselves. In one way or another, the workshop method worked for us. We labor to make it work for our students. We also hang onto Romantic notions of the autonomous writer and "inspiration" and "creativity," however outmoded those may seem in the postmodern English curricula because those are the ideas that continue to empower young writers. Contemporary literary theories that criticize such notions for being naive are resisted by creative writing teachers because they contradict our sense of what Donald Murray called the "natural, magical art of narrative" (103). In the creative writing workshop, art and narratives are nurtured, not analyzed.

"Magic" and "nurturing" are not terms we usually associate with academic theories, so it's no surprise that creative writing has been criticized for being so unlike the rest of the academy, certainly unlike the rest of English studies. Curious about why creative writing and composition didn't share a common pedagogy, Ted Lardner began a search in hopes of "Locating the Boundaries of Composition and Creative Writing," but he concluded that, when it came to creative writing, there was "no *discipline* there" (74). And the reason he offered for finding "no discipline" was that creative writing teachers rarely write about their teaching, and when they do they rarely cite each other's works. In other words, they don't behave like academic scholars. Furthermore, Lardner noted that creative writing remained committed to an "unproblematic notion of an *author* as a unified consciousness at the core of creative production . . . though the poststructuralist critique calls [that] into question" (75). Similarly, Nicole Cooley has argued that while creative writing teachers aim to "foster in students a distinctive voice," they do so without taking into consideration that the "network of assumptions surrounding *voice*" have not been fully examined (99). There you have it: Lardner and Cooley expected to find current literary theories reflected in the teaching of creative writing. But they weren't, still aren't, perhaps never shall be, for the simple reason that creative writing faculty have resisted such theories. We have a vested interest in sustaining the illusion of a "unified consciousness" in order to keep producing creative work, and we may not wish to consider the "network of assumptions" underlying our naive, but highly useful, notions about authorship and voice and creativity and the magic of narrative.

For a couple of years, my department assigned me to teach the introductory undergraduate course in literary theory. I labored mightily to help my students understand why contemporary theorists perceive the text as unstable and why discussion of authorial intention, or authorship at all, might be problematic from a postmodern point of view. But each day, when I left class, I had to turn my back on the very arguments I made in class. I had to build a wall between my intellectual understanding of lit theory and my own writing process. If I hadn't, if I had allowed Roland Barthes to sneak into my consciousness, I wouldn't have been able to finish the play I was working on. I have faith—however naive or unexamined it may be—in the "natural, magical art of narrative" and it sustains my creative work. Literary theories are tools I play with, from time to time, to tease out new possibilities for *literary analysis*, but they are utterly incompatible with my writing process. For that reason, I never bring them up in my creative writing workshops. They do not serve creative writing. I do my best to resist theory.

But the academic trend favoring theory is hard to resist. Almost alone during the great rush to theory of the past thirty to forty years, creative writing has remained, in Patrick Bizzaro's words, "the realm of writers teaching what they and other writers do when they write" (46). The workshop serves as a highly adaptable, craft-centered pedagogical structure in which theory can be ignored, for the most part, and experience given its due.

To be honest, not all creative writing faculty are comfortable resisting theory. Some have wondered if theory shouldn't be included in creative writing classes. Wendy Bishop and Hans Ostrom, in their essay collection *Colors of a Different Horse*, were among the first to reconsider the creative writing workshop. Ostrom asks, in his introduction to their volume, "what might be gained by dismantling the workshop model altogether and starting from scratch?" (xx). Chief among the many criticisms leveled at the creative writing workshop by Ostrom and others (Dawson, Donnelly, Hesse, Irvine, Lim, etc.) is the absence of theory. Kelly Ritter and Stephanie Vanderslice worry that without theory to ground them, practices like the creative writing workshop may outgrow their usefulness.

Dorothy Donnelly worries that the teaching of creative writing may "falter" without some sort of theoretical framework (15).

Yet the field is growing. By all accounts, the number of creative writing programs at the undergraduate and graduate levels continues to increase annually. According to the Association of Writers and Writing Programs, the number of creative writing programs at all levels—A.A.. to Ph.D.—grew ten-fold from 1975 to 2012 (AWP 2012), that is, from 79 programs to 880! The AWP's most recent report (2015) now counts 972 total programs in the U.S. While popularity among students is hardly a defense against charges of lack of theoretical underpinnings, still something is working. The MFA degree and the parallel BA emphasis in creative writing are attracting students and faculty. Apparently, the lack of pedagogical theory has not caused programs to "falter," as Donnelly feared.

Perhaps what some perceive as a lack of theory is a problem of perception, a consequence of *what* they are looking for. If we switch focus from the *literary* theories that creative writing faculty have traditionally resisted to *learning* theories, the creative writing workshop no longer looks so bereft of theory. Learning theory focuses not on a text, but on the learner, specifically *how* the learner learns. The humanistic goals of education were articulated early in the 20th C. by John Dewey, and later endorsed by many teachers/philosophers, including notably Alfred North Whitehead. Both philosophers argue for the kind of student-centered education embodied in the principles of the creative writing workshop.

More recently, the biological theories of Frank Wilson, Robert Ochsner, and Antonio Demasio explore the consequences for writing instruction of current scientific research about the way our bodies shape what we learn and how we learn it. Wilson's studies of how the evolution of the human hand spurred development of the human brain, particularly the frontal lobes necessary for coordination of the hand, lead him to conclude that education should be less about authorized knowledge and more about individual exploration, more child-oriented. In other words, more like the creative writing workshop and less like lecture or teacher-controlled exercises. Ochsner reminds us that there is no language without a body to learn it, hear it and speak it. "Prose originates in a student's body" (28), and the body plays a huge role in the act of composing, a "precognitive" role. Which is to say, we learn to write in large part by doing it over and over again, through an accumulation of experiences, precisely the way writers in a workshop learn from one another. Demasio also advocates for more student-centered pedagogies, with a particular emphasis on "play"—by which he means unstructured activity in which the learners' autonomy is embodied in the decisions they make. While a writers workshop is hardly *un*structured, it is far more loosely organized than most classroom activities, certainly more than the peer review exercises we've been comparing, and sometimes, in the best moments, the workshop conversation rises to the level of "play," voices overlapping each other, laughter spilling across the table or around the room, and we share a sharpened sense of how delightful this playing with words we call "creative writing" can be. It's such moments that Wilson, Ochsner, and Demasio have in mind when they each recommend the workshop approach as one of the best pedagogical strategies for empowering students and enabling learning.

Research into the learning process itself helps us understand why the workshop "works." Neurological studies of how the brain learns new behaviors, like writing, suggest to cognitive researchers like John Bruer that learners benefit when they are given the time and space to struggle on their own to adopt new ideas, new behaviors, new processes. The workshop provides the time, the space, and plenty of new challenges. And recent research into the physiology of the brain by Renate and Geoffrey Caines, among others, reveals what is happening in the brain as we learn to use language. Learning is a much more active process than the traditional lecture method would suggest. Learners need to be engaged in talking, listening, reading, and valuing, the Caines argue, because the human brain learns best by actively *doing*. At its best, the creative writing workshop generates the kinds of conversation that engage learners in talking with fellow writers, listening to readers of their own work, reading a wide range of writing styles, and—of course—deciding what they value and don't value. In creative writing workshops, where authority is decentralized, novice writers can get that kind of rich, engaging, and empowering experience.

The groundwork has been laid for a more appropriate theoretical explanation of the creative writing workshop—not by literary theory, which focuses on analysis of text and context, but by learning theories, which focus on the process of the learner/writer. The more we examine theories *other than* literary theories the more apparent it becomes that the creative writing workshop has persisted in large part *because* creative writing teachers have resisted the general academic trend toward theory, specifically the adoption of literary theories. Like the human brain itself, the workshop thrives by being used, while simultaneously eluding efforts to analyze it.

Part of the criticism of the workshop method derives from mistaken generalizations about what goes on in a workshop, including, for example, assumptions that the purpose of all creative writing workshops is to train professional writers or that competing with one another for status makes students cruel commentators on their peers' work, or that the workshop functions like the traditional mentor-apprentice relationship, with the apprentice working side by side with the master. Certainly, some workshops have as a goal the training of the next generation of creative writers—graduate programs with the status to attract the most ambitious of young writers. But the vast majority of creative writing classes serve students with far less lofty ambitions: students who dream of being writers but don't expect to leave the workshop with a published piece, or students who merely want to become better at something they enjoy doing. When I asked my undergraduate creative writing students if any of them hoped or expected to become professional writers, none raised a hand. A couple chuckled aloud, and one muttered, "Well, maybe . . . someday."

My students are neither competitive nor cruel; in fact there's nothing to compete for, not even the teacher's blessing, since I praise and encourage all of them, no matter how weak their drafts may be, and I steadfastly refuse to grade their work in the optimistic belief that young writers need plenty of encouragement just to keep writing. If they complete the assignments—if they do the writing—they get A's. By being generous, I hope to encourage them to keep writing, to write more. But not all creative writing teachers eschew grades. One of my colleagues, confident in her ability to judge the quality of the students' final manuscripts, assigns grades in a time-honored fashion. Another gives high grades to all those students who take the workshop seriously and whose work shows some sort of development after their pieces were workshopped. Another announces to students and colleagues that he is fulfilling the traditional academic role by evaluating the students' writing but quietly gives nearly all A's, as uncertain about how to judge and as uncomfortable with having to grade as I am. I've made the case elsewhere that grades should have no place in any writing class, but it's particularly out of place in a course where the writers' authority is taken for granted every time the workshop meets. At the end of the term, to suddenly wrest authority from the writers and restore the teacher's institutional power by assigning grades subverts the entire idea of a workshop.

The focus, then, of my workshops is not on the publishable piece but on learning about writing. The shared conversation in the workshop is the heart and soul of that learning process. The pressure of school and jobs, and the values of the university itself, all press against students' desires to write creatively, so I try not to add to those inhibiting forces. Which means, of course, that my classes are far removed from the model of mentor-apprentice. I am not instructing them in how to do something, nor am I modeling a certain kind of writing so they can imitate me. Quite the contrary, like most of the creative writing teachers I know, I encourage my students to develop their own voices, their own strategies, their own processes, and their own goals for writing. I resist telling student writers how to go about doing those things just as I resist grading their work. I would never presume to grade a colleague's latest story or poem, nor do I expect to be graded when I share the draft of a new play with actors and directors. Because I want my students to learn about how professional writers behave, I treat them and their manuscripts the same way.

Which raises the question, why limit workshop pedagogy to creative writing? Wouldn't the workshop approach be just as appropriate for composition classes? I think workshops are appropriate for any writing class, and I'm certain there are teachers out there who continue, in spite of current trends, to run their composition classes as workshops. But most don't, and their reasons for not doing so have nothing to do with the appropriateness or inappropriateness of the workshop and everything to do with the changing culture in which composition teachers are now trained, a culture that emphasizes accountability, measurability, and academic conventions of writing.

For the first half of my teaching career, I used a workshop approach in all my writing classes: freshman comp, introductory creative writing, expository prose, and playwriting. The workshop "worked" in all of them to varying degrees, the degree of success dependent not on the sophistication or age of the student writers but on the particular mix of personalities in any given workshop. I would have continued using workshops in all my writing classes, struggling every semester to make each workshop as effective, as much fun, and as supportive as the last successful one, but the arrival of portfolio grading in the 90s unexpectedly made composition teachers accountable to each other. Where before we read and graded our student papers alone, now we were meeting in groups, reading and scoring *each other's* student essays. The success or failure of your own students in conforming to the expectations—the rubric—of the portfolio scoring team became public and transparent. Everyone knew how everyone else's students were faring. In an effort to help my students improve their scores, I spent less time nurturing the conversation in workshops and more time providing directive feedback myself, or constructing exercises to help students give more useful feedback to each other. With portfolio readers providing a final judgement on the quality of each student's writing, I felt the pressure to help students get better scores. The workshop is not an effective means of raising portfolio scores, so for a time I drifted away from a workshop pedagogy in order to help my students meet the expectations of the portfolio scorers.

There are many benefits to portfolio scoring, and when I was invited to create a brand new composition program for a new campus of the California State University system, I made sure portfolio scoring was at the center of the program, so I'm not criticizing the portfolio system. Nor am I suggesting that portfolios were the primary reason composition shifted away from workshop pedagogy; as noted earlier, there were several movements in academe and graduate composition programs that contributed to the move toward accountability.

But for me personally, it was portfolios that changed my classroom pedagogy. I championed portfolio scoring for composition classes, joined portfolio scoring groups at institutions where they were already in place or set them up in programs where they didn't yet exist. Portfolios were, and are, a boon to composition, but with their arrival, I could no longer think of my composition students the way I did my creative writing students. I needed to help my comp students succeed in the short run, by the end of term, or their grades and student careers might be in jeopardy. No such pressure, no such outside evaluation compelled me to think about the immediate institutional survival of my creative writing students. I continued to nurture their long-term development as writers through workshops, never fretting over the details of a single manuscript but always keeping my eyes on their potential as writers.

If we want students to become writers, and to develop careers as professional writers, then we must treat them as writers, confer upon them the same respect and authority we grant the poets and novelists and playwrights in our departments. That's what makes the creative writing workshop "work": writers talking to writers, not teachers instructing students. One of the chief virtues of the workshop is the multiplicity of kinds of advice writers receive. No one voice dominates, no one kind of advice is privileged. Student writers face what all writers face, a variety of suggestions, often contradictory. Instead of relying on a teacher to decide which advice ought to be followed in the next draft, workshop students have to make those choices themselves, just like writers do. And whether they choose wisely or not, they learn from the experience. They learn how writers think, how writers decide, and how writers behave. That, then, is the promise and the potential of the creative writing workshop.

As I prepare to meet my Creative Nonfiction workshop on Monday, I look over the manuscripts students have submitted. Memoirs. I pair up writers whose memoirs have similarities I think might prompt discussion, or whose style contrasts dramatically with each other. I think about the students who are reluctant to speak and how I might encourage them to participate. I worry about students who've been absent and may need to be reintegrated into the workshop group. In other words, I think about the students and their conversations. I don't mark up the manuscripts, I don't make notes on content, I certainly don't edit or correct or revise any of their work. That's their job. And I don't create the kind of structured review exercise I do in my composition or literature classes. My job in the creative writing workshop is to facilitate *their* conversation, to make it easier for them to talk and behave like writers. And to praise them. For each memoir, I find something that deserves attention and praise, something that we can celebrate in class, something I hope the other students in the workshop will articulate—but if they don't, I am ready to step in and make my contribution: singing the praises of writers. It's a job I relish.

And I wonder, why don't I do this in my composition classes? Has something valuable been lost by replacing workshops with directed peer review exercises? Yes, of course, all change involves some loss. Composition has traded the open-endedness and unpredictability of the workshop dialog for more practical, useful feedback which quite likely helps students succeed in college. Those are noble goals and I'm not suggesting composition abandon them to return to the workshop model. But I am suggesting composition teachers consider if such practical and immediate goals are enough.

The writing process revolution of the 60s and 70s began with big dreams: rethinking entirely the ways we teach writing. Along the way we discovered that treating students as writers—respecting their process and treating their drafts not as minefields full of errors but full of potential—often transformed the writers themselves from reluctant scriveners, revising what they were told to revise and trying desperately to please the teacher, to enthusiastic writers who wanted to write and wanted to share their writing with others.

I can't help but wonder if, in our efforts to improve the writing itself, we compositionists have neglected the writers? By evolving beyond the open-ended workshop model into a more teacher-directed peer feedback model, have we neglected the paradigm-changing insights of the process approach in favor of tangible, but short-term gains? The virtue of many of the teacher-designed peer review activities is that they result in better writing. But do they make better writers? Are students simply following the advice they receive in order to improve their grade, or are they changing the way they think about writing and about their own writing process?

So I conclude this article, and my forty year career as a teacher of both composition and creative writing, with a challenge for compositionists. Look carefully at what students do when they leave our composition classes. Do they voluntarily seek out feedback? Do they think of themselves as writers or students writing? Do they want to write more and hear how others respond to their writing? Because if they resort to older writing habits after the composition class experience, then no matter how wonderful the prose they produce during our classes is, we have failed them. We have given them nothing to carry beyond our classes. We have not transformed them from students into writers.

The virtue of the creative writing workshop is the potential it has for just such conversions.

WORKS CITED

Association of Writers and Writing Programs. *Growth of Creative Writing Programs*. 2012. AWP, Fairfax, VA, https://www.awpwriter.org/application/ublic/pdf/.

Association of Writers and Writing Programs. *Survey of Creative Writing Programs*. 2015. AWP, Fairfax, VA, https://www.awpwriter.org/application/public/pdf/survey/.

Barthes, Roland. "The Death of the Author." *Image/Music/Text*, translated by Stephen Heath. Hill and Wang, 1977, 142–47.
Bishop, Wendy, and Hans Ostrom, editors. *Colors of a Different Horse: Rethinking Creative Writing Theory and Pedagogy*. National Council Teachers of English, 1994.
Bizarro, Patrick. "Workshop: An Ontological Study." *Does the Writing Workshop Still Work?* edited by Dorothy Donnelly, Multilingual Matters, 2010, pp. 36–52.
Bourke, Nike, and Philip Neilsen. "The Problem of Exegesis in Creative Writing Higher Degrees." *TEXT*, vol. 3 (special issue), 2004, http://www.textjournal.com.au/speciss/issue3/bourke.htm.
Bruer, John. *Schools for Thought: A Science of Learning in the Classroom*. MIT Press, 1993.
Bruffee, Kenneth A. *Collaborative Learning*. Johns Hopkins UP, 1998.
Caine, Renate Nummela, and Geoffrey Caine. *Making Connections: Teaching and the Human Brain*. Association for Supervision and Curriculum Development, 1991.
Cooley, Nicole. "Literary Legacies and Critical Transformations: Teaching Creative Writing in the Public Urban University." *Pedagogy: Critical Approaches to Teaching Literature, Language, Composition, and Culture*, vol. 3, no. 1, 2003, pp. 99–103.
Damasio, Antonio. *Descartes' Error: Emotion, Reason, and the Human Brain*. Avon, 1994.
Dawson, Paul. *Creative Writing and the New Humanities*. Routledge, 2005.
Deen, Rosemary, and Marie Ponsot. *Beat Not the Poor Desk*. Heinemann/Boynton-Cook, 1989.
Dewey, John. *Democracy and Education*. Macmillan, 1916.
Donnelly, Dianne. "Introduction: If It Ain't Broke, Don't Fix It; Or, Change is Inevitable, Except from a Vending Machine." *Does the Writing Workshop Still Work?* edited by Dorothy Donnelly, Multilingual Matters, 2010, pp. 1–27.
Elbow, Peter. "Ranking, Evaluating, and Liking: Sorting Out Three Forms of Judgement." *College English*, vol. 55, no. 2, 1993, pp. 187–206.
Emig, Janet. *The Composing Processes of Twelfth Graders*. National Council Teachers of English, 1971.
Gross, Philip. "Small Worlds: What Works in Workshops, If and When They Do?" *Does the Writing Workshop Still Work?* edited by Dorothy Donnelly, Multilingual Matters, 2010, pp. 52–62.
Haake, Katharine. "Teaching Creative Writing If the Shoe Fits." *Colors of a Different Horse: Rethinking Creative Writing Theory and Pedagogy*, edited by Wendy Bishop and Hans Ostrom, National Council Teachers of English, 1994, pp. 77–99.
Harper, Graeme. "Foreword: On Experience." *Does the Writing Workshop Still Work?* edited by Dorothy Donnelly, Multilingual Matters, 2010, pp. xv–xx.
Hecq, Dominique. "Theory." *TEXT*, vol. 15, no. 2, 2011, www.textjournal.com.au/oct11/hecq_poetry.htm.
Hesse, Douglas. "The Place of Creative Writing in Composition Studies." *College Composition and Communication*, vol. 62, no. 1, 2010, pp. 31–52.
Irvine, Colin. "'Its fine, I gess': Problems with the Workshop Model in College Composition Classes." *Does the Writing Workshop Still Work?* edited by Dorothy Donnelly, Multilingual Matters, 2010, pp. 130–45.

Kerr, Jo-Anne. "Writing Workshop and Real-World Learning: A Deweyian Perspective." *The Quarterly*, vol. 21, no. 3, 1999, www.nwp.org/cs/public/print/resource/809

Lardner, Ted. "Locating the Boundaries of Composition and Creative Writing." *College Composition and Communication*, vol. 51, no. 1, 1999, pp. 72–77.

Leahy, Anna. "Teaching as a Creative Act: Why the Workshop Works in Creative Writing." *Does the Writing Workshop Still Work?* edited by Dorothy Donnelly, Multilingual Matters, 2010, pp. 62–77.

Lim, Shirley Geok-lin. "The Strangeness of Creative Writing: An Institutional Query." *Pedagogy: Critical Approaches to Teaching Literature, Language, Composition, and Culture*, vol. 3, no. 2, 2003, pp. 151–69.

Lobb, Joshua. "'They don't flinch': Creative Writing/Critical Theory, Pedagogy/Students." *The Encounters: Place, Situation, Context Papers—the Refereed Proceedings of the 17th Conference of the Australasian Association of Writing Programs*, edited by P. West et al., AAWP Press, 2012, pp. 1–13.

Macrorie, Ken. *Telling Writing*. Hayden, 1970.

———. *A Vulnerable Teacher*. Hayden, 1974.

Mayberry, Bob. *UnTeaching: A Writing Teacher's Odyssey*. CreateSpace, 2017.

Moneyhun, Clyde. "Response to Doug Hesse's 'The Place of Creative Writing in Composition Studies.'" *College Composition and Communication*, vol. 63, no. 3, 2012, pp. 520–27.

Murray, Donald. "Unlearning to Write." *Writing to Learn*. Holt Rinehart and Winston, 1993.

Ochsner, Robert S. *Physical Eloquence and the Biology of Writing*. SUNY Press, 1994.

Ostrom, Hans. "Introduction: Of Radishes and Shadows, Theory and Pedagogy." *Colors of a Different Horse: Rethinking Creative Writing Theory and Pedagogy*, edited by Wendy Bishop and Hans Ostrom, NCTE, 1994, pp. xi–xxiii.

Papert, Seymour. *Mindstorms: Children, Computers, and Powerful Ideas*. Basic Books, 1980.

Pinker, Stephen. *The Language Instinct: How the Mind Creates Language*. William Morrow, 1994.

Ritter, Kelly, and Stephanie Vanderslice. "Creative Writing and the Persistence of 'Lore.'" *Can It Really Be Taught?: Resisting Lore in Creative Writing Pedagogy*, edited by Kelly Ritter & Stephanie Vanderslice, Boynton Cook, 2007, pp. xi–xx.

Smith, Frank. *Insult to Intelligence: The Bureaucratic Invasion of Our Classrooms*. Boynton Cook, 1986.

Swander, Mary, et al. "Theories of Creativity and Creative Writing Pedagogy." *Handbook of Creative Writing*, edited by Steven Earnshaw, Edinburgh UP, 2007, pp. 11–23.

Whitehead, Alfred North. "Aims of Education." *An Anthology*. Macmillan, 1953.

Wilson, Frank R. *The Hand: How Its Use Shapes the Brain, Language, and Human Culture*. Pantheon, 1988.

CHAPTER 3.

A TROUBLED PRACTICE: THREE MODELS OF PEER REVIEW AND THE PROBLEMS UNDERLYING THEM

Christopher Weaver
William Paterson University

Although peer review is a practice that is closely associated with the writing process movement of the seventies and early eighties, it is now widely adopted by both high school and college classrooms without regard to any particular pedagogy. But if peer review has been a constant even as the discipline has changed, it has remained a troubled practice, with both teachers and students often expressing frustration and dissatisfaction with its results. In this chapter, I will argue that this dissatisfaction stems in large part from the problematic nature of the goals underlying peer review. At times, these goals have not been well articulated; at other times, they have not been shared between students and teachers; and finally, these goals, both articulated and unarticulated may not be achievable, particularly within first year composition courses.

In considering the goals and resulting practices of peer review, I will examine it from the perspective of three different models:

1. **The Collaborative Model** which emerged from the writing process movement and posits the goal of peer review as a community of readers helping the writer to discover their meaning.
2. **The Proxy Model** which posits that the goal of peer review is not to help the writer discover their purpose but rather to improve their text so that they will meet the requirements of the instructor. While this model pre-dates the process-movement, it has never been far from high school and college writing instruction, and it has made a resurgence in an era where teachers and administrators are concerned with measurable growth and accountability.
3. **The Disciplinary/Professional Model** which has emerged more recently and posits that the goal of peer review is to familiarize students with a specific rhetorical genre and an academic and professional practice.

The first two models are largely incompatible with each other, though that doesn't mean that they don't co-exist in many writing classrooms where writing teachers have not fully understood and theorized their goals. The third model is a thoughtful and theoretically grounded attempt to work through some of the problems and contradictions of the prior models, though I will argue that it is ultimately unsuccessful in doing so. In spite of their differences, each of these models holds out the same promise of peer review as a transformative practice. Each model is underpinned by the idea that students can learn from each other and that by sharing and responding to each other's writing, they can begin to change their understanding of what writing is and how writing works in a way that would not be possible if they received feedback from their writing instructor alone. However, for each model, this promise runs up against a hard truth: that students, at best, struggle to understand the transformation that is being asked of them and, at worst, resist this transformation.

THE COLLABORATIVE MODEL

Peer review, as it emerged from the pedagogy of the process movement, emphasized the writer's authority over their own text and often insisted that writing instructors needed to diminish their presence in order to make room for the writer to claim this authority. For early advocates of peer review, the authenticity of the writer's relationship with readers was more important than the instructor's expertise, and the teacher's presence posed a danger to the relationship between the writer and readers. Peter Elbow wrote about the power of getting feedback from "fellow students who were no more expert than themselves" (*Writing Without Teachers*, xx). Other compositionists warned that the teacher's presence posed a danger to writers seeking reactions from readers. Donald Murray stressed that "The teacher must give the responsibility for the text to the writer, making clear again and again that it is the student, not the teacher, who decides what the writing means" (34). Lil Brannon and C.H. Knoblauch warned that the "normal and dynamic relationship between a writer's authority and a reader's attention" is likely to be disrupted by "the peculiar relationship between teacher and student" (158). These composition scholars' concern with writers claiming authority and readers helping them to do so without the undue interference of instructors was crucial to creating the dynamics of peer response groups in the era of process pedagogy. The label most often associated with such a process was "writing workshop," a term that evoked graduate programs in creative writing where writers shared and reacted to each other's work. In addition to borrowing some of the pedagogy of these workshops, the term also worked to confer a sense of agency and prestige that was absent from freshman composition at the time.

The importance of student-to-student collaboration was emphasized by Kenneth Bruffee, who, in his 1984 article, "Collaborative Learning and the 'Conversation of Mankind,'" attempted to articulate the theoretical underpinnings of peer review by focusing on the term "collaborative learning." Like the process theorists before him, Bruffee highlighted the importance of students learning from each other. Still, he also articulated the social constructionist perspective that knowledge in a discipline is not passed down by instruction but created through community life. The key to community, Bruffee suggested, is conversation. "What students do when working collaboratively on their writing is not write or edit, or, least of all, read proof. What they do is converse" (Bruffee 645).

But what *kind* of conversation was likely to lead to the outcomes these compositionists desired? For Elbow, at least, the answer was a conversation that valued both the goals and intentions of the writer and the richness and complexity of the writing process itself. Elbow, in particular among the process theorists, has been labeled (sometimes derisively) an expressivist for his interest in student writing that centers on thoughts and experiences. However, where Elbow is most clearly an expressivist is not so much in the kind of writing he advocates (for he also encourages student writing that grapples with ideas) but in the language he uses for describing the writing process itself and in his suggestions for forms of response that take place in peer review. He relies heavily on metaphors, comparing the writing process to cooking (*Writing Without Teachers*) and to wrestling with a snake without killing it (*Writing with Power*), and he also encourages students to use metaphor in their responses to each other's writing (*Sharing and Responding*). Furthermore, Elbow asserts that the kind of feedback students often need most is descriptive feedback—not judgments about whether their writing is good or not but an account of how their writing affects readers. (This position is most clearly articulated in *Sharing and Responding* by the feedback technique that Elbow and Belanoff call "Movies of the Reader's Mind.")

There is much in this collaborative model of peer review that speaks to teachers like me who began their careers influenced by process pedagogy: the idea of empowering students to claim agency over their own learning, the prestige of writing as the kind of rewarding activity that is practiced in creative writing workshops, and the framing of the writing process as something rich and complex rather than rote and formulaic. Yet many of us have found that centering a first-year composition class around the collaborative model of peer review is highly problematic. One problem comes from the artifacts we create in order to guide peer response groups. While we may envision our prompts and worksheets as open-ended and encouraging writerly conversations, they may be more controlling than we think. Mark Hall describes just such a discovery in his article, "The Politics of Peer Response" when he looks at his own worksheet and tries to analyze it not as a set of neutral prompts that allow students to discover the meaning within their texts but rather as a document whose ideological agenda is hidden. Read through this lens, he concludes that "the entire worksheet shows evidence—not of the liberating, student-centered pedagogy I intend—but of the worst sort of controlling and domesticating educational practice" (6) and that "students may be so busy serving my interests in filling out the worksheet that peer response fails to meet their need to talk and to listen actively to each other about their writing" (8). By insisting that student response be guided by his questions, Hall realized that he was substituting his authority for their goals and values and cutting off the kind of student-centered conversation necessary for real collaboration. In an article about students' perceptions of peer review, Charlotte Brammer and Mary Rees come to the same conclusion: that handouts with lists of questions lead to "a lot of writing but little interaction" (79). In response to this problem, Hall, speculates on the possibility of students being asked to create their own set of questions for peer review.

In my experience, however, the difficulty with trying to guide students through the peer review process is not so much a problem of me imposing my goals and values on them as it is their reluctance to embrace the idea of writing as a collaborative act. Rather than viewing writing as a process of discovering and working out their own ideas, sharing those ideas with each other, and entering a conversation about how meaning is made, they hold onto the current-traditionalist view of writing that has been reinforced by textbooks, high school teachers, and standardized tests. They see writing as a set of static forms and features such as narrative or persuasive essays and introductions, thesis statements, transitions, and conclusions. Far from appropriating their texts, when I give them prompts that ask them to describe and respond to each other's writing, they simply ignore my questions and default to their earlier view of writing by either proofreading each other's papers or badly approximating their idea of teacher talk: making one-size-fits-all suggestions such as "add more details" or "use more examples." While it might be argued that as a writing teacher my job is to help them leave this old model of the writing process behind and replace it with a more dynamic one, this sort of persuasion is an uphill battle to say the least. Not only are most students more comfortable with directive feedback than they are with the ambiguity of a writerly conversation; their entire experience with education has been in support of this type of learning. Moreover, even if I could persuade them to see writing differently, the university at large does not support a collaborative model of learning and does not reinforce the idea that writing is a way of making meaning. Teaching students using a collaborative model of peer review contradicts the social and institutional spaces in which they have been raised and in which they will be asked to do their work. It is no wonder then that when they are asked to participate in peer review activities, they react with a mixture of confusion, frustration, apathy, or occasionally even hostility.

As to Hall's suggestion that students be invited to create their own set of questions for peer review, this idea pre-supposes both that students have a framework for imagining such questions in the first place and that, in the second place, they would be willing participants in this process if they could be. In fact, I have tried something similar: having students construct their own rubrics for articulating their goals and evaluating their own writing. My students were confused and frustrated by this process because they were used to writing assignments where the goals were established by the instructor. They lacked a vocabulary and conceptual framework for articulating goals and criteria, and when after some initial hesitation and confusion about what I was asking them to do, they completed the assignment, their rubrics mimicked overly general goals that they had been required to meet in previous assignments such as "having clear ideas," "writing without mistakes," and "conveying my point." In short, the advocates of the collaborative model of peer review all emphasize the role of conversation among students who identify themselves and each other as writers with a sense of agency and authority, but my experience has been that the students themselves are unlikely to understand the terms or share the goals of this kind of conversation.

THE PROXY MODEL

In this model of peer review, the goal is not for students to collaborate with each other in order to work out the meaning of a text but rather to read each other's writing and reach an approximation of the teacher's goals and values. Students' judgments of their peers' writing are proxies for the judgments of their instructor, and the goal of peer review is not a conversation about how writing works on multiple readers but rather a judgment about how well writing reflects the instructor's values and meets their standards. Thus, the prompts for the proxy model of peer review are likely to be aimed at identifying strengths and weaknesses and at augmenting the former and fixing the latter.

This model of peer review reflects a kind of traditionalist instruction that pre-dates the process movement but that, in truth, continues to be present in high school and college writing classes. While writing courses have adopted peer review as a practice, they may not have adopted the goals and values of Elbow, Bruffee et al. In fact, in his reconsideration of the history of writing groups, Kory Lawson Ching suggests that in spite of the process movement's focus on student collaboration, "peer response may not have emerged so much out of a move to decenter classroom authority but instead as a way for students to share some of the teacher's burden" ("Peer Response" 308).

But whether the goal is burden sharing or teaching students to understand and imitate institutional values, the proxy model of peer review does not align well with the theories of discourse and knowledge creation described by theorists like Bruffee. However, as the writing process movement has faded into the romantic past and with the move towards standardized testing, rubrics, and institutional accountability, this model has gained traction and even a certain amount of credibility, if not in the discipline of composition and rhetoric, then at least in schools of education. In particular, I've noticed over the last decade how the term "actionable feedback" has entered the lexicon in education. I first encountered this term in a 2012 article by Grant Wiggins in the journal *Educational Leadership* entitled "Seven Keys to Effective Feedback." Wiggins argues that an essential quality of good feedback is that it must be "actionable":

> Effective feedback is concrete, specific, and useful; it provides actionable information. Thus, 'Good job!' and 'You did that wrong' and B+ are not feedback at all. We can easily imagine the learners asking themselves in response to these comments, What *specifically* should I do more or less of next time, based on this information? No idea. They don't know what was "good" or "wrong" about what they did. (4–5)

Wiggins' article has been widely cited by teaching blogs as well as by articles and consultants in business management that aim to improve employees' performance by providing them with more efficient feedback. Underlying the idea of "actionable feedback" is the assumption that the eventual goal, both in the classroom and the workplace, is to help the student or employee to improve in the opinion of their teacher/supervisor. "Actionable" means that the person receiving the feedback can make changes in order to improve their standing in the eyes of the person doing the evaluating. Whereas the collaborative model emphasizes student agency and warns against the teacher appropriating the student's text, the proxy model accepts the teacher's institutional authority and sees peer review as a tool for teaching students to reproduce their values and judgments about writing in order to achieve academic success.

While it abandons the student-centered pedagogy of the collaborative model, the proxy model has the advantage of more closely aligning with the goals of many students, particularly those in freshman writing classes. When I ask my students at the beginning of each semester what they expect to happen in my college writing course, most of them say that they want and expect to receive feedback that will make their writing better. I always end each course that I teach by giving students a survey where I list a number of activities we have done over the semester and ask them to rate the usefulness of each. In the twenty years I have been giving this survey, not a single class has rated the usefulness "peer feedback" as equal to or greater than the usefulness of "feedback from the instructor." Students tend to see the role of feedback as to improve their performance, and since I am the evaluator, they value my feedback more highly than that of their peers. In other words, even after a semester in which I use the language of process pedagogy and in which I try to complicate the model of the writing process that they have brought with them from high school, they continue to align themselves with the proxy model rather than with the collaborative model. For this reason alone, in spite of its shortcomings, the proxy model may be worth writing teachers' reconsideration.

Of course, a major difficulty of this model of feedback is that students do not make good proxies for teachers. They do not possess the same evaluative criteria that we do, and they often misinterpret or misapply those criteria when they give feedback. This gap, however, can be a useful opportunity for teachers to examine and make explicit the criteria that we use to evaluate student writing. I have found that within limited circumstances, the proxy model of peer review can improve students understanding of specific disciplinary conventions and rhetorical moves.

One example of this has been the kind of peer review process I have used in my introductory freshman literature course. I ask student groups to review each other's rough drafts against a specific set of criteria that is particularly relevant to the genre of literary analysis. The first time I used this process, I outlined four different criteria for students to evaluate. However, students struggled so much with this feedback that I quickly cut the criteria to two items. I ask reviewers to identify a thesis or, if no thesis is clear, to suggest one that the rest of the draft might point to. And I also ask them to identify specific places where the writer analyzes the readings as well as places where they merely summarize, pointing to specific examples of each.

Students post their drafts and their feedback to their classmates online so that I can read them. I don't respond to the draft at this stage of the writing process, but I do give each student's feedback to their classmate a score from 1–4 as well as a brief explanation for my score. The scores do not count towards the students' grades, but I tell them that they are important because they indicate an understanding (or lack thereof) of the criteria I will apply to their final drafts. I tell them that if they score a 3 or 4, then they are well underway to understanding my requirements for success in their papers. If they score lower than that, then they should review those criteria, and possibly we should meet to discuss their misunderstanding. Depending on the class I am teaching, students go through this peer review process 3–4 times over the semester.

Looking back over the six classes that I have taught using this method, I can see that between their first peer review group and their final one, the average student's feedback score improved from 1.9 to 2.8, not a dramatic improvement, perhaps, but a significant one. However, in addition to seeing students become better peer reviewers, the class benefited from a more thorough discussion of some of the criteria that were central to success in the papers that students wrote for the course. The process of peer review became the vehicle through which students and I defined and applied the criteria I articulated as the key to success for the genre. This process harnesses students' preconceptions that it's the instructor with expertise that they need to look to for guidance while also valuing the process of peer review group as the site for understanding and applying these criteria. It also mitigates students' concerns that their classmates do not know enough to give good peer reviews by letting them know that I am overseeing the process and entering the discussion after the reviews have been given. At this point in the process, I respond only to the reviews and not to the drafts themselves.

The advantage of assessing peer reviews rather than initial student drafts is that it conveys that the idea that peer review is valuable not for its ability to offer the *writer* useful advice that will improve her paper but for the opportunity it presents to the *reviewer* to see and to assess the variety of strategies that other student writers deploy and to understand the criteria for successful writing so that they might apply it to their own drafts. Indeed, this peer review benefit is emphasized by a number of contemporary scholars. In her article, "Peer Review for Peer Review's Sake: Resituating Peer Review Pedagogy," E. Shelley Reid emphasizes this shift in focus "from the possible products of peer review . . . to the gains made during the *process* of peer review itself" (218). Reid argues that reviewers benefit as much or more than writers because "they learn to understand a new writing task the way professionals learn, by closely reviewing multiple examples in the genre" (220). Melissa Meeks picks up on Reid's shift in focus from writer to reviewer, referring to reviewers' ability to understand and apply specific criteria for success as "giver's gain," and concluding that "Students who can talk to peers about the criteria are best able to apply them to their own work" (Meeks, "Give One, Get One").

However, although the proxy model can have some benefits, it also has significant limitations. For one, although some scholars complain that peer review may have become an entrenched practice for overworked teachers as a form of labor sharing, the process I have described certainly does not have that advantage. Peer review is only labor saving if it requires less intervention from instructors than reading and responding to student drafts. This process required me to read all of my students' drafts as well as all of the feedback given by their classmates. I usually put students into groups of 3–4, so that meant reading 2–3 peer reviews for every draft. Admittedly, these were short, initial drafts, and I didn't respond to the drafts themselves but only the peer reviews. Still, this process took somewhat longer than simply responding to each draft alone. A common refrain in the scholarship on peer review is that it requires more time spent training students in how to read and respond to each other, and this was clearly true in my classes. Moreover, in order for my version of peer review to succeed, I had to limit its focus to understanding and improving particular genre features. While these review criteria were useful in the context of a literature classroom, it's debatable whether they would transfer to another writing situation. Formulating and supporting a thesis is a highly disciplinary activity, and to the degree that this kind of proxy feedback is useful in a literature course, it is probably much less so in a class like freshman writing that attempts a wider variety of writing tasks.

Finally, this kind of peer review crowds out other writing issues, including a more freewheeling discussion of the content of their writing. Even focusing on just four criteria proved overwhelming to my students and forced me to narrow my focus to the two above. An investment in certain types of peer feedback is also a decision not to spend time on other aspects of a class, an opportunity cost that any teacher must consider. And, of course, the proxy model defines writing almost entirely as meeting the expectations of an evaluator—itself an impoverished view of the writing process and one that minimizes student agency.

THE DISCIPLINARY/PROFESSIONAL MODEL

In the past two decades, some composition scholars have sought to address the conflicting goals of the collaborative and proxy models. These scholars seek to reframe peer review neither as a path for the student to claim authority and agency as a writer nor as an unquestioning submission to teacher authority, but rather as an academic and professional practice that students can analyze and emulate. There is substantial work being done from this perspective, but I would like to address articles by three scholars whom I think make interesting suggestions and whom I think are fairly representative of this new approach to peer review: Elizabeth Parfitt, Mark Hall, and Kory Lawson Ching.

In "Establishing the Genre of Peer Review" Elizabeth Parfitt outlines a class in which short writing assignments exist in large part as springboards at first for peer reviews of those assignments and later for longer written assignments where students rhetorically analyze their own peer reviews. Through analysis and discussion of their own reviews, the students learn what an effective example of the genre looks like. Parfitt justifies her emphasis on this genre over others by arguing that peer review best exemplifies the kind of professional activity that students may encounter outside of the writing classroom:

> Framing peer review as a genre with its own rhetorical components allows students to begin thinking about their writing as professional. When professional writers receive reviews of their work, they are presented with multiple voices, opinions, and often requests asking the author to respond by prioritizing statements of critique they deem most useful for the given purpose and audience. (2)

I mentioned Mark Hall earlier in this chapter as a teacher who realized that his attempts to guide students through prompts and worksheets were not liberating but rather overly controlling. In "The Politics of Peer Review," Hall replaces them with a series of "gateway activities" that he believes will lead the class to an examination of peer review as a practice. He first asks students about their prior experiences with peer review and has them compile a list of what sorts of feedback are effective or ineffective. Then he selects student texts and gives feedback to them alongside of his students, and he asks them to compare his comments and responding strategies with theirs. Finally, he has them revisit to and revise their original list of criteria for effective responses. Like Parfitt, Hall wants to make the practice of peer review more central to the writing classroom. He believes that this series of activities makes the process of peer review visible and open to interrogation.

Kory Lawson Ching is another scholar who argues for making the practice of peer feedback explicit and visible. Like Hall, Ching argues that instructors can never really remove their authority from peer review groups because their presence will always be felt through their evaluative criteria and reproduced in peer review groups by "(problematic and incomplete) mimicry" (24). Whereas Hall creates "gateway activities" to initiate students into a discussion of peer review strategies, Ching suggests that replacing peer-only groups with instructor-led groups creates a "contact zone" where the norms and practices of peer response can be exposed and questioned. Ching explains how having the instructor lead peer review groups builds on familiar relationships in the writing classroom (reviewer-writer and instructor-writer) by adding a new relationship (instructor-reviewer). He argues that this relationship "potentially complicates received notions of authority, autonomy, and ownership" (21) by highlighting the instructor's dual role as both collaborator and guide:

> Part of this relationship is collaborative (or at least cooperative), in that both the instructor and the student-reviewers are mutually engaged in the activity of offering feedback to the writer. But this

> relationship is also instructional, in that another objective of the peer conference is that reviewers learn, with guidance and assistance from the instructor, how to generate that feedback. (23)

These scholars share a number of assumptions and practices that differentiate them from the earlier collaborative and proxy models. They all recognize that students bring with them outmoded and ineffective approaches to peer review and believe that these approaches must be replaced through explicit instruction. In order to do so, they present models of practice that increase the time spent on peer review in a writing class, often arguing that the peer review assignment should receive equal or greater attention than the "real" texts that are reviewed. The quotation marks around the word "real" appear in Parfitt's article and demonstrate these scholars' rejection of the idea that peer review is ancillary to other types of writing rather than a legitimate genre itself. For them, there is no writing activity more real than peer review. These scholars recognize the issue of student authority as problematic, but they reject both the collaborative model's belief that student agency will be enhanced if the instructor's role in response is effaced and also the proxy model's implicit assumption that peer groups can replicate the teacher's values and standards without first understanding peer review as a disciplinary practice that is rhetorically situated. They respond to the problem of authority by adopting peer review strategies that make the practice and the teacher's modes of responding more visible and thus subject to questioning and analysis. To this end, they not only make the practice the subject of scrutiny but also analyze the "review" as a specific genre of writing. Finally, they note that older practices of peer review have failed because they have not generated the kind of conversation that Kenneth Bruffee claimed was necessary for collaborative learning to take place. When such conversation is missing, peer review becomes merely an exercise in copy editing. Contemporary peer review theorists address the problem of "conversation" by attempting to model and initiate students into a particular *kind* of conversation—not the "writerly" conversation of early peer review advocates like Elbow and Murray, but a conversation shaped and guided by instructors and one which represents peer review as a disciplinary and professional practice.

There is much about this new approach to peer review that I find interesting and admirable. I have a great deal of respect for these scholars' honesty about the problems of collaboration and authority and their attempts to make these issues visible and subject to questioning. However, it seems to me that the disciplinary/professional model of peer review is no more likely to persuade students to adopt it than earlier models. It recognizes that in order for peer review to work, teachers need to engage students in a conversation about writing, but its success depends upon students being any more interested in the kind of conversation that it proposes than they were in the kinds of complex conversations about writing favored by the collaborative model. Rather than asking them to imagine themselves as writers pursuing their own goals, it asks them to imagine themselves engaging in the discourse practices of other kinds of communities—academic and professional. Based on my experience with students, particularly freshmen, the idea that they can be enticed to join a conversation because it represents the discourse of the academy or of some imagined eventual employer strikes me as unrealistic. Perhaps recognizing the enormity of this task, the proponents of the disciplinary/professional model advocate making training in peer review the central focus of the writing class and devoting much more time to it. But this means spending less time focusing on other aspects of the writing process, and it means entirely reframing the process of sharing and responding to each other's writing around a set of goals that students may be reluctant to embrace.

CONCLUSION

All three models of peer review have drawbacks that may be insurmountable because teachers and students simply do not share the same goals for peer review, and persuading students to adopt a new set of goals and practices is extremely difficult work. Despite teachers' best efforts, students hang on to their "practical" model of peer review. They tend to want reliable, authoritative, "actionable" feedback that allows them to make specific changes to a draft in order to get a better grade on the next one. Moreover, while many peer review advocates have argued that teachers should devote more time in their classes to train students in peer review and that the process should occupy a more central focus in the classroom, this shift in emphasis comes at a cost: it crowds out other kinds of writing and other activities that writing teachers view as useful.

Yet, despite these problems, peer review deserves to be an important part of any writing class. Peer review deadlines force students to commit less than perfect writing to the page and to share their works-in-progress with an audience. The act of hearing your words read to others is an important part of the writing process even with less than perfect feedback or with none at all. As Elbow puts it, "Surely what writers need most is the experience of being heard . . ." (3). An additional benefit is that whatever feedback and discussion emerges from peer review groups can be a window for teachers into how students are grappling with writing assignments. When teachers can access this feedback, either by observing peer review groups in the class, collecting written reviews, or by overseeing peer review groups online, we can adjust our planning in the rest of the course to more effectively meet students where they are. And finally, as writing scholars like E. Shelley Reid and Melissa Meeks remind us, the process of peer review may be more important for the student giving feedback than the student receiving it. By reading other students' work and considering what responses to give, students come to understand the writing assignment and to consider various ways of responding to it that potentially benefit their own writing.

All of these are good reasons to continue to make ample use of peer review. However, none of them require us to adopt the stance that so many scholars have advocated over the history of all of these models—that we need to devote more time to peer review and make training a more central focus of the writing classroom. Instead, we ought to admit that trying to shift students' modes of peer response through worksheets, training, modeling, rhetorical analysis, or any other technique is unlikely to succeed. This admission allows us up to stop worrying that peer review will yield the kind of results that we insist on and frees us up to reap the benefits of peer review listed in the paragraph above.

Moreover, it also addresses the problems of agency and authority that have plagued peer review since its inception. When teachers stop trying to impose a set of practices or responses on peer review groups, it allows us to be more transparent about our authority at other stages of the writing process. In my writing classes, I have students discuss their experiences with peer review, and when the inevitable reservations come up and they say that they don't trust themselves or their classmates to give good advice, I tell them not to worry about it. I tell them that it's my job as a teacher to give them that advice, which I will do in conferences and in my written comments, and that they should use peer review groups as a chance to share their writing and test it out on readers.

In spite of my early allegiance to the collaborative model of peer review, I accept the lesson of the disciplinary/professional model that we cannot efface our own authority nor expect that our absence will somehow coax students into a more authentic ownership of their own writing. The three models of peer review above all attempt to persuade students to adopt a particular set of goals and practices—although some of these models are more transparent about their agendas than others. I have come to believe that peer review is a poor venue in which to try to enact this kind of persuasion and that it is more useful to envision the writing class in terms of different spaces: the peer review group, which is relatively free of my prescriptions for particular kinds of feedback, and the rest of the class (including readings, discussion, other writing activities and assignments, and my comments to student writing) in which I can be clear about my values, beliefs, and expectations.

This past semester I asked students in my freshman writing class to write a reflective piece about how their writing was affected by readers in different stages of the revision process. In their reflection, one of the students distinguished between the responses they received in their peer review group and the responses they received from me. They wrote: "Your reaction as a teacher guided me towards where I should be going as in comparison where my classmates are only able to give me the feedback as to where I currently am." This student's use of the word *only* indicates the preference common among students for the "usefulness" of teacher feedback to steer them towards a better grade. But while I used to view such an attitude as a failure of peer review as a collaborative process, I now see it as a useful distinction. If the student can rely on my guidance and authority in the future ("where I should be going,") then they are more likely to listen to readers discuss his writing in the present ("where I currently am"). By not placing pressure on peer review to enact the kind of conversation that I want, I hope to create a space where students can share their writing and where conversation may happen on their own terms.

WORKS CITED

Brannon, Lil, and C. H. Knoblauch, "On Students' Rights to Their Own Texts: A Model of Teacher Response." *College Composition and Communication*, vol. 33, no. 2, 1982, pp. 157–66.

Brammer, Charlotte, and Mary Rees, "Peer Review from the Students' Perspective: Invaluable or Invalid?" *Composition Studies*, vol. 35, no. 2, 2007, pp. 71–85.

Bruffee, Kenneth A. "Collaborative Learning and the 'Conversation of Mankind.'" *College English*, vol. 46, no. 7, 1984, pp. 635–52.

Ching, Kory Lawson. "The Instructor-Led Peer Conference." *Peer Pressure, Peer Power: Collaborative Peer Review and Response in the Writing Classroom*, edited by Steven J. Corbett et al., Fountainhead Press, 2014, pp 15–28.

———. "Peer Response in the Composition Classroom: An Alternative Genealogy." *Rhetoric Review*, vol. 26, no. 3, 2007, pp 303–19.

Elbow, Peter and Patricia Belanoff, *Sharing and Responding*. McGraw-Hill, 1999.

Elbow, Peter. "About Responding to Student Writing." Memo. Greenrooftechnologies. net. 31 May 2015.

———. *Writing Without Teachers*. Oxford UP, 1973.

———. *Writing with Power*. Oxford UP, 1981.

Hall, Mark. "The Politics of Peer Response." *The Writing Instructor*, July 2009, https://files.eric.ed.gov/fulltext/EJ890609.pdf.

Meeks, Graham Melissa. "Give One, Get One." *The Eli Review Blog*, December 8, 2016, https://elireview.com/2016/12/08/give-one-get-one.

Murray, Donald M. "Making Meaning Clear, The Logic of Revision." *Journal of Basic Writing*, vol 3, no. 3, 1981, pp. 88–95, https://doi.org/10.37514/JBW-J.1981.3.3.04.

Parfitt, Elizabeth. "Establishing the Genre of Peer Review to Create New Rhetorical Knowledge." *Compendium2*, vol. 5, no.1, 2012, pp. 1–8.

Reid, E. Shelley. *Peer Pressure, Peer Power: Collaborative Peer Review and Response in the Writing Classroom*, edited by Steven J. Corbett, et al., Fountainhead Press, 2014, pp. 217–31.

Wiggins, Grant, "Seven Keys to Effective Feedback." *Educational Leadership*, vol. 70, no.1, Sept 2012, pp. 10–16.

PART TWO. PEER REVIEW: RHETORICALLY SITUATED

CHAPTER 4.

INTERROGATING PEER REVIEW AS "PROXY:" REFRAMING PEER RESPONSE WITHIN CONNECTIVE PRACTICE

Kay Halasek
Ohio State University

Although among the most common pedagogical methods employed in U.S. writing classes, peer review is a classroom practice about which composition scholars and researchers have devoted relatively little attention in recent years. Elizabeth Flynn, for example, reports only fifteen articles on peer review in *College Composition and Communication* and six in *College English* between 1970 and the early 1990s, supporting her claim that "research on the topic arising out [of] mainstream composition studies, for the most part, tapered off in the early 1990s and was replaced, within composition studies, by research focusing on peer review using technology" ("Re-viewing," np). A survey of research on peer review after 2011 affirms Flynn's claims—both her observation about the relatively little attention paid to peer review in scholarly journals and books in composition studies and the direction of that published scholarship, which continues to focus on ELL writers, technologies for peer review, or a combination of the two. (There are, of course, exceptions since 2011, including work in composition studies by Bedore and O'Sullivan and Corbett et al.) As was the case in 2011 when Flynn composed her survey, much of the scholarship on peer review between 2011 and 2017 appears in educational journals, ELL and ESL journals, international journals, and journals devoted to disciplinary writing pedagogies. In *College Composition and Communication* between 2011–2017, for example, only two articles take up peer review (Weiser; Selfe and Hawisher), and both take up *scholarly* peer review, not student peer review. The most relevant dissertations, such as Kristen J. Nielsen's 2011 *Peer Evaluation and Self Assessment: A Comparative Study of the Effectiveness of Two Complex Methods of Writing Instruction in Six Sections of Composition*, come out of other disciplines. In Nielsen's case, the Boston University College of Education.

DOI: https://doi.org/10.37514/PER-B.2023.1961.2.04

Working both from alongside and against recent work on peer review in composition studies and from across disciplines (Brammer and Rees; Corbett et al.; Nielsen; Patchan et al.; Walsh et al.), I propose a means of reframing peer *response* as a connective practice encompassing a range of purposes, modalities, and locations that attends to both generative and formative value. I then address a particular assumption in composition studies that complicates and perhaps even compromises peer response as a connective practice by examining and challenging our own and our students' implicit (and sometimes explicit) belief that peer review is a "proxy" for instructor feedback. In examining peer response as connective practice, I situate it in and refer to data and student examples from the teaching and research that colleagues and I have undertaken since 2013 in several iterations of the second-year writing course at Ohio State in hybrid, face-to-face, and MOOC instructional spaces. I chose these locations in part because the instructional development teams intentionally constructed those courses (offered between Spring 2013 and Spring 2016) with peer response as a defining feature using a locally-developed and locally-administered online platform, WEx, The Writers Exchange.

Before beginning our WEx-based approach to peer response in 2013, those of us on the instructional team regularly employed peer review in our face-to-face courses: designing peer review methods, creating peer review sheets, and modeling for students the kinds of collaborative review we practiced in our own work as writers. We were also aware of the divided nature of research on peer review as early as the 1970s, with some studies demonstrating that peer review had little to no effect on the quality of student writing and others showing gain across a number of skills and affective areas (Griffith 17–20). And, like many writing teachers and scholars (Bedore and O'Sullivan; Brammer and Rees; McKendy), we also often felt disappointed at the inconsistency in the quality and efficacy of peer review in our courses and students' abilities to engage in meaningful, substantive, constructive commentary with one another about their reviews. We also aligned ourselves with John Bean, who argues that without adequately structured peer review activities and instructional support, "peer reviewers may offer eccentric, superficial, or otherwise unhelpful—or even bad—advice" (295). And, we often reflected on the wisdom of Kenneth Bruffee, who told compositionists many years ago, "[p]eer criticism is the hardest writing most students will ever do" (78)—a point that reminded us of the complexity of peer review and the challenge facing students who are asked to engage in the practice.

The hybrid courses and MOOCs gave us the opportunity to both test our assumptions about peer review and extend students' engagement with it. If it were–as we had experienced in face-to-face classrooms–a less than satisfactory activity with unpredictable outcomes for students, why did we continue to include it in our courses? One answer, however unsatisfactory, is disciplinary habit. Peer review has long been a customary and staunchly defended practice in composition studies, with Anne Ruggles Gere dating some of the earliest classroom uses of peer review to the 1880s (17). Coming of age in the 1980s and supported by the work of Piaget and Vygotsky through the social constructivist movement, peer review has stood—if not unassailable (as many of us experience and express concern and frustration about it)—as a ubiquitous practice in college writing classrooms.

REFLECTING HISTORICALLY ON PEER REVIEW

A first step in taking up a historical review of the scholarship on peer review is to acknowledge that the terminology around the practice is inconsistent—both historically and in contemporary scholarship. Although peer "review" appears to be the most frequently used term, peer "evaluation," peer "assessment," peer "criticism," peer "grading," and peer "response" are also common. Throughout this chapter, I use peer "review" to connote those activities most commonly aligned with the practice: in-class written or spoken feedback on or assessment of a piece of writing typically guided by instructor-developed guidelines and feedback forms. I distinguish peer "review" from peer "response," a much broader term that encompasses other forms of feedback with much broader ranges of purpose, modality, and location. Given this distinction, peer "review" is a *form* or *type* of peer response but not synonymous with it.

Even after the early work on peer review in the 1970s, 1980s, and 1990s, in which researchers situated peer review as one means of establishing exigency for conversation and creating authentic social contexts and audiences for writing (e.g., Bruffee; George; Grimm; Holt; Newkirk), peer review has rarely been valued as a rhetorical act of knowledge making or textual production in and of itself. Instead, more often than not, peer review is positioned almost exclusively in service to "real" classroom writing, those compositions for which students receive a grade. Whereas the audience for peer review may be more "real" (that is, not simply the teacher), the contexts, investments, and stakes rarely are, relegating the activity to a role as an ancillary practice. Moreover, it is not a practice defined or enacted in composition studies scholarship in terms of universal or participatory design. Peer review–if completed during a single class session in which students read and comment on one or more peers' drafts–is not an accessible practice for students who, under the pressures of time constraints, socio-emotional stressors, and other factors, may not perform to their highest ability, an actuality students themselves report. The PIT Core Publishing Collective, for example, relates several students' apprehensions and the impact of their past experiences with peer review as affecting their view of peer review, noting, in particular, the challenges to students of "time-driven" in-class processes that mitigate against "quality-driven" responses (108).

Complicating matters even further, the scholarship regarding students' valuing of peer review is—like much scholarship on the subject—not definitive. Peckham claims that students prefer their peers' responses over instructors (62), while more recent research (especially in L2 contexts) suggests otherwise (Braine; McCorkle et al.; Ruecker). Peer review has been, to my knowledge, almost exclusively a teacher-conceived and teacher-monitored practice, a point made by others, as well (Nielsen). Certainly, other scholars in the past forty years have argued for a richer, more engaged and connective understanding of peer review (DiPardo and Freeman; Ellman; Newkirk, "How Students"). Some scholars (Ede, Nielsen, Griffith) also call into question the proxy model, but by-and-large, the disciplinary understanding and deployment of peer review remains informed by the proxy model, wherein student peer review stands in for or supplements instructor feedback and evaluation.

Moreover, as a discipline, we harbor a kind of collective uncertainty about the value and effectiveness of peer review and have not come to a consistent understanding of just what it is we want peer review to do—or even how it should be deployed in our classrooms (Ashley et al.). The most frequent understanding, however, is that of peer review as proxy for teacher commentary and evaluation, an understanding, I argue, that problematically limits the possibilities of peer response as a connective practice, subordinating it and ignoring its possibilities both as substantive commentary and rhetorical practice. In short, when student writers, student peer reviewers, and teachers conceive of peer review as a proxy for teacher feedback on writing, peer review will fall short of expectation and fail to function as a constitutive feature of instruction and learning.

The problems with proxy are numerous. When assuming the role of proxy, students attempt to mimic evaluative "teacher talk," responding in ways they *believe* teachers would respond (Griffith). They often focus their comments on discrete elements (LOCs, or lower-order concerns) and on correcting error. Because they do not have (and *realize* they do not have) authority as "teacher," they also often have little confidence about their own and their classmates' abilities to provide sufficient (i.e., accurate) response. As a consequence, writers often ignore or discount peers' responses. Peer reviewers are also burdened by the perception that they can't live up to the expectation. They're not teachers, after all. Even when asked to "respond as readers" or as "members of the intended audience," the specter of the teacher continues to overshadow peer reviewers' contributions. Finally, by assuming the proxy role, students essentially distance themselves from their own expertise and perspective, which in turn limits the range of the feedback they provide.

I argue, in short, that when students (as well as teachers) conceive of peer review as a proxy for teacher commentary—peer review is all but bound to fall short of our own and students' goals. To make matters worse—or at least more likely to compromise the value of peer response—how, when, and where we situate peer review in our classrooms also undermines its potential affordances. Peer review that is immediately followed by teacher commentary, for example, is subordinated by that teacher commentary as students reasonably turn to the teacher's response for guidance for revision because attending to teacher commentary is more important to improving grades (PIT Core).

Fundamental to my developing thinking on proxy is Kevin Griffith's 1992 dissertation, *Metalanguage about Writing and the Transition from K-12 to College: The Written Responding Processes of Six First-year Students Entering the University.* In his study, Griffith examined the written peer reviewing practices of first-year college students before they had entered a composition course at the university. His hypothesis—informed by a Bakhtinian understanding of the word as always already partly someone else's—was that students brought with them practices informed by their previous schooling and the habits and voices that dominated that schooling. In short, he "hypothesized that the students' responding behaviors would have clear roots in past experience," and his research bore out that hypothesis as students' "responding language" was "not 'their own' as they entered the university" and the voice most dominating their responses was that of an authoritative "past 'teacher'" (249). With that hypothesis in hand, Griffith's goal was to examine the tendencies and practices students brought with them to the university and the possible sources for those tendencies and practices.

The Bakhtinian has always struck me as a meaningful frame through which to examine composition pedagogy and what our pedagogies and materials relate to students or what students might well infer from our pedagogies and materials (Halasek). Griffith's examination into the voices that populate the narratives students bring with them about peer review serves as a meaningful point of departure for demonstrating that the narrative is one of proxy: The role of students is to mimic (insofar as they are able) the voice of authority, of critic and teacher. Shifting students away from this narrative into the narrative I propose—that of connective practice set within ecologies of writing—entails extending the scope of peer response by enacting practices and creating opportunities for the dialogic that demonstrate the connective nature of writing, responding, and learning and emphasize the qualities of meaningful peer response that Kenneth Bruffee articulated over forty years ago: Clarity, tact, honesty, truthfulness, thoroughness, and helpfulness (78). Another way of putting this is to move from a product- to a process-oriented understanding of peer response (Griffith 5) *and* to extend it beyond responding to drafts of students' formal compositions.

PEER REVIEW AS "PROXY": THE EFFICIENCY ARGUMENT

One of the recurring arguments in the conversation in the scholarly literature about peer review that implicitly situates the student as proxy for the teacher is that of efficiency. The argument, in short, suggests that peer review be implemented in the classroom as a means of lightening instructors' workloads. Both shortly after the turn of the twentieth century and again in the 1970s and later, scholars proposed peer review as a means of reducing instructor workload (Bright, Cook, Ellman, Hardaway, Peckham; Wagner). In fact, these articles make no secret of their positions. Cook's article, for example, is entitled "Reducing the Paper-Load" and Wagner's "How to Avoid Grading Compositions."

Griffith, in critiquing the proxy assumption, cites two studies by Newkirk, giving voice to the opinion (in Newkirk) that the goal of peer review is to mimic teacher response: "Without . . . training, students may respond differently from their teacher, in unpredictable and unsatisfactory ways" (qtd. in Griffith 26). Certainly, training in peer review—even extensive training and repeated practice—is a productive pedagogical intervention, but that training should not take as its end training students to read and respond as teacher. Nielsen makes an observation similar to Griffith's, noting that scholars such as McLeod et al. argue for peer review as a means of managing instructional demands (12). In other words, scholars continue today to leverage the efficiency argument, as Nielsen notes, as we can see demonstrated in numerous locations, such as the "Peer Review and Scaffolded Assignments" on the CUNY-Staten Island writing across the curriculum site, which suggests peer review as a way for teachers to "manage the stress and time of scaffolded assignments" by "divid[ing] the labor" (n.p.).

At the same time the efficiency argument situates peer review as a substitute for teacher feedback, it also subordinates the value of peer evaluation to teacher evaluation. Francine Hardaway demonstrates this contradiction in "What Students Can Do to Take the Burden Off You" when she both argues that "[a]ll the actual work . . . is done by the students" and teachers serve only as a "resource—not as a fount of specious authority" and that "individual conferences are a necessity" for the teacher both as a means of corroborating (certifying) the peer evaluation and as a kind of final check for "special problem[s], or matters not identified by the student evaluators (578). In other words, students' may relieve some of the burden, but—as laborers—they still require managerial supervision and oversight.

Rather than being efficient, the practice as Hardaway outlines it is, in effect, duplicative and therefore massively *inefficient*, not to mention exploitative. If our primary (or even secondary) goal is to reduce our workload and make it more efficient, and if our primary means of accomplishing this is to use students as free labor (essentially as graders), we're exploiting students. Scholars do not acknowledge this material reality of peer review, instead focusing on whether peer review is valid and reliable, whether it stands the test as a marketable commodity. By focusing our attention on determining whether peer review is valid and reliable, we miss the opportunity to ask our research questions differently, to examine, for example, the affordances of students responding from their own experiences, perspectives, and expertise, even if (or perhaps even *because*) those responses don't mimic or align with teacher response. Griffith rightly notes, in my mind, that asking training students to read "according to what the teacher expects they should say . . . reduces peer responding to mere parceling of the teacher's task" (27). Peer review in this model is no more than a convenient means of distributing labor away from the instructor and on to the students.

Let me point out that it's not as if only Griffith, Nielsen, and I question what I'm calling the proxy model, but efforts debunking the proxy model are far less common than representations of peer review as proxy. Nonetheless, productive efforts to reframe peer review are worth acknowledging. A quick review of textbooks like those used in the Second-year Writing Program at Ohio State University, for example, demonstrates that compositionists relate to students the various and productive means by which they might engage peer response. Stephen Wilhoit distinguishes productively among various roles for peers reviewing their classmates' work: "average reader," "adviser," and "editor" (307). Jordynn Jack and Katie Rose Guest Pryal encourage students to realize that they have valuable contributions to make if they "draw on [their] own experience as a reader and writer" (482). Lisa Ede explicitly warns students, "Don't attempt to play teacher." "Your job is not to evaluate or grade your classmates' writing but to respond to it" (355). Ede's use of "respond" rather than review is a critical distinction as it signals the critical turn I wish to make in moving away from proxy, as even "review" carries with it suggestions of evaluation, of grading. Moving away from proxy is facilitated by this subtle shift in peers' roles: They respond rather than review.

But other locations in which peer review is described or enacted give conflicting advice. Ede's recommendation and those of Wilhoit and Jack and Pryal contrast with other representations about the purposes and focus of peer review, as with the CUNY-Staten Island website and Peerceptiv, a digital peer review platform, which in its promotional video characterizes peer review as "improv[ing] learning by placing students in the role of the teacher, making assessment part of the learning process." Its website banner also recalls those early efficiency arguments: "Eases Instructor Workload" (Peerceptiv). These are among those many voices students encounter as they are asked to conduct peer review.

MOVING FROM PROXY TO CONNECTIVE PRACTICE

As I mentioned earlier, we also catch glimpses from past scholarship that both question the proxy model and provide a more expansive vision of peer response, as with Anne DiPardo and Sarah Warshauer Freedman, who write,

> Indeed, where group work is seen as a parceling of tasks normally completed by the teacher, any digressions from a given instructor's response norms might be seen as a major flaw; but where groups are conceived as having more fully collaborative life of their own, *providing an extended social context in which to give and receive feedback*, failure to match a teacher's response mode perfectly does not present such a consuming concern. (140; cited in Griffith 32–33; emphasis added)

DiPardo and Freedman's observation emphasizes the value of understanding and enacting peer response as situated within an "extended social context" of the classroom, a defining characteristic of what I term "connective practice." Connective practice is an approach to teaching based on the assumption that all elements of a writing course—from learning outcomes, assessments, and content to classroom activities—circulate around and connect through students' engagement with and responses to those elements. Connective practice integrates peer response fully into all aspects of a course, presents peer response as a rhetorical practice, creates the means through which students understand it as a genre situated within particular contexts and serving particular purposes, and creates the means through which students may construct reflective and cumulative understanding of their writing, peer response, and learning.

Based in part on the principles of backward design (Wiggins and McTighe), connective practice takes peer response as the central means through which knowledge is generated and course objectives are met. Within connective practice, peer response stands, as it does for Steven Corbett, the "prime pedagogical mover" of the course ("More is More" 173). Peer response as connective practice means connecting peer response to and engaging it through all facets of a course and curriculum—not limiting it to commenting on students' more formal compositions. Instead, peer response is enacted throughout a course in multiple forms and modalities for multiple purposes and engages course materials and the theories that inform them. In other words, when enacted as a fully connective practice, peer response is no longer a "stand-alone," "time-driven," "mindless and repetitive task[. . .]," or "evacuated form that lacks substance" (PIT Core 107–8). Instead, it becomes a critical organism, a kind of connective tissue in the ecology of the writing classroom.

In invoking the ecological, I mean to illustrate the reach and impact of peer response as connective practice. Like Marilyn Cooper, I recognize writing as a dynamic social activity and wish to extend that understanding explicitly to peer response, noting in particular that peer responses, like all forms of writing and interpersonal engagements "through which a person is continually engaged with a variety of socially constituted systems," "both determine and are determined by the characteristics of all other writers and writings in the system" (367–368). In terms of peer response as constitutive of connective practice, the ecological model at once acknowledges and demands that the peer response be understood as means through which "writers connect with one another" (369). Given this understanding, to limit peer response to only drafts of formal compositions or peer review to proxy is to deny the critical social functions of response throughout the ecology of the writing and learning taking place in the classroom.

The concept of connective practice draws in small part from Jenny Corbett's work (2001) in special education, which describes "connective pedagogy" as "a form of teaching which opens up creative possibilities to learn" (56). Connective practice also shares characteristics with Dana Lynn Driscoll's "connected pedagogy," which advocates for creating and making explicit connections for students across their learning. Unlike Driscoll's connected pedagogy, however, which focuses on transfer and the importance of connecting learning in first-year writing courses to other courses and students' lives (2013, 70), my focus is decidedly local in that I propose that we examine the connectiveness among the various practices *within* our courses, including how peer response functions with that classroom ecology. Despite the differences between the frames through which we conceive connectiveness, I share with Driscoll two critical observations relevant to connective practice as I conceive it. First, we must debunk the assumption that "students [in their writing courses] are able to make connections . . . themselves," absolving teachers from responsibility to articulate those connections. Second, connectiveness should reside in all elements of a course: "activities, readings, class discussions, writing assignments, metacognitive reflections, and student research" (2013, 71). The practices Driscoll suggests in her work—scaffolding assignments and creating assignments that promote student inquiry, not assuming that students will make connections on their own, and "building in metacognitive reflection . . . and having students monitor their own learning" (2013, 73, 75–6)—are integral principles that guide my concept of connective practice.

I think of connective practice—both within a given cycle of peer response and across an entire course or curriculum—as ecologies informed by Barry Commoner's tenet that "Everything is connected to everything else." Peer response occupies a particular niche in the system but also extends across and throughout a course to multiple kinds of texts with multiple purposes.

Understood as connective practice set within a classroom ecology, peer response can then take on more complex roles and serve greater ends in the classroom as sites of learning about writing, rhetoric, and course content, contributing to the classroom ecology in these "reciprocal, mutually dependent roles" (Nystrand et al., 61). As such, peer response becomes the hub of a "dynamic and integrated system of resources for learning" in a context in which "development in one area often impacts and/or possibly inhibits development in another" (Nystrand et al., 63). In making this claim, I follow the lead of contributors to Corbett et al.'s *Peer Pressure, Peer Power* who articulate the value of connecting peer response to and deploying it throughout all facets of writing courses and situating it as a pivotal practice (Ashley et al., Steven Corbett, LaFrance, PIT Core).

PEER RESPONSE AS CONNECTIVE PRACTICE

Interestingly, some of the most innovative work in peer response that I would identify as connective practice is taking place across the curriculum and being reported in disciplinary pedagogy education journals such as *Teaching Philosophy* and *Assessment & Evaluation in Higher Education*. For example, Kate Padgett Walsh et al. found that a semester-long curriculum that engaged students in a series of peer review (their term) activities surrounding a scaffolded research project improved student writing performance, especially among the least skilled writers (482). Their two-year study demonstrated not that peer review alone but that the integrated (I would say *connective*) practice of scaffolding the research paper into "manageable pieces so that students can practice the skills specific to each task" *along with peer review* of each of these products *together* had the positive effect (482). The study also demonstrates another element of connective practice: separating peer response from grading. Padgett Walsh et al. required students to complete each of the scaffolded assignments and the peer review associated with each (for which they received completion points) (484), but only the final product received a grade from the instructor (483). Although they articulate efficiency as its primary value, the "multiple rounds" of peer review Padgett Walsh et al. built into their scaffolded research paper are critical to the kind of formative feedback peer response offers. Working in cross-ability writing groups and using instructor-developed rubrics, students were prompted to "offer constructive criticism on how to improve the writing" and address strengths and weaknesses in the writing (486). While still closely tied to the traditional concept of peer review, the scaffolded nature of the research project and peer reviewing in peer writing groups created an ongoing exchange between reviewers and writers that facilitated a different understanding of peer review. Students worked in peer writing groups sustained over the term and instruction around the research project aligned with the scaffolded tasks and reviews students composed. For example, instruction in drafting thesis statements preceded a task in which students were asked to review their peers' thesis statements (486). In other words, the content instruction in the course and expectations for the assignment aligned with and informed the peer review tasks students were asked to complete, creating a connective approach that integrated content knowledge, writing task, and peer response.

As has been our experience in using peer response as connective practice here at Ohio State, Padgett Walsh, et al. report that many students in their study commented that they "benefitted more from *giving* feedback, and that they found exposure to the writing of others to be of great value" (493; emphasis added). Steven Corbett describes this disposition toward the value of peer review (as benefitting the reviewer who encounters peers' texts) as a critical point of understanding for students ("More is More" 179). Kristi Lundstrom and Wendy Baker report similar results from their study in which "givers" (those who reviewed peers' writing but did not receive peer review on their own writing) "made more significant gains in their own writing" than "receivers" (those who received review of their writing but did not review their peers' writing) (30). In interpreting their results, Lundstrom and Baker posit (citing Rollinson) that in being taught to conduct peer review and then undertaking peer review, the "givers" were able to "critically self-evaluate their own writing in order to make appropriate revisions" while the receivers, who were instructed only in how to interpret feedback, did not realize the same degree of success in revision (38). The work of Padget Walsh et al. and Lundstrom and Baker point to the importance of understanding peer response as an *exchange*, as a reciprocal act comprised of distinct actions and skills. Their work also anticipates another critical element of peer response as connective practice: understanding and enacting peer response not only as active but also constructive and interactive practices (Chi).

Michelene T. H. Chi's work on conceptual frameworks for learning activities has been instrumental to our instructional team as we have reflected on peer response as connective practice. Distinguishing among passive, active, constructive, and interactive activities, Chi argues convincingly for the value of leveraging the active (making or doing something such as composing a summary or manipulating objects) to the constructive (extending the making or doing by inferring or integrating, elaborating, justifying, linking, reflecting) and elevating it to the interactive in which students dialogue with one another or the instructor in joint learning or creating knowledges, processes, and understanding (77). In terms of peer response, this entails engaging the practice as reciprocal exchange and dialogue—something that goes beyond simply producing a peer review and instead uses reflection to synthesize peer reviews and, ultimately, engages students in dialogue about peer response, which in the connective practice described here takes the form of helpfulness scores and responses.

TOWARD CONNECTIVE PRACTICE: THE "RHETORICAL COMPOSING" MOOC

Between 2013–2016, I was a member of an instructional team that designed and offered the MOOC, "Rhetorical Composing," a second-level writing course. The team for the MOOC initially included Professors Susan Delagrange, Scott Lloyd DeWitt, Ben McCorkle, Cynthia L. Selfe, and me. Ph.D. students on the initial team were Kaitlin Clinnin and Jen Michaels. Our programmer was Cory Staten. In subsequent years, the research team expanded to include Ph.D. Students Michael Blancato and Chad Iwertz. Chase Bollig, Chad Iwertz, and Paula Miller also contributed substantively to developing and delivering the course in hybrid platform. Built intentionally (and out of necessity given the thousands of persons enrolled) as a site in which responses to writing fell entirely to the participant writers in the course, we constructed a systematic approach and digital platform to accommodate peer response. (See Clinnin et al. 2017; Clinnin et al. 2018; Halasek et al.; McCorkle et al. 2016; and McCorkle et al. 2018 for detailed discussions of the Rhetorical Composing MOOC and WEx.) Figure 4.1 depicts the cycle of peer response in the WEx-based MOOC and later hybrid second-year writing courses at Ohio State.

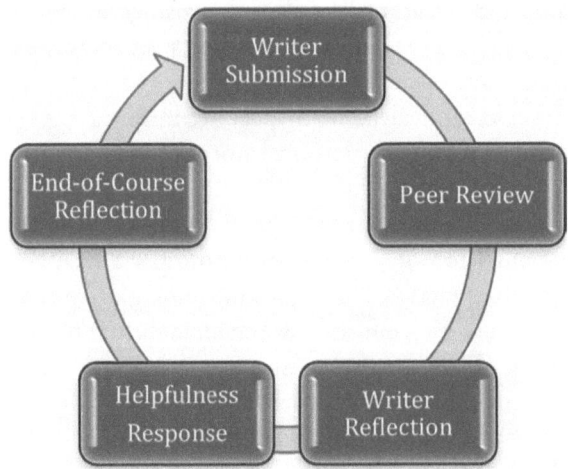

Figure 4.1. The cycle of peer response in WEx.

Students submitted assignments (syntheses, multimodal public service announcements, research-based projects) to WEx, The Writers Exchange, that were randomly assigned to and read by other MOOC participants or students in one of five hybrid sections of our second-year writing course. Once completed, peer reviews were electronically distributed back to authors, who then completed reflections on the peer reviews and created working revision plans based on them. After completing the reflections, authors were prompted to respond to their peer reviewers with feedback on their reviews and provide a rating (1–5) reflecting the helpfulness of the individual reviews. At the end of the term, students also completed end-of-course reflections that engaged all assignments, reviews, self-reflections, and helpfulness scores (both helpfulness scores they both received *and* gave), engaging them in assessing themselves both as writers *and* reviewers. By situating review and response as a system of reciprocal exchange, we sought to engage students in the kind of purposeful reflection that Michelle LaFrance (268) recommends by having writers respond back to peer reviewers with feedback on whether and in what ways their reviews were helpful to the writers as they reflected and began framing revision plans. As we note (McCorkle et al.), Chi's framework provided a means of assessing the degree to which we created constructive and interactive opportunities for peer review in the MOOC. In short, while the peer review stage engaged students actively and the reflection stage allowed students to engage in individual constructive activities, the cycle of peer review represented in Figure 4.1 did not allow for interactive engagement (63). However, interactive engagement *did* occur in course discussion forums and were largely initiated by the participants.

To introduce the goals of response as connective practice, the instructional team created *The WEx Guide to Peer Review*, a digital instructional manual designed to introduce students to the peer response process (DeWitt et al.). The *WEx Guide* employs a Describe-Assess-Suggest model that aligns with recommendations from Bean and others who advocate for descriptive—rather than judgment-based—responses to peers' writing (297). *The WEx Guide* also includes a teaching module, which serves as an informal means of calibrating peer response through an anchor paper. It's important to note, however, that unlike CPR (calibrated peer review) systems, the WEx platform neither prohibits students from completing peer review if their scoring deviates from the norm nor statistically adjusts their scores as in SWoRD (now Peerceptiv). Moreover, the "helpfulness scores" in WEx are not (as in SWoRD or Peerceptiv) "computed from . . . back reviews" (Bean 302) but are assigned directly *by the writers themselves*. Rather than focus our attention on whether students' reviews stood in as a successful proxy for instructor feedback or aligned with other reviewers' scores, we asked students to relay back to peer reviewers whether reviews were "helpful." We gave no specific definition of helpfulness and provided no rubric for scoring helpfulness, instead asking students to "rate each of the reviews . . . received for helpfulness": "The Helpfulness rating is based on how useful the feedback in the peer review was, not necessarily how flattering the review was or how much you agree with the review" (DeWitt 27). We did encourage students to consider when assigning helpfulness scores features of the reviews (as opposed to their content) such as its clarity and specificity and whether the review included "concrete, practical advice to improve your paper" (*WEx Training Guide* 27).

Although this chapter does not provide detailed description or analysis of the MOOC and hybrid data sets, the data sets from which I select examples and in which I situate claims include 140 assignment submissions, peer reviews for those submissions, peer review scores, reflections, helpfulness scores and course evaluations from students in five sections of the hybrid course; 12 focus group interviews with students in the hybrid sections; 1200 submissions, peer reviews of those submissions, peer review scores, reflections, and helpfulness scores from participants in the MOOC; and 327 MOOC participant discussion forum posts. These data are part of "Writing II: Rhetorical Composing in MOOC Environments," an IRB approved research project at Ohio State (2013B0076).

STUDENTS COMMENT ON PEER RESPONSE

The final two stages of peer review in WEx—writers' reflections and helpfulness responses—stand as the critical elements in the WEx cycle of peer response as connective practice. These two stages stand in contrast to more traditional deployments of peer review in which the cycle is significantly truncated—with writers handing their assignments to peers who complete the peer review and return it to the writer. Peer reviewers receive no feedback on their feedback. Unless classmates informally relate information to reviewers about their reviews, reviewers have no means of knowing whether their feedback was helpful. Moreover, instructors using peer review in these face-to-face contexts will likely not even see peer reviews until the writers turn in their final versions. WEx has demonstrated to those of us on the OSU instructional team that when situated as that "prime pedagogical mover," a robust, extensive, and integrated approach to peer response enhances students' writing experiences, their writing, and their conceptual understanding of writing, rhetoric, and course content.

One student exchange in WEx that illustrated for me the power of self-reflection as a critical part of peer response as connective practice is one between a peer reviewer and writer. In response to a draft of a synthesis assignment the peer reviewer wrote the following (anonymously and in part) to a writer in a different section of the hybrid course: "This writer's style seems distractingly pretentious and deters me from wanting to read the essay. Loosen up! If you're more casual with the essay stylistically, that'll get more people to connect with your essay and your cause." The peer reviewer closed the review by granting the assignment a score of 2 out of 5 ("not very well") for the criterion that asked reviewers to rate how well authors "composed a critical synthesis that is . . . engaging and compelling, created critical reflections, and utilized meaningful evidence to make a claim about the narratives."

In her reflection (which included a response to the peer reviewer who assigned her a "2" on the criterion noted above), the author composed (in part) the following:

> [M]y last peer review noted that my writing style is "distractingly" pretentious and a few others [peer reviewers] said it was difficult to read at times. After reviewing the analytics on WEx, I noticed that I have a high rating for the average characters per word, grade level, and reading ease [elements of descriptive analytics reported through WEx]. I thus think that I need to be conscious of loosening the formality of my writing and word choice. I also need to revise my sentences and recognize which run on and cause confusion.

After composing her reflection, the writer responded with a helpfulness score to the "distractingly pretentious" peer review, assigned it a "5" ("Extremely helpful"). I find several elements of this exchange compelling. First, the peer reviewer describes both the writer's style *and its impact on him as a reader*. Second, he then suggests that by relaxing her style she may also reach more readers, allowing them to "connect" to her piece and the social cause about which she is writing. Third, the writer, rather than take a defensive stance in the reflection, situates the reviewer's comments in terms of others' (who found it "difficult to read") responses and the features of her discourse, concluding with a focused revision plan that attends to these elements of the collective reviews.

By asking students to both reflect on the peer reviews they received and then assign helpfulness scores and compose responses to their peer reviewers, many conversations (meditated through WEx) like the one above ensued, giving both reviewers and writers opportunities to extend the conversation *beyond* the peer review. These two steps created critical opportunities connective practice, for peer reviewers to learn how their reviews were being received (and rated) by writers. Particularly in instances when reviews were not as thorough that depicted in the exchange above, writers were willing in the discursive comments that accompanied helpfulness scores to encourage—even request—more substantive and critical responses from their peer reviewers, as in the following example:

> Peer Review Prompt: Please take the time to share a few overall thoughts with this writer about how you read this essay as an audience member, what you felt was done well and how this writer might improve this piece of writing.
>
> Peer Reviewer's Overall Rating of the Essay: 4 ("Very Good")
>
> Peer's Explanation of Rating: I think this blog post is great. As someone who doesn't know much about neutral net your blog post not only gave me information about it but made it easy to read and understand! I like how you threw in your own feelings about it but also gave straight facts.

Responding with a helpfulness rating and explanation, the author of the blog on net neutrality assigned the review a "3" ("Helpful"). The writer thanked the reviewer for the "kind words" but went on to note,

> [T]here is very little constructive criticism in your review. Criticism, to me, is more helpful than just talking someone up. It is nice to know that my hard work was recognized, but don't be afraid to tell me what I did wrong either. Also, you don't have very strong reasons for giving me the scores that you did. . . . I don't mind receiving 4's, but please tell me what to do to improve my writing in the future. . . .

This kind of exchange—in which a peer reviewer assigned an overall score of "4" or "5" on an assignment but provided feedback that writers felt was average or below average in helpfulness—was not unusual in the hybrid course or MOOC and became a point of focused conversation in class and on discussion forums among the students and between students and the instructors. What the exchange above illustrates for me is the critical nature of that penultimate stage, of the author informing the peer reviewer that the review was only marginally helpful and why. The reviewer (who received helpfulness scores and comments from all of the peers whose work he reviewed) was then in a position to reflect on and synthesize those scores and comments before engaging in the next round of peer reviews. As a final stage in the cycle of response, students completed final course reflections in which they self-assessed both their work as writers and reviewers, allowing a longer holistic view and assessment of their work in the course.

A WORK IN PROGRESS: IMPLEMENTING PEER RESPONSE AS CONNECTIVE PRACTICE

As I reflect on the MOOC and assess our subsequent hybrid implementations of "Rhetorical Composing" through the lens of peer response as connective practice, I see we fell well short in some respects and succeeded in others. As we conceived of peer response and intentionally employed it in the classes, we limited it largely to responses to submitted drafts of assignments. In other words, we did not construct opportunities for peer response that moved outside of the traditional model—although we did deploy a dialogic, active, and reciprocal process of peer response in WEx by including reflections and helpfulness as features. Largely because of the affordances of the technologies available during the MOOCs, however, peer response did, in fact, inform participants' learning outside of WEx as participants themselves engaged in constructive dialogue about writing and learning and connective practice on discussion boards and in a participant-initiated and participant-led Google Community (Halasek et al.; McCorkle et al. 2018).

Elevating peer response to connective practice cannot, however, be left to chance. It must be systematic and intentional. As I note earlier, connective practice entails integrating peer response fully into all aspects of a course, discussing peer response as a rhetorical practice, creating the means through which students understand it as a genre situated within a particular context and serving a particular purpose, and creating the means through students may construct reflective and cumulative understanding of their writing, peer response, and learning, as illustrated in Figure 4.2.

As I reconceive my own teaching in writing courses in hybrid and face-to-face contexts to move fully toward peer response as connective practice, I ask myself five critical questions that prompt me to move beyond peer response as peer review:

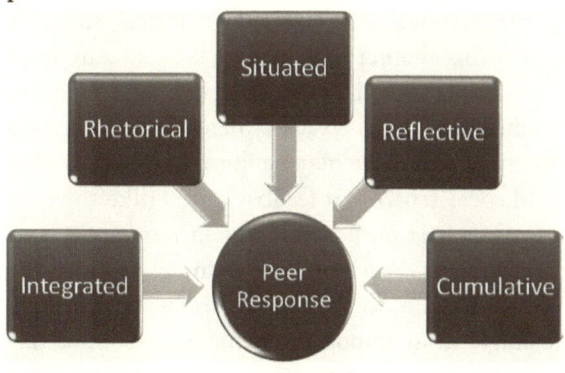

Figure 4.2. Peer response as connected practice

- In what ways might I better introduce, instruct about, and create more and better *integrated* approaches to peer response throughout my course? Specifically, how might I integrate it with other elements, activities, and goals that inform the course?
- What does it mean (and what does it look like to students and to me) to describe peer response as a *rhetorical* act? What pedagogical and scholarly sources might facilitate this understanding?
- What pedagogical strategies can I use, and what activities can I create that will demonstrate to students the *situated* nature of and purposeful nature of peer response?
- How might I encourage a *reflective* understanding of peer response—especially the value of having students reflect on what they learn about their own composing and learning by seeing and commenting others' work?
- As we near the end of the term, what kinds of exercises, activities, or assignments might I craft that will encourage students to reflect in a *cumulative* fashion on the various ways they've engaged peer responses during the term?

Peer response as connective practice, in other words, not only includes but also goes beyond implementing conventional best practices such as offering instruction in peer review, providing guidelines, modeling, using rubrics, incentivizing review, and articulating the objectives of peer review (Corbett et al. 6). Connective practice requires careful, consistent, and repeated efforts to *demonstrate* and guide students toward a new understanding of peer response as integral to and integrated into the whole of the classroom ecology. Even as our MOOC instructional team strived to create opportunities for peer response, we were still employing practices that did not enable students to achieve the level of engaged learning and peer response that we sought. What does it look like to understand and deploy peer response as integrated, rhetorical, situated, reflective, and cumulative? In fact, this chapter has already taken up a number of these elements, noting, for example, the situated, reflective, and cumulative nature of peer response, reflections, and self-assessment. What it means to articulate peer response as rhetorical practice may be illustrated by the *WEx Guide*, in which students are told consistently that feedback itself (like any type of communication) is "rhetorical" as it is purposeful, audience-oriented, and defined by a particular context (DeWitt). Peer response, as integrated into the whole of the classroom and its curriculum, as the "prime pedagogical mover" (Corbett 173), is perhaps the single most important element in demonstrating how peer review is so much more than proxy. By situating peer response alongside and within the particular pedagogical and theoretical frames of our courses, we elevate peer response.

In our hybrid classrooms and later iterations of the MOOC, we have begun to be much more intentional about situating discussions of and building opportunities for peer response in terms of scholarship on revision and research-based writing, both of which were integral parts of the writing objectives for the course. In short, we recognized the importance of making instruction in and practices of revision and research-based writing integral to the peer response objectives for the course. From Joseph Bizup's "BEAM: A Rhetorical Vocabulary for Teaching Research-based Writing," we now emphasize in peer response for the final research-based project the value of responding in terms of the rhetorical uses of sources as background, exhibit, argument, and method. Doing so allows students to both compose using Bizup's framework for research-based writing and respond from and through that same framework, creating opportunities for students to develop a greater familiarity and facility with the critical terms and strategies Bizup outlines. From Joseph Harris' *Rewriting*, we take the set of questions he proposes for writers as they draft and deploy them as peer response questions (98): *What's your project? What works? What else might be said?* and *What's next?*

Linking peer response in these explicit ways to the content of the course (as well as to rhetoric more generally) creates a connective practice in which peer response informs and is informed by theories of writing, research, and rhetoric—not simply that stand-alone," "time-driven," "mindless and repetitive task" or "evacuated form that lacks substance" (PIT Core 107–8).

Reconceiving peer response as connective practice and integrating it fully into the ecology of the writing class entails focusing on the various ways it can be productively deployed beyond typical peer review activities. By understanding both the ecology of peer response and its connections to larger practice and ecology of the writing classroom, we can begin to nudge students (and ourselves) away from the belief that the goal of peer review is to emulate teachers' evaluations or serve as proxies rather than provide helpful, responsive feedback. In effect, a pedagogy that engages peer response as connective practice will shift the focus from evaluating a single piece of writing to ongoing exchanges in which peer responses themselves are understood, engaged, and rated for their helpfulness to writers *as defined by those writers*.

WORKS CITED

Ashley, Hannah, et al. "Apertures and Opportunities: Hanging Peer Review on Our Rubric." *Peer Pressure, Peer Power: Theory and Practice in Peer Review and Response for the Writing Classroom*, edited by Steven J. Corbett et al., Fountain Head, 2014, pp. 195–208.

Bean, John C. *Engaging Ideas: The Professor's Guide to Integrating Writing, Critical Thinking, and Active Learning in the Classroom.* 2nd ed., Jossey-Bass, 2011.

Bedore, Pamela, and Brian O'Sullivan. "Addressing Instructor Ambivalence about Peer Review and Self-Assessment." *WPA,* vol. 34, no. 2, 2011, pp. 11–36.

Braine, George. "ESL Students in First-year Writing Courses: ESL Versus Mainstream Classes." *Journal of Second Language Writing,* vol. 5, no. 2, 1996, pp. 91–107.

Bizup, Joseph. "BEAM: A Rhetorical Vocabulary for Teaching Research-based Writing." *Rhetoric Review,* vol. 27, no. 1, 2008, pp. 72–86.

Brammer, Charlotte, and Mary Rees. "Peer Review from the Students' Perspective: Invaluable or Invalid?" *Composition Studies,* vol.35, no. 2, 2007, pp. 71–85.

Bright, M. Aline. "Pupil Participation in Theme Correction." *The English Journal,* vol. 15, no. 5, 1926, pp. 358–67. *JSTOR,* https://www.jstor.org/stable/802167.

Bruffee, Kenneth A. "Collaborative Learning: Some Practical Models." *College English,* vol. 34, no. 5, 1973, pp. 634–43. *JSTOR,* https://www.jstor.org/stable/375331.

———. "Two Related Issues in Peer Tutoring: Program Structure and Tutor Training." *College Composition and Communication,* vol. 31, no. 1, 1980, pp. 76–80.

Chi, Michelene T.H. "Active-Constructive-Interactive: A Conceptual Framework for Differentiating Learning Activities." *Topics in Cognitive Science,* vol. 1, no. 1, 2009, pp. 73–105.

Clinnin, Kaitlin, et al. "The MOOC as a Souk: Writing Instruction, World Englishes, and Writers at Scale." *Global Communication: Applications for International Communication Exchange,* edited by Kirk St. Amant and Rich Rice, Utah State UP. 2017, pp. 140–60.

Clinnin, Kaitlin, et al. "Meeting Students Where They Are: Practicing Responsive Pedagogy." *Writing for Engagement: Responsive Practice for Social Action,* edited by Mary P. Sheridan et al., Lexington Press, 2018, pp. 225–38.

Cook, Luella B. "Reducing the Paper-Load." *The English Journal,* vol. 21, no. 5, 1932, pp. 364–70. *JSTOR,* https://www.jstor.org/stable/804804.

Cooper, Marilyn M. "The Ecology of Writing." *College English,* vol. 48, no. 4, 1986, pp. 364–75.

Corbett, Jenny. "Teaching Approaches which Support Inclusive Education: A Connective Pedagogy." *British Journal of Special Education,* vol. 28, no. 2, 2001, pp. 55–59.

Corbett, Steven J. "Great Debating: Combining Ancient and Contemporary Methods of Peer Critique." *Kairos,* vol. 19, no. 2, 2015. https://praxis.technorhetoric.net/tiki-index.php?page=PraxisWiki%3A_%3AGreat+Debating.

———. "More is More: Making Guided Peer Response the Center of Our Writing Pedagogy." *Peer Pressure, Peer Power: Theory and Practice in Peer Review and Response for the Writing Classroom,* edited by Steven J. Corbett et al., Fountain Head Press, 2014, pp. 171–81.

Corbett, Steven J., et al., editors. *Peer Pressure, Peer Power: Theory and Practice in Peer Review and Response for the Writing Classroom.* Fountainhead Press, 2014.

DeWitt, Scott Lloyd, et al. *The WEx Training Guide.* Unpublished training manual, Ohio State University, 2014.

DiPardo, Anne, and Sarah Warshauer Freedman. "Peer Response in the Writing

Classroom: Theoretic Foundations and New Directions." *Review of Educational Research*, vol. 58, no. 2, 1988, pp. 119–49.

Driscoll, Dana Lynn. "Connected, Disconnected, or Uncertain: Student Attitudes about Future Writing Contexts and Perceptions of Transfer from First Year Writing to the Disciplines." *Across the Disciplines*, vol. 8, no. 2, 2011, https://doi.org/10.37514/ATD-J.2011.8.2.07.

———. "Connected Pedagogy and Transfer of Learning: An Examination of Graduate Instructor Beliefs Vs. Practices in First-year Writing. *Journal of Teaching Writing*, v. 28, no. 1, 2013, pp. 53–83.

Ede, Lisa. *The Academic Writer: A Brief Guide*. 3rd ed., Bedford/St. Martin's, 2013.

Ellman, Neil. "Peer Evaluation and Peer Grading." *English Journal*, vol. 64, no. 3, 1975, pp. 79–80.

Falchikov, Nancy, and Judy Goldfinch. "Student Peer Assessment in Higher Education: A Meta-Analysis Comparing Peer and Teacher Marks." *Review of Educational Research*, vol. 70, no. 3, 2000, pp. 287–322.

Flynn, Elizabeth A. "Re-Viewing Peer Review." *The Writing Instructor*, Dec. 2011, ERIC. Accessed 6 May 2023, https://files.eric.ed.gov/fulltext/EJ959705.pdf.

———. "Students as Readers of Their Classmates' Writing: Some Implications for Peer Critiquing." *The Writing Instructor*, vol. 3, no. 3, 1984, pp. 120–28.

Fosmire, Michael. "Calibrated Peer Review: A New Tool for Integrating Information Literacy Skills in Writing-intensive Large Classroom Settings." *Libraries and the Academy*, vol. 10, no, 2, 2010, pp. 147–63.

George, Diana. "Working with Peer Groups in the Composition Classroom." *College Composition and Communication*, vol. 35, no. 3, 1984, pp. 320–26. *JSTOR*, https://www.jstor.org/stable/357460.

Gere, Anne Ruggles. *Writing Groups: History. Theory and Implications*. Southern Illinois UP, 1987.

Griffith, Kevin Robert. "Metalanguage about Writing and the Transition from K-12 to College: The Written Responding Processes of Six First-year Students Entering the University." Dissertation, Ohio State University, 1992

Grimm, Nancy. "Improving Students' Responses to Their Peers' Essays." *College Composition and Communication*, vol. 37, no. 1, 1986, pp. 91–94. *JSTOR*, https://www.jstor.org/stable/357386.

Halasek, Kay. *A Pedagogy of Possibility: Bakhtinian Perspectives on Composition Studies*. Southern Illinois UP, 1999.

Halasek, Kay, et al. "A View from a MOOC: How MOOCs Encourage Us to Reexamine Pedagogical Doxa." *The Invasion of the MOOCS*, edited by Steven Krause and Charlie Lowe, Parlor Press, 2014, pp. 156–66.

Hardaway, Francine. "What Students Can Do to Take the Burden Off You." *College English*, vol. 36, no. 5, 1975, pp. 577–80.

Harris, Joseph. *Rewriting: How to do Things with Texts*. Utah State UP, 2006.

Holt, Mara. "The Value of Written Peer Criticism." *College Composition and Communication*, vol. 43, no. 3, 1992, pp. 384–92. *JSTOR*, https://www.jstor.org/stable/358229.

Jack, Jordynn, and Katie Rose Guest Pryal, *How Writing Works: A Guide to Composing Genres*. Oxford UP, 2014.

LaFrance, Michelle. "An Example of Guided Peer Review." *Peer Pressure, Peer Power: Theory and Practice in Peer Review and Response for the Writing Classroom*, edited by Steven J. Corbett et al., Fountain Head Press, 2014, pp. 267–76.

Lundstrom, Kristi, and Wendy Baker. "To Give is Better than to Receive: The Benefits of Peer Review to the Reviewer's Own Writing." *Journal of Second Language Writing*, vol. 18, no. 1, 2009, pp. 30–43.

McCorkle, Ben, et al. "Teaching and Surprise in MOOCs: Developing Responsive Pedagogy at Scale." *Writing for Engagement: Responsive Practice for Social Action*, edited by Mary P. Sheridan et al., Lexington Press, 2018, pp. 209–24.

McCorkle, Ben, et al. "Negotiating World Englishes in a Writing-based MOOC." *Composition Studies* Special Issue on "*Composition's Global Turn: Writing Instruction in Multilingual/ Translingual and Transnational Contexts.*" Guest edited by Brian Ray and Connie Kendall Theado. *Composition Studies*, vol. 44, no. 1, 2016, pp. 53–71.

McKendy, Thomas F. "Legitimizing Peer Response: A Recycling Project for Placement Essays." *College Composition and Communication*, vol. 41, no. 1, 1990, pp. 89–91. *JSTOR*, https://www.jstor.org/stable/357886.

McLeod, Stephen G., et al. "Improving Writing with a PAL: Harnessing the Power of Peer Assisted Learning with the Reader's Assessment Rubrics." *International Journal of Teaching and Learning in Higher Education*, vol. 20, no. 3, 2008, pp. 488–93.

Newkirk, Thomas. "Direction and Misdirection in Peer Response." *College Composition and Communication*, vol. 35, no. 3, 1984, pp. 301–11.

———. "How Students Read Student Papers: An Exploratory Study." *Written Communication*, vol. 1, no. 3, 1984, pp. 283–305.

Nielsen, Kristen J. "Peer Evaluation and Self Assessment: A Comparative Study of the Effectiveness of Two Complex Methods of Writing Instruction in Six Sections of Composition." Dissertation, Boston University, 2012.

Nystrand, Martin, and Deborah Brandt. "Response to Writing as a Context for Learning to Write. *Writing and Response: Models, Methods, and Curricular Change*, edited by Chris Anson, National Council of Teachers of English, 1989.

Nystrand, Martin, et al. "On the Ecology of Classroom Instruction: The Case of Writing in High School English and Social Studies." *Writing as a Learning Tool: Integrating Theory and Practice*, edited by Påivi Tynjålå et al. *Studies in Writing*, vol. 7, series edited by Gert Rijlaarsdam, Boston: Kluwer Academic Publishers. 56–81.

Padgett Walsh, Kate, et al. "Building a Better Term Paper: Integrating Scaffolded Writing and Peer Review." *Teaching Philosophy*, vol. 37, no. 4, 2014, pp. 481–97.

Patchan, Melissa M., et al. "A Validation Study of Students' End Comments: Comparing Comments by Students, a Writing Instructor, and a Content Instructor." *Journal of Writing Research*, vol. 1, no. 2, 2009, pp.124–52.

Peckham, Irvin. "Peer Evaluation." *English Journal*, vol. 67, no. 7, 1978, pp. 61–63.

"Peer Review and Scaffolded Assignments: A Suggestion from John Bean." Writing across the Curriculum @ The College of Staten Island (CUNY), 15 November

2013, https://statenislandwac.wordpress.com/2013/11/15/peer-review-and-scaffolded-assignments-a-suggestion-from-john-bean/.

"Peerceptive Overview." *Peerceptiv,* Panther Learning, 2013, https://youtu.be/dhfAjE4CyhU. Accessed 15 September 2016.

Peerceptiv. Panther Learning, 2013, peerceptiv.com. Accessed 15 September 2016.

PIT Core Publishing Collective. "Peersourcing: A Definition, Justification, and Application." *Peer Pressure, Peer Power: Theory and Practice in Peer Review and Response for the Writing Classroom,* edited by Steven J. Corbett et al., Fountain Head Press, 2014, pp.107–24.

Ruecker, Todd. "Analyzing and Addressing the Effects of Native Speakerism on Linguistically Diverse Peer Review." *Peer Pressure, Peer Power: Theory and Practice in Peer Review and Response for the Writing Classroom,* edited by Steven J. Corbett et al., Fountain Head Press, 2014, pp. 91–105.

Rollinson, Paul. "Using Peer Feedback in the ESL Writing Class." *ELT Journal* vol. 59, no. 1, pp. 23–30.

Selfe, Cynthia L., and Gail Hawisher. "Methodologies of Peer and Editorial Review: Changing Practices." *College Composition and Communication,* vol. 63, no. 4, 2012, pp. 672–98.

Wagner, Eileen. "How to Avoid Grading Compositions." *English Journal,* vol. 64, no. 3, 1975, pp. 76–78.

Weiser, Irwin. "Peer Review in the Tenure and Promotion Process." *College Composition and Communication,* vol. 63, no. 4, 2012, pp. 645–72.

Wiggins, Grant, and Jay McTighe. *Understanding by Design.* Merrill Prentice Hall, 1998.

Wilhoit, Stephen. *A Brief Guide to Writing from Readings.* 6th ed., Longman, 2011.

CHAPTER 5.

PEER PERSUASION: AN ETHOS-BASED THEORY OF IDENTIFICATION AND AUDIENCE AWARENESS

Courtney Stanton
Rutgers University-Newark

Peer review continues to puzzle writing teachers and researchers. Despite its intuitive appeal and an abundance of discussion regarding its potential benefits as an effective tool of process-driven pedagogy (Ching; Lam; DiPardo and Freedman; Kirby and White; Harris), there is little denying the gaps which often exist between the intended benefits and actual results of peer review (Diffendal; Brammer and Rees; Covill; Lam). We need, for example, to reject the deceptively alluring notion that if we teach students how to provide useful feedback, this feedback will, in turn, be recognized by their peers, and successful revisions will ensue.

In general, existing research offers few encouraging responses to the question of whether students actually revise in direct response to peer comments, as valuable peer-peer exchanges often do not translate into productive revisions. Most available studies of peer review tend not to evaluate the latency period, focusing primarily on the immediate interactions between students, and those that do typically suggest that feedback received does not, as we might expect, necessarily correlate to revisions made (see Topping; Lam; Kaufman and Schunn; Walker). Of course, peer comments lose a great deal of value when student writers do not take them up; there is value in *providing* feedback on the part of the reviewer, but clearly, much value is wasted when comments are ignored and the reviewer, despite his or her best efforts, has little to no influence on revision. By underpinning peer review with rhetorical theory, then, I hope to challenge this lack of influence by showing that to question the extent to which students revise based on peers' comments is to question the extent to which students are *persuaded*, by their peers, to revise.

In foregrounding its persuasive nature, I also resist the inclination to conceive of peer review as an exercise in student independence. Instead, I argue, we need

DOI: https://doi.org/10.37514/PER-B.2023.1961.2.05

to recognize and find ways to more effectively acknowledge that student-student reviews, like any writing experiences, are audience-*de*pendent and that despite the moniker, the instructor is a central figure of the peer review audience. To build this argument, I first examine the basic rhetorical makeup of peer review, using the Aristotelian framework of persuasive modes to illustrate that ethos is conspicuously absent from peer review, as students express a lack of trust in one another's reviews. I argue that we need to recognize the instructor's ethotic position as a source for this lack of trust between students, and from this, I suggest that we foster identification, as defined by Kenneth Burke, between instructor and students, as a means to extend this ethos to students. More pointedly, I argue that to be persuaded to revise, students must identify their reviewers with the instructor, as it is through this identification that the reviewer establishes a more productive sense of ethos, making the review process more persuasive. Rather than retreat from the instructor's central role in the classroom audience, a theory of peer ethos based on identification acknowledges that this role continues even during peer review sessions and offers a way forward for instructors to more actively mitigate the persistent lack of trust between students. I end with some practical suggestions based on my experience with building students' identification-based ethos and offer some important reminders about the need to ground identification-building activities in broader discussions of audience.

THE BREAK(ING)DOWN OF PERSUASIVE APPEALS

Aristotle's modes of persuasion—pathos, logos, and ethos—are a useful place to start when trying to understand peer review as a failure to persuade, for several reasons.

They offer a succinct framework for understanding the rhetorical situation, and they stem from the fundamental concern with audience which Aristotle perceived and which, I argue, is crucial to understanding peer review. In the first chapter of his *Rhetoric*, Aristotle distinguishes between the truth-seeking purpose of dialectic, which is "to discern the real and the apparent syllogism," and the more audience-based purpose of rhetoric, which is "to discern the real and the apparent means of persuasion" (7). While dialectic is concerned with reason and truth, and typically engaged only by those with the proper training, Aristotle realizes that "before some audiences not even the possession of the exactest knowledge will make it easy for what we say to produce conviction" (6). As such, he sees rhetoric as a means to appeal to public audiences, using not just reason and truth but other means of persuasion as well, and from this assumption he develops his modes. The modes thus speak to the enduring significance of audience—especially audience as a varied, public entity—in any attempt to understand rhetorical situations, including peer reviews. More specifically, they also highlight the fundamental audience issue already reflected, implicitly, in the existing research on peer review, namely that a lack of revision based on peer feedback stems in part from a lack of peer-peer trust.

Most scholarship on peer review indicates students' general ability and willingness to appeal to pathos, to "dispos[e] the listener" by exciting emotions conducive to persuasion (38). Aristotle writes at length about friendliness being especially favorable to persuasion, as a friendly audience is one that sees its own beliefs and wishes reflected in those of the speaker/writer and is thus more receptive to the latter's ideas (125). Friendly feeling suggests a perceived sense of honesty and sympathy, both of which are intended to make a speaker/writer more well-disposed to his or her audience. Research suggests positive peer-peer emotions are fairly common, as there is no evidence that malice or antagonism exists within peer assessment relationships in any generalized way. Indeed, students may find themselves demonstrating an *excess* of emotional appeal, as they offer an overabundance of praise to their peers. In her discussion of student attitudes toward peer revision, for instance, Lee Ann Diffendal observes that a "common impediment to effective peer revision is students' ambivalence about criticizing their peers," as they often feel that "honest feedback should not supersede common courtesy" (35; 36). Students tempering feedback in the interest of maintaining cordial relationships or protecting self-esteem is a fairly common observation, and this is a trend not generally perceived as malicious or intentionally misleading by reviewees. Rather, this excessive praise is more likely an appeal to emotions which is overzealous to the point that it can, inadvertently, become counter-productive, when concerns about friendliness supersede concerns about reviewees' best academic interests. Yet, the basic intention to appeal to the reviewee's emotions is a wise one, rhetorically speaking; praise is detrimental only if it takes the place of constructive criticism.

The type of appeal Aristotle was most interested in was that of logical reasoning, and logos is relevant to peer review primarily as it relates to the presentation of "the truth or the apparent truth," (39) as by "showing or seeming to show something" (38). These qualifications that proof need not be infallible or universal are essential to composition pedagogy, as the contextuality of writing precludes recourse to any sense of absolute "correctness." The appearance of truth, which we might equate to the sense of "truth" defined by the particular facets of a given writing context, is more relevant to peer review processes than any absolute standard of truth Aristotle may have had in mind. Terms like "reliable" and "valid," when used by scholars to describe peer feedback, speak to the logos of the particular context. They indicate the extent to which students' comments are *true*—to the instructor's expectations, the assignment criteria, etc. Various empirical studies have scrutinized the reliability of students' marks and indicate that, when asked to evaluate the work of their peers, whether by attaching an actual grade or providing comprehensive feedback for revision, students are able to do so with a fair amount of accuracy (see Topping; Patchan, Charney, and Schunn; Patchan et al.). Students are able to present feedback which is reflective of sound judgment and consistent with—true to—the rationale of a given writing context.

This is particularly important in light of evidence of students' negative perceptions of peer abilities (see Kaufman and Schunn; Brammer and Rees; Covill; Bhullar et al.). Student reviewers can and do exhibit the logos necessary for persuasion, yet students' perceptions do not necessarily reflect this. In their study of student attitudes toward peer review, for example, Charlotte Brammer and Mary Rees found that a majority of students did not trust their peers to review their papers, particularly because they did not trust their peers' writing skills. They observed that of the student survey, "comments that focused on the quality of the reviewer, most expressed concerns about classmates' dedication and ability to peer review" (80). Students expressed doubts about peers' emotional investment and intellectual ability, and the sample comments offered by the authors emphasize ability as the primary concern. A student admits, "I don't trust my peers to review my paper. I don't think they can do it competently, just like I don't think I can give a good Peer review b/c I am a horrible writer" (80). Another student laments: "If [my peers] can't write a good paper, why do I want them to correct mine?" (80). Students express a general suspicion that the feedback offered is, even if well-meaning, to some extent inaccurate.

Thus, despite the evidence indicating the presence of logical and emotional appeals in student responses, students do not necessarily trust their peers to offer them useful feedback. In short, the *presence* of logos and pathos does not correlate positively with students' *recognition* of them, a discrepancy which potentially cancels out their persuasive value and explains why students may not consistently revise in response to peer feedback. Thus, instructional focus on just the quality of peer comments is inadequate, as such focus mistakenly assumes that the quality of feedback correlates to a writer's use of it, avoiding the simple fact that a lack of peer-peer trust has the power to cancel out feedback value. As such, I argue that we need to place much greater emphasis on establishing ethos within peer assessments.

DETERMINING THE SOURCES OF CLASSROOM ETHOS

In the second book of his *Rhetoric*, Aristotle explains that because rhetoric "is concerned with making a judgment," the speaker must not only "look to the argument, that it may be demonstrative and persuasive" but must also "construct a view of himself as a certain kind of person" (112). A speaker who demonstrates, in addition to logic and expressiveness, an ethos—broken down by Aristotle into three core elements: practical wisdom, virtue, and good will—is "necessarily persuasive to the hearers" (113). He asserts that these three elements are those qualities that "we trust other than logical demonstration" and which make "speakers themselves . . . persuasive" (112). In his brief elaboration of the terms of ethos, Aristotle suggests that they are predicated in large part upon the perceived correlation of what one believes with what one claims to believe. Those lacking virtue, for instance, "though forming opinions rightly . . . do not say what they think," and those lacking goodwill choose "not to give the best advice although they know [what] it [is]" (113). Aristotle's conception of ethos is based on a perceived correlation between speech and knowledge/belief. One establishes authority by conveying the sense—whether genuine or not—that what one says or recommends is an accurate reflection of one's knowledge/belief, and this sense is informed by occurrences beyond the bounds of the immediate rhetorical situation. What one expresses in the immediate situation must correlate to something beyond it—one's past actions, for instance.

Yet, to what should students' words correlate? As they express themselves and offer feedback to peers during review sessions, what is there beyond the bounds of the immediate session, to lend weight to their words? Aristotle provides us a useful definition for ethos, but not necessarily any reasonable means to achieve it. His statements about what people "really think" and what they "know" suggest a kairotic situation which extends beyond the words themselves, to the knowledge the audience members believe they have about the speaker, apart from his actual speech. He makes clear that varied authority dynamics may precede one's speech, but his guidance for how to manage these dynamics range from statements like "praise is based on actions" to the assertion that education and goodness of birth are "attendant" to persuasion (79–80). He makes clear that the words of the immediate situation are not all that determine one's ethos, but once we identify that ethos is the missing facet of the peer review experience, he offers us and our students only limited means to move forward. His understanding of ethos is clearly informed by the social stratifications of his time, and while fitting one's words to one's actions remains a wise bit of advice, it is not of much specific use in the context of a writing course. Moreover, the specific context of peer-peer assessments is more complicated than the speaker-audience dynamic implied in classical definitions of ethos, in that there is the additional presence of the instructor—and, by extension, the parameters of the course itself—acting upon the situation. It would be easy to interpret the Aristotelian conception of ethos as suggesting that ethos emanates primarily from the speaker and his/her choices and that the appeal occurs solely between the speaker and audience, but neither is the case within student-student feedback experiences.

Roger Cherry's distinction between ethos and persona is useful to illustrate the limitations of the classical perspective toward ethos. Cherry argues that while ethos refers to a rhetor's portrayal of self in the attempt to establish credibility, persona is more closely associated with fiction and refers to an "intentional 'mask'" adopted by the writer. One produces or fabricates a persona but merely expresses or exhibits ethos. He attempts to clarify the distinction with the example of writing tasks which ask students "to assume the identity of a fictional personage and create a text appropriate for that individual," saying that such assignments require students to create both a "persona appropriate for the fictional rhetorical situation" and an "ethos . . . appropriate for the real (i.e., evaluative) rhetorical situation." The difference in terms seems fairly clear here, as students construct a character acknowledged by both reader and writer as imaginary, but what happens in the face of writing tasks lacking an explicitly fictional rhetorical situation? An assignment asking students to analyze an author's argument, for instance, offers no explicitly fictionalized entity for students to embody but does in some sense require them to construct a new identity—a voice that reflects the standards of the course and the expectations of the instructor. Such a voice may be less overtly fictional than that of a character in an imagined narrative, but this does not necessarily equate to it being objectively "real." Like Aristotle, Cherry appeals to the assumption that students must rely on themselves—whether by appealing to some element of their background or by tapping into some sort of genuine self—in order to establish their writerly ethos. For the writing student, however, this instruction is of minimal use, as the situated and discursive nature of writing makes any sort of essential self tough to identify or stabilize in any meaningful way.

Expecting students to exhibit ethos entirely on their own is unrealistic for various reasons, not least of which is that they are in a generally unfamiliar environment. Moreover, this classroom environment is one in which their sense of ethos is automatically challenged, by virtue of their position as students being evaluated and graded by an instructor. In our role as instructors, we are the ones expected to teach; this is not only a reason to extend our ethos to them but also an explanation why, if we do *not* extend it, they are unlikely to trust one another.

Typically—there are exceptions, of course—the instructor occupies a position of considerable classroom authority, and the research shows that, even in the face of valuable peer feedback, students are understandably concerned primarily with this authority. In the context of the more practical goals of most courses—successful completion, a strong grade—the instructor plays a much more substantial role than do peers, and students of course understand this.

Various scholars have explored the dynamics of classroom authority and argue that instructor authority is an inevitable, and in fact a necessary, reality of the classroom (see Bizzell; Gale; Pace; Lutz and Fuller; Bedore and O'Sullivan; VanderStaay et al.). Through this lens, however, the instructor is easily construed as the "true" or "ultimate" audience for any writing students produce, and subsequently peers are often left to occupy a pseudo-audience position which inevitably limits their influence. The instructor's ethos, in other words, may hold great enough sway to potentially overshadow student ethos and undermine the persuasive power of the peer reviews.

I do not mean to suggest through this observation that instructors are unimpeachable or that their authority is indicative of some sort of intrinsic merit. As various scholars mentioned above attest, there are important differences between authority and other more stringent concepts like power and control. However, by virtue of their role as instructors, they *do* have inherent influence over students' work. We may bristle at the dangers of instructor-student power relationships, but there is little denying the influence which comes along with acting as an audience. Aristotle certainly understood this, offering various observations on the importance of audience, among them the adage from Socrates, that "it is not difficult to praise Athenians in Athens" (136). Kenneth Burke likewise understood, further extending the classical understanding of the audience's role. For Burke, rhetoric is not simply a matter of finding the right audience for one's ideas; the audience actually participates in shaping them, as "an act of persuasion is affected by the character of the scene in which it takes place and of the agents to whom it is addressed" (62). In more recent years, composition scholarship has been continually informed by discussions of audience, like Lisa Ede and Andrea Lunsford's influential "Audience Addressed/Audience Invoked." Seen through their more focused framework, the instructor plays an increasingly complicated role in the peer review audience. In the practical terms of address, she is the concrete figure who will eventually rate the draft; she is also invoked by students, as peer reviews are guided by students' sense of what the teacher wants.

These examples are simply meant to illustrate that audience has always been a central element of persuasion, and that if we are willing to acknowledge the instructor's unique role as not just an audience member but typically the one whose authority is most perceptible and of greatest consequence, and to consider how this authority necessarily carries over to peer reviews, then the expectation that students will simply discover or build their own sense of ethos is decidedly unreasonable. Moreover, it also implies a certain level of powerlessness on the part of the instructor. It suggests that while we can work to improve their appeals to logos and pathos—guiding them about what sorts of comments to give and how best to express them—we cannot work to establish trust, that this must come from the students. Yet, the existing research on peer review suggests that this point in the rhetorical setup is precisely where we need to more actively involve ourselves. Thus, an alternative method for establishing ethos is necessary. I propose that we conceptualize student ethos—in the context of peer review, specifically the reviewer's ethos—as an extension of instructor ethos. Doing so not only highlights the contextuality of the peer review experience but also offers us a foundation from which to intervene and build greater student-student trust within the peer review experience.

FOSTERING IDENTIFICATION, BRINGING STUDENTS INTO THE CONCEPTUAL DISCUSSION

What we need to do, then, is extend our influence to reviewers, using our ethos to build theirs, through the process of identification. Burke writes in *Rhetoric of Motives* that "If, in the opinion of a given audience, a certain kind of conduct is admirable, then a speaker might persuade the audience by using the ideas and images that identify his cause with that kind of conduct" (55). Through the process of identification, "A is not identical with his colleague, B. But insofar as their interests are joined, A is *identified* with B" (20). Using the terms of peer review, the reviewer (A) can better persuade the reviewee (the audience) when he "identif[ies] his cause" with that of the instructor (B). Burke further explains that "In being identified with B, A is 'substantially one' with a person other than himself. Yet at the same time he remains unique" (21). Through this consubstantiality the reviewer is at once a unique peer and a reflection of the instructor, and given that the instructor is the locus of classroom ethos, this identification is bound to heighten the ethos of the reviewer. Through this identification the reviewer becomes associated more closely with that audience which the reviewee recognizes as most authoritative; with this closer association the reviewer can more actively engage the audience dynamic which already exists between reviewee and instructor, inserting him or herself into the dynamic as an active participant. Rather than a pseudo representation of the audience, the reviewer becomes an extension of it.

Some may push back against the idea of inserting the instructor more actively into peer-peer interactions, based on the assumption that such interactions are meant to represent a transferring of authority away from the instructor. Yet, the notion that students are working independently of teachers when they engage in assigned peer assessments is fallacious, most fundamentally because such activities originate from and are monitored by the instructor. The instructor occupies a relatively stable, normative position in the classroom, and rather than ignore this fact, this concept of reviewer-instructor identification embraces it. In identifying with the instructor, the reviewer is acknowledging a dual audience—the reviewee, who values this instructor-based identity, and the instructor herself, whose evaluation system informs the reviewer's own. As such, through identification the reviewer can address the initial audience-based glitch in the peer review process, namely that the reviewee considers the instructor the only relevant audience, by developing a closer association with said audience. This framework acknowledges the uncomfortable reality that the teacher is the ultimate source of classroom ethos, and at the same time it accomplishes the tricky task of affording instructors the opportunity to actually disrupt this reality.

Acknowledging that peer review is not an independent student experience need not force us into the opposite conclusion, that it is merely another instance of a troubling power dynamic. In proposing identification as the route to peer review success, my intention is not to simply get students to trust one another by making them appear as conduits for the instructor, as I realize that asking students to parrot an instructor's comments uncritically is of little lasting value to students. The gap between reviewer and instructor needs to be bridged, certainly, in order for feedback to be persuasive, but the arguably larger benefit of this framework is that it has the potential to actually reinforce certain fundamental principles of composition, in ways that have great long-term value for students. Indeed, viewing peer review through the frame of identification and consubstantiality allows us to see peer review as a means of developing the shared language and shared context of the classroom. Coupled with meaningful discussions about the concept of audience, identification-building can be useful to not only immediate review scenarios but also writing experiences in later coursework.

This encouragement of meaningful discussion stems from my broader assumption that composition is a discipline with content and, subsequently, that we should share this knowledge with students. I agree with Linda Adler-Kassner and Elizabeth Wardle, who assert in their collection on threshold concepts for composition that "writing is not only an activity in which people engage but also a subject of study," and that the more transparently we discuss the content of composition with students, the more successful they will be (15). The concept of audience is a crucial facet of this content, so rather than avoid discussions of audience—and implicitly reinforce the spurious monolith of "good" writing—we should help students better understand how we function as a specific audience for their work and how identification enters into this relationship. In guiding students to identify with us, we need not present our language or values as the "right" or "correct" ones in any sort of universalized way. We can present them as *ours* and talk with students about how language and values are inevitably situated and how they will need to make different decisions for the different audiences they face in the future. We can, in short, teach them about a *specific* audience, ourselves, and about the *concept* of audience. Various concepts explored in the encyclopedic first section of Adler-Kassner and Wardle's collection could easily serve as starting points for these classroom discussions.

Discussing the dynamics of identification with students also allows us an opening to further disrupt students' perceptions of "good" and "bad" writing. Burke explains that "Identification is compensatory to division. If men were not apart from one another, there would be no need for the rhetorician to proclaim their unity. If men were wholly and truly of one substance, absolute communication would be of man's very essence" (22). In the terms of composition, there would not be so many different textbooks, methods, and schools of thought on how to write effectively if we actually had one definition of "effective" upon which we could all agree. By establishing the terms of the classroom, those with which she hopes to see her students identify, the instructor can actively acknowledge that differing terms exist. As such, her ethos—and by extension, the students'—is established some way apart from the artifice of objective value, in a way that de-prioritizes distinctions between "good" and "bad" writing. Instructors can help students to reconceptualize the label "good writer" as a designation not of correctness but of identification with a particular audience of value, in this case the instructor. If we instead try to minimize ambiguity and clarify for students the (supposed) distinctions between "good" and "bad" writing, we will be no closer to understanding effective peer review. Such attempts perpetuate non-existent ideals, and they disregard the existing research, which shows that even if students *could* achieve absolute "correctness" in their reviews, this in no way necessarily leads to the employment of these reviews. Objectively "good" writing is not just an arbitrary and rather meaningless label; even if a reviewer *were* to exhibit it, the lack of ethos in the peer review setup would strip it of any impact anyway. Conceiving of ethos instead as a function of identification grounds it fundamentally in a particular audience, and exposing this dynamic to students works to offset their expectations of an objective or universal "good."

Moreover, this framework builds on existing research suggesting that students are more successful when they understand and interact with the specific criteria by which they are being evaluated. Various scholars have observed that asking students to engage directly with evaluative criteria typically leads to students' greater comfort with and accurate application of said criteria (see Leydon, Wilson, and Boyd; Ashton and Davies; Yucel et al.; McLeod et al.; Bird and Yucel; Hawe and Dixon; Li and Lindsey; Chong). In short, students understandably do better when they recognize what is being asked of them, and guiding students to more actively identify with the instructor builds on this observation in at least two ways. Practically speaking, students must progress from knowing the criteria to actually employing it within their own feedback to their peers; moreover, they ideally gain a greater conceptual understanding, as they move beyond just identifying the criteria to understanding their varied purposes. Again, the key to making this effort most successful is to partner this call for identification with discussions of those concepts mentioned above, like audience and "good" writing, so as not to turn peer review into an exercise in mimicry. Hawe and Dixon hint at this particular risk when they note that "Students cannot be blamed for thinking they have been successful in their work once each element is 'ticked off' as present" if "they have been inducted into the notion that quality resides in the presence of properties identified in the criteria" (76). Writing instructors have the responsibility not only to foster identification but also to guide students away from an understanding of peer review as a simple checklist of desired qualities.

Striking this balance, between establishing specific expectations and challenging the objectivity of these expectations, is not necessarily an easy task for instructors, though. Perceiving this balance may be difficult for students, too, particularly those in the early stages of their development as writers and academics. Forwarding a concept of ethos as identification demands a greater sense of how this identification might actually be fostered, so it is useful to briefly consider some ways that instructors can translate this theory of ethos building into classroom practice.

SUGGESTIONS FOR MINDFUL PRACTICE

The correlation of ethos and identification foregrounds the importance of community within the writing classroom in various ways, as it is only through the power of *shared* language that the reviewer-instructor link can be forged and recognized by the reviewee. Burke argues that "you persuade a man only insofar as you can talk his language by speech, gesture, tonality, order, image, attitude, idea, *identifying* your ways with his," and thus only through a process of shared recognition by all three parties—reviewer, reviewee, and instructor—can persuasive identification occur (55). It is not enough for the reviewer to take steps to identify him or herself with the instructor; the reviewee must be able to recognize this consubstantiation as well. For the instructor, the task becomes more than just building the link between herself and reviewers; she must also ensure that all participants are able to perceive and take part in this association. As such, the most effective methods for fostering identification will start at the level of the classroom, with the goal of establishing a shared knowledge among its many participants. There are plenty of ways to approach this knowledge-building, and to couple it with meaningful discussions focused on long-term value for students.

One of the more obvious, intuitive ways to encourage identification is to engage students in extended analyses of instructor comments, ideally as applied to samples of student writing. Reviewing samples with students is nothing new, but more often these are used as a means to analyze the student writing rather than the comments provided in response to it. Moreover, there is plenty of scholarship examining instructors' feedback methods (for recent examples, see Dixon and Moxley; Vincelette and Bostic; Laflen and Smith; Ferris) and how students make use of the individualized comments given to them (McGrath and Atkinson-Leadbeater; McMartin-Miller; Ruegg; Daniel, Gaze, and Braasch; Calhoon-Dillahunt and Forrest), but there is little discussion of how approaching instructors' comments as an ongoing text for *students* to analyze is valuable. By asking students to critique sample comments, instructors can encourage students to see their feedback as an additional text to critically examine and understand and ask them to rhetorically analyze things like wording, style markers, and the priorities implied by the instructor's various choices.

For instance, the instructor could give students a pair of samples and ask them to analyze sentence-level marks and consider any differing patterns between them. If one sample contains significantly more structural and conceptual weaknesses than the other, students will likely notice fewer sentence-level notes, and more global ones, in the former. This conclusion can then be used as an opportunity to discuss layers of priority students have to grapple with when reviewing and precisely how the instructor prioritizes different strengths and weaknesses. They can discuss, for example, the practical reasons a more global comment about evidence usage might supersede marks on run-on sentences which the instructor would otherwise offer and try to emulate this reasoning in their own reviews. As the students provide feedback to peers and make decisions about what to focus on and what to postpone, they can speak back to these conversations, aligning their decisions with the instructor's. In my own classes, I try to review numerous examples like this over the course of the semester, typically just prior to peer review sessions. I actively encourage students to draw comments from the samples we review together, always being careful to frame this drawing as engagement with a particular audience, me, rather than simple copying. An instructor's approach to the analysis of samples will be crucial in maintaining this distinction, as the question of *what* the instructor says via feedback is not nearly as important as the question of *why* she says it. Focusing too much on *what*—identifying choices and patterns without considering contextual purpose—would likely lead to uncritical parroting.

Along with offering feedback to analyze, instructors can also work more directly toward building a shared vocabulary, emphasizing it as the representation of the unique lexicon of their specific classroom. That shared vocabulary is a means toward greater pedagogical effectiveness is a common assumption, and I suggest instructors can magnify the significance of this sharing by highlighting the distinctions between their classroom vocabulary and others'. Showing students the different definitions and connotations of words underscores the specific expectations of the instructor and, in the long term, the need for them to understand their intended audience; most importantly for peer review, it helps to imbue their own use of these words, as reviewers, with more precise meaning. One way to build this vocabulary is for the instructor to compile a list of words that she uses often in her feedback and to review her meanings as well as other possible meanings students may encounter. Words like "clear" and "unclear" would be obvious choices, as the instructor could discuss the different meanings that they take on within her own feedback—e.g. how a "clear" sentence does not necessarily signify the same thing as a "clear" idea—as well as how clarity often differs from one disciplinary context to the next. This could even serve as an opportunity for the instructor to refine her own language. "Clear," for example, was a word that I used to use quite often—and admittedly quite vaguely—in my own comments to students, until a class discussion about its meanings helped me to better understand my true intentions for the term. I tended to use "clear" in the context of thin analysis, when I noticed that a student needed to in some way further flesh out an idea, yet through various discussions with students I came to realize that while *I* understood that my goal was to encourage further explanation from students, this wasn't necessarily coming across in my choice of words. Subsequently, I have worked to become more aware of my own references to clarity when writing to my students, and I now make a point of analyzing my definitions of clarity with students, so that when I *do* use this terminology, they have a better understanding of my intentions and can try to put my comments to better use.

When it comes time for peer review, these discussions may then impact students' language as well. Whereas "clear" tends to be a popular go-to word for students to use, as marking text as clear or unclear can serve as a simple stand-in for more substantive comments, I typically notice that, as the course progresses, students use these terms in isolation less and less frequently. This general trend has proven true with other terms that I discuss with students as well, words like "awkward" and "good." The more I mention them in class and we analyze them for specific meaning, the more students tend to qualify and contextualize their uses of them, saying things like "awkward word choice" instead of just "awkward" and "good—quote really fits your point here" instead of just "good." Interestingly, I have seen that over time my students also start to challenge each other's usage, pushing for more specifics when their reviewers fall back into vague terminology. They begin to see, it seems, that when they push beneath the surface definitions, they can find deeper feedback that is incredibly valuable to them as writers.

An example of a more individualized means of building reviewer-instructor identification, to be engaged ideally after large-scale activities like those above, is to ask students to draw on previous comments from the instructor to the reviewee as they build their reviews. Ideally reviewees would be willing to simply share previous papers with reviewers, but in the case that students prefer not to do so they could also offer reviewers a written or verbal summary of the feedback they have received. Either way, reviewers can then try to speak to these comments as much as possible as they craft their assessments of their peers' work. For example, if a student was given comments regarding a lack of textual evidence on a previous paper, the reviewer can critique the current work with an eye toward this particular issue and can actively cite the instructor's previous remarks as he/she comments on the peer's use of evidence in the current work. I do this in my own courses and find that referring to my comments as they are reviewing is fairly easy for most students and may, interestingly enough, encourage them to offer more pointed feedback, most likely because references to me act as a reassurance that their own remarks are on target. As the reviewer indicates recognition and understanding of the comments and is able to apply them to the current text, he/she acts as an extension of the instructor, deepening his/her identification. So, I have seen students progress, for instance, from general comments like "need topic sentence" to "remember her [my] comment on last paper—need to say paragraph's main point here," and from "put quote here" to "last paper didn't have enough evidence so remember to put quote for this." Behind every comment the reviewee receives is more weight, buttressed as each one is by the instructor's ethos.

It is important to highlight here as well that, just as my students' feedback tends to improve in various ways, my observations suggest that their engagement with said feedback also becomes more active and thoughtful. As mentioned at the start of this piece, a huge moment in the peer review process that remains ripe for greater exploration is that latency period after peer comments have been offered and recorded, and efforts to build stronger identifications with instructor feedback have immense potential to enrich that time. In addition to students pushing one another for greater detail, I typically notice a general increase in students' engagement with peer comments. In the past, unless given explicit instructions from me to do otherwise, students would typically shelve their peer comments once the review was over, usually only addressing peer feedback with me in those cases when comments were minimal or tough to understand; I would rarely see them much at all, beyond any assigned tasks I might ask them to do with the feedback. In contrast, I now find that students engage not only each other more often but me as well, asking me questions about the feedback and, in many cases, making peer-inspired changes and reviewing them with me during office hours or after class. Further investigation is needed to draw conclusions about how, if at all, this greater involvement translates into more successful final drafts, but the influence on student engagement reflected in my own experiences is certainly promising.

These few strategies are by no means the only ones that can be used to extend the instructor's ethos to students, but my hope is that they illustrate the relative ease with which this ethos-based theory can be put into practice and, even more importantly, the instructor's responsibility to engage students in meaningful discussion of the larger purposes and goals of their classroom work. It would be rather easy to adopt any of the activities above in a superficial sort of way, incorporating them into peer review sessions as matters of routine or general busywork and not considering how they work to reinforce, or perhaps even challenge, one's existing pedagogical perspective. For them to have meaningful impact—meaningful not just in terms of students' immediate critical engagement but also in terms of their transfer potential—strategies aimed at extending instructor ethos need to be grounded in a much broader conceptual perspective. There is certainly more research needed to further support this identification theory, but my experiences support the notion that these strategies work *best* when one continually emphasizes to students those concepts like audience and purpose which are central to mindful writing and review processes.

CONCLUSION

Students already realize that peer review, in all its forms, involves—or is at least supposed to involve—some vague sense of working with others, but this recognition is not equivalent to an awareness of the principles of rhetoric and composition underpinning the necessary distinctions between identification and correction. If instructors can frame the peer review process as an activity grounded in identification, rather than correction, and explore different ways to establish this frame for students, they can hopefully disrupt the rhetorical relationships which exist between students and infuse them with the greater trust required for effective reviews. Again, I use the term "frame" deliberately here for its connotation as an entire conceptual outline; in contrast, terms like "method" or "strategy" do not quite capture the scope of the necessary changes. Instructors could devise various "methods" for building a shared classroom vocabulary, for instance, but if they do not talk with students about why such steps are important and how they tie to larger concerns about audience, the emphasis remains on regurgitation rather than on mindful employment. Shared terms could be simplified into shallow markers of "right" and "wrong," in line with the corrective, checklist model of peer review, and thus the persuasive problems with the process would remain, which is why the broader frame is so crucial.

At a most basic level, what this ethos-based theory of peer review is meant to do is simply increase the chances that students will actually consider and incorporate peer feedback during the latency period. For all the research we have on what happens during the immediate process, we have yet to exhibit any great influence on the time to follow, when students grapple with—or more pointedly, *avoid* grappling with—the feedback they have received. Knowing that feedback quality is not necessarily correlated with revision quality should compel us to closely consider precisely what is missing, what is needed to make the time *after* the initial review a time of more active, conscientious engagement.

The entire peer review process constitutes a unique rhetorical situation for students, and while conventional wisdom may suggest that it is an experience during which the instructor is meant to temporarily cede or withdraw her authority, I instead argue that is actually an experience calling for greater intervention. Seen through the lens of the most basic modes of persuasion, it is clear that trust is an issue which trumps other rhetorical considerations at play in peer assessments. Without trust between students, any otherwise persuasive feedback they receive is of little consequence, and to make our students' peer reviews more effective we need to embrace our own roles in establishing this peer-peer trust. Instructors are not merely responsible for providing the venue for peer review, pairing students up in certain ways and then passively waiting for success under the assumption that such "independent" work is useful for them. Students fail to establish ethos among one another in part because they recognize the already-established dynamic between themselves and the instructor and understandably perceive her as the overriding source of ethos in the classroom. Rather than recede from this recognition, instructors should more actively extend their ethos to students; doing so is an opportunity not only to achieve more effective reviews but also to strengthen students' grasp of the fundamental concept of audience.

WORKS CITED

Adler-Kassner, Linda, and Elizabeth Wardle. "Metaconcept: Writing Is an Activity and a Subject of Study." *Naming What We Know: Threshold Concepts for Writing Studies,* edited by Linda Adler-Kassner and Elizabeth Wardle, Utah State UP, 2015, pp. 15–16.

Aristotle. *On Rhetoric: A Theory of Civic Discourse.* 2nd ed. Translated by George Kennedy. Oxford UP, 2007.

Ashton, Scott, and Randall S. Davies. "Using Scaffolded Rubrics to Improve Peer Assessment in a MOOC Writing Course." *Distance Education,* vol. 36, no. 3, 2015, pp. 312–34.

Bedore, Pamela, and Brian O'Sullivan. "Addressing Instructor Ambivalence About Peer Review and Self-Assessment." *WPA: Writing Program Administration - Journal of The Council of Writing Program Administrators*, vol. 34, no 2, 2011, p. 11.

Bhullar, Naureen, et al. "The Impact of Peer Review on Writing in a Psychology Course: Lessons Learned." *Journal on Excellence in College Teaching*, vol. 25. no. 2, 2014, pp. 91–106.

Bird, Fiona L., and Robyn Yucel. "Feedback Codes and Action Plans: Building the Capacity of First-Year Students to Apply Feedback to a Scientific Report." *Assessment & Evaluation in Higher Education*, vol. 40, no. 4, 2015, pp. 508–27.

Bizzell, Patricia. "Classroom Authority and Critical Pedagogy." *American Literary History*, 1991, p. 847.

Brammer, Charlotte, and Mary Rees. "Peer Review from the Students' Perspective: Invaluable or Invalid?" *Composition Studies*, vol. 35, no. 2, 2007, pp. 71–8.

Burke, Kenneth. *A Rhetoric of Motives*. University of California Press, 1969.

Calhoon-Dillahunt, Carolyn, and Dodie Forrest. "Conversing in Marginal Spaces: Developmental Writers' Responses to Teacher Comments." *Teaching English in the Two-Year College*, vol. 40, no. 3, 2013, pp. 230–47.

Cherry, Roger D. "Ethos Versus Persona: Self-Representation in Written Discourse." *Written Communication*, vol.15, no. 3, 1998.

Chong, Ivan. "How Students' Ability Levels Influence the Relevance and Accuracy of Their Feedback to Peers: A Case Study." *Assessing Writing*, vol.31, 2016, pp. 13–23, https://doi.org/10.1016/j.asw.2016.07.002.

Covill, Amy E. "Comparing Peer Review and Self-Review as Ways to Improve College Students' Writing." *Journal of Literacy Research*, vol. 42, 2010, pp.199–226.

Diffendal, Lee Ann. "Peers Respond to Peer Revision." *Inside English*, vol. 32, no. 1, 2004, pp. 31–8.

DiPardo, Anne, and Sarah Warshauer Freedman. "Peer Response Groups in the Writing Classroom: Theoretic Foundations and New Directions." *Review of Educational Research*, vol. 58, no. 2, 1988, pp. 119–49.

Dixon, Zachary, and Joe Moxley. "Everything Is Illuminated: What Big Data Can Tell Us About Teacher Commentary." *Assessing Writing*, vol.18, 2013, pp. 241–56. *ScienceDirect*, https://www.sciencedirect.com/science/article/abs/pii/S1075293513000330.

Ede, Lisa, and Andrea Lunsford. "Audience Addressed/Audience Invoked: The Role of Audience in Composition Theory and Pedagogy." *College Composition and Communication*, vol. 35, no. 2, 1984, pp.155–71.

Ferris, Dana R. "Responding to Student Writing: Teachers' Philosophies and Practices." *Assessing Writing*, vol. 19, 2014, pp. 6–23.

Gale, Xin Liu. *Teachers, Discourses, and Authority in the Postmodern Composition Classroom*. State University of New York Press, 1996. eBook Collection.

Harris, Muriel. "Collaboration Is Not Collaboration Is Not Collaboration: Writing Center Tutorials vs. Peer-Response Groups." *College Composition and Communication*, vol. 43, no. 3, 1992, pp. 369–83.

Hawe, Eleanor M., and Helen R. Dixon. "Building Students' Evaluative and Productive Expertise in the Writing Classroom." *Assessing Writing*, vol. 19, 2014, pp. 66–79.

Kaufman, Julia H., and Christian D. Schunn. "Students' Perceptions about Peer Assessment for Writing: Their Origin and Impact on Revision Work." *Instructional Science*, vol. 39, no. 3, 2011, pp. 387–406.

Laflen, Angela, and Michelle Smith. "Responding to Student Writing Online: Tracking Student Interactions with Instructor Feedback in a Learning Management System." *Assessing Writing*, vol. 31, 2016, pp. 39–52, https://doi.org/10.1016/j.asw.2016.07.003.

Lam, Ricky. "A Peer Review Training Workshop: Coaching Students to Give and Evaluate Peer Feedback." *TESL Canada Journal*, vol. 27, no. 2, 2010, pp.114–27.

Leydon, Joseph, et al. "Improving Student Writing Abilities in Geography: Examining the Benefits of Criterion-Based Assessment and Detailed Feedback." *Journal of Geography*, vol. 113, no.4, 2014, pp. 151–59.

Li, Jinrong, and Peggy Lindsey. "Understanding Variations Between Student and Teacher Application of Rubrics." *Assessing Writing*, vol. 26, 2015, pp. 67–79.

Lutz, Jean, and Mary Fuller. "Exploring Authority: A Case Study of a Composition and a Professional Writing Classroom." *Technical Communication Quarterly*, vol. 16, no. 2, 2007, pp. 201–32.

McGrath, April, and Karen Atkinson-Leadbeater. "Instructor Comments on Student Writing: Learner Response to Electronic Written Feedback." *Transformative Dialogues: Teaching and Learning Journal*, vol.8, no. 3, 2016, pp.1–16.

McLeod, Stephen G., et al. "Improving Writing with A PAL: Harnessing the Power of Peer Assisted Learning with the Reader's Assessment Rubrics." *International Journal of Teaching and Learning in Higher Education*, vol. 20, no. 3, 2009, pp. 488–502.

McMartin-Miller, Cristine. "How Much Feedback Is Enough?: Instructor Practices and Student Attitudes Toward Error Treatment in Second Language Writing." *Assessing Writing*, vol. 19, 2014, pp. 24–35.

Pace, Judith L., and Annette Hemmings. "Understanding Authority in Classrooms: A Review of Theory, Ideology, and Research." *Review of Educational Research*, 2007, p. 4.

Patchan, Melissa M., et al. "A Validation Study of Students' End Comments: Comparing Comments by Students, a Writing Instructor, and a Content Instructor." *Journal of Writing Research*, vol. 1, no. 2, 2009, pp. 124–52.

Patchan, Melissa M., et al. "The Effects of Skill Diversity on Commenting and Revisions." *Instructional Science: An International Journal of The Learning Sciences*, vol. 41, no.2, 2013, pp. 381–405.

Ruegg, R. "The Effect of Assessment of Process After Receiving Teacher Feedback." *Assessment and Evaluation in Higher Education*, vol. 41, no. 2, 2016, pp.199–212.

Topping, Keith. "Peer Assessment Between Students in Colleges and Universities." *Review of Educational Research*, vol. 68, no. 3, 1998, pp. 249–76.

VanderStaay, Steven L., et al. "Close to the Heart: Teacher Authority in a Classroom Community [Excerpt]." *College Composition and Communication*, vol. 61, no. 2, 2009, pp. 262–82.

Vincelette, Elizabeth Jackson, and Timothy Bostic. "Show and Tell: Student and Instructor Perceptions of Screencast Assessment." *Assessing Writing*, vol.18, 2013, pp. 257–77.

Walker, Mirabelle. "The Quality of Written Peer Feedback on Undergraduates' Draft Answers to an Assignment, and the Use Made of the Feedback." *Assessment & Evaluation in Higher Education*, vol. 40, no. 2, 2015, pp. 232–47.

White, Theresa L., and Brenda J. Kirby. "'Tis Better to Give Than to Receive: An Undergraduate Peer Review Project." *Teaching of Psychology*, vol. 32, 2005, pp. 259–61.

Yucel, Robyn, et al. "The Road to Self-Assessment: Exemplar Marking Before Peer Review Develops First-Year Students' Capacity to Judge the Quality of a Scientific Report." *Assessment & Evaluation in Higher Education*, vol. 39, no. 8, 2014, pp. 971–86.

CHAPTER 6.

POSITIONING PEER REVIEW FOR TRANSFER: AUTHENTIC AUDIENCES FOR CAREER READINESS AND WORKPLACE COMMUNICATION

Nora McCook
Bloomfield College

> By [critiquing] my peers work, it gives me different ideas on how to proofread my own writing and comparing it to their writing. Such as, noticing what their weaknesses and what their strongest points are. If my weaknesses are their strongest points or if my strongest points are their weaknesses and take notes on how they express their ideas.
>
> – First-Year Student's Reflective Portfolio Letter

Peer review has long occupied a discrete writing stage in college composition courses. It has helped convey a process-oriented view of writing as recursive and unfinished as well as promoted revision that responds to audience feedback. While peer review continues to occur as a common step in ePortfolio development, no other writing pedagogy since the process movement has placed significant emphasis on peer review praxis. In many areas of writing courses and curricula, peer feedback has lost its prior prominence and alignment with emerging writing pedagogies. As the field of writing studies has moved on from process pedagogy—even with many of its instructional practices still in place, there are new pedagogical vantage points through which to utilize peer review. In particular, exigencies related to job market pressures for students and graduates and new emphases on learning transfer provide a rich new arena in which to consider and reposition peer review in writing courses. Instead of viewing peer review as process-informed student-to-student instruction that recenters student writing and exchange (over current-traditional and "banking" or instructor-focused teaching), we can recognize peer feedback as a workplace genre that cultivates several transferable writing and inter/intrapersonal skills. To do this, writing instructors should first identify the ways that peer review translates into the workplace and then utilize transparent teaching and an updated approach to peer review reflection to facilitate learning transfer.

In the excerpt at the beginning of this chapter, a first-year writing student describes several different angles of analysis she used when she read both her peers' drafts and their feedback. She measures her "strengths" and "weaknesses" and also infers "proofreading" strategies from her peers' work. She pays attention to "how" her peers "express their ideas." Her comparative rhetorical approaches to her peers' texts offer useful tools for adapting to new writing demands and forms in work and community spaces. I argue that we should recognize that this writer is developing skills beyond typical peer feedback tasks of providing "readerly feedback" or suggestions on her peer's writing or discussing the effectiveness of her or his rhetorical choices. Instead, she is practicing "soft" or inter -and intrapersonal skills of peer benchmarking strategies that she can use not just in future writing courses but also when she produces unfamiliar workplace genres. These future contexts for applying rhetorical, interpersonal, analytical, and writing skills associated with peer feedback present an opportunity to encourage meta-awareness and transfer of these skills through peer review. Cultivating this student's perceptiveness into both her own and her peers' writing involves a "teaching for transfer" approach to peer review. Teaching for transfer (TFT) draws upon several process-inspired pedagogical roles for peer review and reflection but offers a clearer purpose for peer review that addresses growing demands for learning transfer and learners' own interests in preparing for workplace writing. Despite these connections between peer review and TFT, which this chapter explores, practitioners of transfer pedagogy as a whole have not identified an explicit role for peer review.

Concerns over whether learners are transferring skills and knowledge arise from multiple locations, including classroom-based and program assessment (via instructors and administrators) and also students, families, and employers. Current research into learning transfer paints a murky picture of the afterlife of college writing skills (Moore; Yancey et al.; Jarratt et al.). First-year writing courses have come under scrutiny for adhering to vague, school-based writing situations that fail to provide rich rhetorical contexts and audiences that can foster meta-cognitive skills and transfer (Wardle). Upper-level writing courses similarly raise concerns about students' abilities to apply rhetorical choices that appropriately address community and non-academic audiences (Bacon). Meanwhile, employers are reporting a desire to hire new graduates who can make use of skills and learning beyond the classroom. Hart Research Associates report, "just 14% of employers think that most of today's college students are prepared with the skills and knowledge needed to complete a significant applied learning project before graduation" (6). The same 2015 Hart Research Associates study of employers and college graduates found a disparity between the two groups' confidence in college students' preparation overall for the workforce: "College students are notably more optimistic about their level of preparedness across learning" compared to their employers (11). These troubling views of writing transfer and other workplace-applied skills open new possibilities for peer review as a multifaceted writing activity that we can leverage for its potential to foster professional writing and interpersonal skills and self-awareness.

In practice, one of the first obstacles writing instructors face with peer review is student resistance to "fixing" other peers' work. This perception derives from two common misconceptions about instructors' aims for assigning peer feedback; both are legacies of peer review's historical dexterity as a pedagogical tool in writing. The first is the vestige of peer review as a feedback-and workload-management strategy for instructors wanting students to have additional opportunities for personalized feedback in large writing classrooms. The second is the association peer review has—for instructors and for students—with high school or first-year (lower level) writing courses. As I will discuss, these are important legacies of peer review's long stronghold in composition courses. David Perkins and Gavriel Salomon's backward- and forward-reaching reflections are useful strategies for encouraging students (and instructors) to reevaluate their understanding of peer feedback, its purpose and value, and to anticipate workplace applications that will aid in their skill transfer. We can update our own and our students' approaches to peer review by being transparent about how peer review applies to workplace writing and career readiness and by implementing backward- and forward-reaching reflection to encourage transfer.

Influential educational researchers David Perkins and Gavrial Salomon proposed in 1988 that transfer of learning could be facilitated by reflecting on both prior and future experiences engaging with related tasks and skills. In this chapter, I adopt these TFT pedagogy concepts on two levels in order to examine the practice of peer review first through a lens of backward- and forward-reaching reflection, considering both historical legacies (reflecting backward) and future/forward-looking uses of peer review. This broad framework enables a second level of application for Perkins and Salomon's concepts: implementing a TFT approach to peer review. On a larger scale of re-examining peer review, when writing instructors look *back* on peer review's historical development, we see that legacies of academic labor constraints combine with documented declines in the use of peer feedback in more advanced college writing courses to confine perceptions of peer review as a school-based and even remedial genre. By contrast, looking *forward* to community and to workplace writing applications for peer review can amplify peer review's role in cultivating inter- and intrapersonal skills associated with career readiness. As a classroom TFT strategy, forward-reaching reflection involves students explicitly discussing future uses for certain writing skills and genres. Backward-reaching reflection involves students evaluating their own prior experiences with and beliefs about writing or learning and considering how they can be applied to a current writing task. Taking this forward- and backward-facing examination of peer review as a framework, I aim to show that peer review as a whole can be productively re-examined through TFT. Furthermore, I encourage writing instructors across colleges and universities to utilize a TFT approach to implementing peer review using backward- and forward-reaching reflection and transparent learning goals. TFT helps reposition peer review as a significant professional genre through which learners can reflect and transfer writing and rhetorical skills as well as "soft" or "intangible" inter/intrapersonal skills that can prepare confident and well-rounded writers and thinkers after college.

LEGACIES OF PEER REVIEW'S HISTORY FOR TEACHING 21ST-CENTURY TRANSFER

Peer review as a teaching strategy and writing activity has more than a century of precedent, but the process movement of the 1970s and 80s remains the most prominent articulation of peer review praxis in writing studies. Even with recent attention to writing portfolios re-emphasizing peer review, process pedagogy and its expressivist and social constructionist theoretical underpinnings continue to be the dominant pedagogical approach to implementing peer feedback. Process approaches to peer review over the past forty years have productively foregrounded students' writing and insights and have underscored the value of addressing "authentic" audiences and obtaining feedback in writing classrooms. Much less emphasized in process-informed peer review practice is what learners should do with these peer audience encounters and with crafting and utilizing feedback beyond the classroom or assignment. Teaching peer review from a standpoint of transfer, as the next sections will explore, guides students to anticipate professional applications more intentionally for many skills gained in peer review. Before considering how TFT can utilize transparency and backward- and forward-reaching reflection to facilitate learning transfer, this section proposes that some of the lack of fresh scholarly and pedagogical attention to peer review—and indeed decline in the uses of peer feedback in college writing classrooms overall—is due to two significant historical legacies of integrating peer feedback into writing instruction: using peer review, first, as a labor solution for crowded classrooms and, second, for the purposes of remediation.

Today, many current practitioners of peer review were influenced by process pedagogy, which urged students to write to "real" peer audiences and to learn from one another as they worked together to improve drafts. Expressivist and social constructionist orientations emphasize certain aspects of peer feedback, such as developing reading and revision strategies, hearing from audience members, and building knowledge and writing/rhetorical tools collaboratively. Rebecca Moore Howard summarizes peer response as a collaborative pedagogy, highlighting the pedagogical interests envisioned by peer review practitioners hailing from these theoretical vantage points: "[. . . T]o encourage students to articulate their readerly responses is to offer writers an understanding of the effects of their work. Equipped with this understanding, the writer can then better anticipate and provide for readers' needs and expectations" (61). As writing studies scholars pressed to establish their insights as a scholarly, praxis-based field of study, peer review presented a recognizable departure from models of correctness policing, lecturing, and instructor-directed writing practiced by many literature-dominated English departments (Tobin).

The main assumptions that process approaches to peer review conveyed were that students would derive writing insights from one another and that this learning opportunity would highlight the process (not product) of writing and share some of the power in evaluating student work. These interventions successfully targeted tired and even unjust classroom dynamics that had frequently foreclosed student voices and insights into writing. Yet, for all of its disruption and championing of students, process approaches to peer review fail to theorize the usefulness of engaging in this practice beyond the writing classroom.

Citing Muriel Harris' differentiation between peer review and peer tutoring, Rebecca Moore Howard summarizes, "Peer response focuses on general writing skills; tutoring, on the skills of one individual" (60). The primary set of skills process-trained peer reviewers obtain are "understanding the effects of their work" on actual peer audience members and crafting readerly "responses rather than [. . .] judgements" (Howard 61; 60). As a form of collaborative learning, Kenneth Bruffee argues that peer review "harnessed the powerful educative force of peer influence" in which "Students' work tended to improve when they got help from peers; peers offering help, furthermore, learned from the students they helped and from the activity of helping itself" (418). Bruffee describes that peer feedback might involve commenting on a paper's structure and areas for improvement as well as negotiating "consensus," both of which are valuable writing and thinking skills, but process pedagogy fails to provide students a means through which to utilize these skills beyond the immediate classroom context. As Linda Flower suggests:

> Many of the arguments for using peer response presume that the group will affect the cognition of the individual student: groups intervene within and can affect the writing process itself; they prompt students to work collectively to discover ideas;

> they create a live audience to which students can respond, which, it is argued, leads the individual to an internalized sense of how readers respond; and finally, they shift the emphasis in a classroom from product to process and from teacherly evaluation to writers' goals and readers' responses. (741)

As Flower's description underscores, process pedagogy utilized peer review to address perceived inadequacies of the classroom and prepared students to work together to hone drafts, all of which were aimed at cumulatively improving student writing. How and where should students transfer these writing skills? This question was of less interest to writing studies theorists during the process movement; it has become a central concern of writing instructors and learners today.

Since the process movement's challenges to "traditionalist" composition pedagogies, peer review and its role in decentering conversations about student writing have had a less clear pedagogical mandate. Teaching for transfer provides a new impetus and framework for engaging in peer review that addresses present-day demands for learning transfer as well as learner interests in workplace readiness. This lens for revisiting peer review as preparation for dynamic twenty-first-century workplace writing environments presented here has its own early predecessor. Lynée Lewis Gaillet excavated the writings of George Jardine, who taught philosophy at the University of Glasgow between 1773 and 1826. Jardine's argument for peer assessment assignments stands out in its assertion that peer critique engages rhetorical approaches which anticipate participation in the public sphere by (male) students from different class backgrounds (Gaillet 104). In Jardine's model, student examinations and feedback of one another's writing "prepares students for normal discourse in business, government, and the professions, which is both written within and addressed to status equals" (Gaillet 105). Like the late-eighteenth-century logic classroom, today's writing students debate and hone one another's rhetorical choices, whether text-based or multimodal, in manners similar to what they can deploy in community and workplace settings.

Jardine's early peer review praxis that considered ties to students' civic and professional lives was not the dominant framework for peer review over the next couple of centuries. Several prominent scholars in writing studies have made linkages between past peer review practice to more recent student-centered writing pedagogies. Newer scholarship is calling attention to the messier motivations and pedagogical goals that inspired early versions of peer writing feedback. Late-nineteenth and early-twentieth-century writing instructors faced growing logistical and instructional challenges as new demographics of students entered college classrooms (Kitzhaber; Connors). Some of the responses to using peer review with more diverse and increased numbers of students have relegated this writing practice to being associated with "busy work" and more general, lower-level writing classes. Both of these connections to peer review developed historically and pose obstacles today for students and instructors envisioning the long-term transferability of skills developed during peer review.

One difficulty forward-reaching TFT faces with peer review is a misconception that peer review replaces instructor feedback in order to lighten the grading load on faculty. This notion, it turns out, has deep historical roots in academic labor challenges. Many writing studies-trained practitioners are familiar with Anne Ruggles Gere's account of non-curricular writing groups developing a model of fruitful critical exchange amongst peers that took shape as writing workshops in the late nineteenth and early twentieth centuries. Kory Lawson Ching challenges Gere's genealogy by reviewing the primary sources upon which *Writing Groups* was based to show that peer review practice was at least as interested in reducing the teacher's workload amidst a challenging recitation and correction pedagogy as it was in elevating students' authority in the writing classroom. Ching reminds modern observers of centuries-old pedagogical tracts that our perceptions are "shaped by [their] own historical moment," just as Gere's history of writing groups during the "zenith" of peer review interest (303–304). The process-dominated 1980s lens Gere brought to nineteenth-century extra-curricular collaborative writing highlighted the absence of teachers during a contemporary interest in reevaluating power dynamics in writing classrooms (Ching 306). Conversely, Ching asserts that a "refiguring of history suggests [. . .] that peer response may not have emerged so much out of a move to decenter classroom authority but instead as a way for students to share some of the teacher's burden" (308). The demand for college writing instructors to accommodate more students under a strict pedagogy of correctness led to the adoption of peer review in many 19th-century U.S. classrooms. In this setting, students were asked to emulate the teacher's grading and correction approaches (311)—skills that had little relevance beyond the immediate writing course. Peer review has since undergone several other pedagogical transformations, but the idea of students sharing the grading or feedback load of instructors persists and may impact students' motivations for engaging in peer review and their ability to recognize its connections to collaborative writing in workplace contexts. Instructors who assign peer feedback must continue to be transparent about the purpose of this activity. We must be clear that we are not asking students to take on the role of a teacher. Replacing the instructor's feedback on drafts is a lingering misconception of past peer review pedagogical settings that prevents students who do not plan to be writing instructors from envisioning future applications of the skills they develop through peer exchange.

Another obstacle to implementing forward-reaching peer review practice is a more recent prominence of peer review in predominantly lower-level writing courses. Formal peer review of student writing is no longer as prominent in college classrooms, especially in upper-level courses. This decline presents the second major historical challenge to engaging with peer review through the lens of transfer today. In 2010 Joanne Addison and Sharon James McGee analyzed several large-scale surveys of writing instruction in college and high school. Two major trends they observed were that "college faculty are far less likely than high school faculty to (1) provide opportunities for informal, exploratory writing or (2) have students read/respond to other students' work" (Addison and McGee 157). The authors' own study of several different types of high schools and colleges/universities recorded that "have students read/respond to other students' work" was among the least frequently used "deep learning" practices by high school and college faculty, but slightly lower in college (157–8). Two studies they report on also indicate that students participated in peer review less frequently in their fourth year of college compared to their first year. These include Stanford University's institutional survey, which shows a 75% decline (156), and the 2002–2003 National Survey of Student Engagement of high school and college instructors, which shows 40% fewer assigned peer feedback on drafts (154). In all, these studies capture an emphasis on peer review in high school and first-year courses. One implication may be that students (and perhaps faculty) associate peer feedback with early writing classes in high school and college careers rather than with capstone, community, or workplace writing. Transfer of peer review skills will be less obvious to learners because of this trend.

Peer feedback on writing has lost some steam as a teaching practice, perhaps due to the lack of pedagogical underpinning connecting peer review to the central work and learning of the writing classroom since the process movement. In light of questions about transfer, connections to workplace writing, and emphasis on inter/intrapersonal skills, peer review offers renewed pedagogical exigencies for writing students today. Explicit effort is needed, however, to overcome lingering beliefs held by students and instructors that peer review is simply a way to give the instructor a break from "grading" or giving feedback and is not as worth the time and effort for more specialized, upper-level writing classes. TFT shifts the orientation of peer review from the writing classroom to explicitly anticipate professional contexts and transfer itself.

REFRAMING PEER REVIEW AS TRANSFERABLE SKILLS AND WORKPLACE WRITING GENRE

To reconsider peer review as a rich and relevant teaching and learning activity in and beyond twenty-first-century writing classrooms, we can start by examining its forward-reaching applications in workplaces. Peer review involves learners exchanging drafts and crafting responses, feedback, and suggestions in an oral, written, or multimodal format. With the support of transparent teaching and reflection, learners can greatly expand upon this interaction by building awareness of how their own approach to the writing task compares to their peers' drafts, how their concerns and reactions to the feedback they receive can inform rhetorical decisions about crafting feedback to others; how to most effectively communicate responses to a peer's work with attention to others' feelings, and how well their peers' feedback on their own drafts navigated these rhetorical and interpersonal dynamics and could serve as models for future peer suggestions. Encouraging students to recognize the complexities of writing for real audiences in peer review promotes the development of inter- and intrapersonal skills that they can leverage in post-graduation workplace and community writing settings.

This section continues to adopt the meta-framework of examining backward- and forward-reaching connections of peer review by identifying peer review skill applications beyond the classroom. To facilitate forward-reaching reflection on peer review for learning transfer in our own classes, instructors must also be ready to describe specific forward-reaching interpersonal skills, be transparent about how these are useful and desirable traits in professional settings, and introduce peer feedback as a workplace writing genre.

Writing instructors have several resources they can utilize to draw forward-reaching connections between peer review and marketable intra/interpersonal workplace skills. With pressure to both anticipate types of skills that will serve graduates in their careers and lives and to measure learners' accomplishments, educational researchers and practitioners have begun to emphasize intra and interpersonal often referred to as "soft" or "invisible" skills in addition to technical and disciplinary learning (Dorman and Brown). Several organizations have sought to define the types of soft skills most needed for twenty-first-century workplaces in the past decade. The National Association of Colleges and Employers (NACE) identifies eight "competencies that broadly prepare college graduates for a successful transition into the workplace" ("Career Readiness Defined"). These competencies include (1) critical thinking/problem solving, (2) oral/written communication, (3) teamwork/collaboration, (4) digital technology, (5) leadership, (6) professionalism/work ethic, (7) career management, and (8) global/intercultural fluency. Several of these competency descriptions highlight intra- and interpersonal skills, such as "The individual demonstrates integrity and ethical behavior, acts responsibly with the interests of the larger community in mind, and is able to learn from his/her mistakes" for Professionalism/Work Ethic. The American Association of Colleges & Universities surveyed employers in 2013. Reflecting on the AAC&U study they led, Finley and McNair explain:

> [Ninety-five] percent of employers agree (and 57 percent strongly agree) that "their company puts a priority on hiring people with the intellectual and interpersonal skills that will help them contribute to innovation in the workplace." Employers "place the greatest degree of importance on the following areas":
>
> Ethics: "Demonstrate ethical judgment and integrity" (96 percent important, including 76 percent very important)
>
> Intercultural Skills: "Comfortable working with colleagues, customers, and/or clients from diverse cultural backgrounds" (96 percent important, including 63 percent very important)
>
> Professional Development: "Demonstrate the capacity for professional development and continued new learning" (94 percent important, including 61 percent very important). (26)

As we look forward to the tools and skills that college graduates will need to utilize in their careers, working conscientiously with others rises prominently within such categories as "ethics," "professionalism," and "leadership" as well as more obvious "teamwork/collaboration" and "intercultural fluency/skills."

Several components of participating in peer review can target these workplace interpersonal skills; however, instructors must facilitate these connections. Some specific writing and inter/intrapersonal skills that peer review can facilitate include: comparing and evaluating the effectiveness of works-in-progress and of feedback; applying comparative insights towards revising own draft; organizing actionable feedback for an authentic (peer) audience; reflecting back on and applying own experiences as receivers of peer feedback to rhetorical strategies and content of feedback; empathy; developing and integrating emotional awareness into effective oral or written feedback; and evaluating and anticipating future applications of a multifaceted approach to peer exchange of writing in subsequent workplace or community writing settings. These valuable intra and interpersonal skills also prepare learners for workplace writing and thinking. Peers can gain sophisticated rhetorical insights simply by comparing their own work to their group members. Keith Topping suggests that this activity amounts to "norm referencing," which "enabl[es] a student to locate himself or herself in relation to the performance of peers and to prescribed learning targets and deadlines" (255). This comparative reflection helps students identify areas to improve on their current writing projects but should also be cultivated as a transportable benchmarking strategy for understanding how one's own products compare to colleagues' and whether any of their approaches might be adopted or improved upon.

There are multiple "soft" skills we can choose from to address through peer review. I encourage instructors to consider NACE, AAC&U, their own institution's employer and alumni research, and other data and recommendations on desirable inter/intrapersonal skills for graduates. We can also look to our current and former students for guidance about which skills matter. In my own classes, I currently emphasize applying comparative draft insights, organizing feedback for peers, and anticipating specific future applications of peer exchange. I aim to achieve these by explicitly explicitly stating these goals in my peer letter prompt and when I introduce peer review assignments as well as through reflection assignments at the end of major projects that have included peer review. The reasons I chose these specific intra- and interpersonal skills to focus on are that they build upon approaches I already see my students undertake (comparing their drafts to their peers; see the epigraph at the beginning of this article for an example of this), and they also make explicit often implicit knowledge about how to communicate feedback or use classroom-based peer review in professional contexts. I'll expand on my own practices in the next sections about transparent teaching and reflection, including why we should consider transparency in terms of access and inclusion. Here I wish to underscore that instructors must strategically engage in forward-reaching reflection about how peer review applies to workplace skills and make sure that we can identify and explain how these skills are valuable and applicable to future professional writing contexts.

In addition to fostering inter- and intrapersonal skills, peer feedback itself is a pervasive workplace genre. Topping and Van den Berg et al. all call attention to the realistic ways peer feedback anticipates workplace genres such as feedback and evaluations. Ineke Van den Berg et al. assert that "peer assessment of students' writing presents them with an authentic task" (342). The authors connect this experience to students' post-graduation lives, claiming that peer assessment "closely resembles students' future professional practice at the level of a higher education graduate, in which their texts will be assessed and commented upon by colleagues or, for example, by editors of a journal" (342). Peer review prepares writers to exchange documents with colleagues in professional settings. Topping calls further attention to some of the auxiliary skills that students build through peer review which also apply to workplace writing. He summarizes that "[l]earning how to give and accept criticism, justify one's position, and reject suggestions are all forms of social and assertion skills" and then observes, "practice in peer evaluation could facilitate subsequent employee evaluation skills" (Topping 256). Both of these studies confirm that the central writing scenario of peer review, giving and receiving suggestions to another writer or colleague, exists in workplaces and certainly beyond writing classrooms. As writing instructors, we have a huge opportunity to encourage students to attend to the rhetorical and meta-awareness skills they deploy during peer review and anticipate how to adapt and transfer this knowledge to post-graduation writing settings.

Because of the historical legacies of peer review as "busy work"—making responding to drafts easier for instructors—and as a remedial writing activity, positioning peer review as both cultivating inter/intrapersonal skills and practicing a workplace genre requires reframing peer review for our students. Ensuring that we are clear about the transferable skills we are targeting with peer review is the first step towards TFT. Transparent teaching practice begins to implement a TFT approach to peer review, and reflection helps students envision applying this learning to their future lives and careers.

IMPLEMENTING TEACHING FOR TRANSFER THROUGH TRANSPARENCY

Despite what may appear to be obvious correlations between giving a classmate feedback on a draft assignment and offering suggestions to a colleague in a workplace setting, we should not assume that students anticipate this transferred application. For one, student participants in transfer studies frequently overlook ways that writing outside of the classroom relates to writing they complete within the classroom setting (Shepherd; Brent; Beaufort). Furthermore, with peer review specifically, students may view this exchange as preliminary or secondary to other assigned writing in their classes. They may even view peer feedback as a school genre with few analogies in other rhetorical settings. Many of these beliefs about peer review are rooted, as discussed above, in past implementations of peer feedback in college writing courses. As with any activity that we want students to transfer beyond the particular activity in which it is assigned, we must encourage students to recognize the larger uses of peer review. Our task as instructors is to make learners aware of forward-reaching applications for the writing and intra/interpersonal skills they develop in peer review once we have identified the transferable skills on which we want to focus.

One of the most straightforward actions we can implement is being specific and direct about the skills we want students to transfer from peer review and in what contexts they will apply. According to Ryan Shepherd, "Transparency is key to the process of facilitating transfer. Students should be aware of the connections we want them to make and why we want them to make the connections" (112). Threshold concepts have made the goals of writing pedagogies explicit and have encouraged instructors to design learning experiences, such as portfolio assignments, to directly support engagement with threshold concepts (Downs and Wardle; Adler-Kassner et al.). Recent scholarship in teaching and learning has similarly emphasized transparency as an approach to assignment design and a teaching method that facilitates learning for low-income and historically excluded college students (Winkelmes et al.). Transparent teaching includes "teaching students about more than just the course subject matter. It means telling students about your rationale for how and why you've chosen to shape their learning experiences" (Winkelmes "Transparency in Teaching and Learning").

In introducing peer review assignments in my first-year writing classes, I take two main approaches to transparency. First, I share how my own experiences with grant writing for a nonprofit inform my emphasis on peer review as a useful workplace writing genre to practice. Second, I spell out my intended purpose, skills, and knowledge for peer letter feedback on my assignment prompt using Winkelmes' Transparent Assignment Template (see Appendix). I have implemented the first strategy for the past decade since teaching my very first college-level writing course. I found that I could get students' attention and even motivate them to draft thoughtful peer feedback by explaining that peer review had been one of the only forms of writing I produced in college which I used again in my job after I graduated. I then discuss how stressful writing grants became when I began my position as an AmeriCorps VISTA at a literacy nonprofit just before the recession hit in 2008. As a result, our small organization cranked out one grant and solicitation after another, constantly commenting on each other's words. I sometimes share that this mode of peer writing learning and adaptation was so influential that I had a hard time switching back to formal academic writing when I began graduate school. Early in my master's program, one professor kindly pointed out that I was using bolding, underlines, and italics not realizing that this font weighting was not as effective as it was in the skimmable grant requests I was so used to drafting.

This way of opening up about how influential the practices of peer feedback and benchmarking with my colleagues' writing were directly out of my undergraduate degree helps me be up-front about my motivation for spending time and devoting assignments to peer letters and face-to-face feedback in small groups. Even before I more actively encourage students to consider how their future workplaces might share and value colleague feedback, this early start to being transparent about my aims of teaching workplace-applicable writing through peer review helps foster trust in the assignment and motivation to offer more careful feedback through peer review. I do not have a comparison to "before" I shared this personal anecdote and how it affected students' peer letters or evaluation of peer review in my classes. I can offer two observations: (1) that it has energized my own experience of introducing peer review in my classes and (2) that I have never received a set of course evaluations that did not mention peer review as a valuable learning experience in the course.

Since my early "luck" with implementing peer review in my writing courses, I have developed a more robust approach to transparency which includes clearly stating the learning objectives and, more recently, the purpose, skills, and knowledge of my peer letter assignments using the Transparent Assignment Template. The appendix shares my most recent version of a peer review prompt for an online first-year writing class. Research into "transparency" by Mary-Ann Winkelmes and her collaborators suggests that sharing the pedagogical aims and rationales with students for assigned work helps reduce confusion and guesswork that marginalized and underrepresented students in particular face in college projects ("Transparency"). In a 2014–2015 experimental study of sixty-one college courses and 1,174 students, researchers determined that "students who received more transparency reported gains in three areas that are important predictors of students' success: academic confidence, sense of belonging, and mastery of the skills that employers value most when hiring" (Winkelmes et al.). The skills valued by employers (based on Hart Associates findings) were "learning on your own," "applying knowledge and skills to different contexts," "writing effectively," "considering opinions or points of view different from your own," and "judging the strengths and weaknesses of ideas" (Winkelmes et al.). Being transparent about the skills, knowledge, and purpose of our assignment reinforces several of the skills that we want students to acquire through peer review, including transferring knowledge and skills to new contexts. Clearly explaining these larger purposes of peer review will help students reflect on how they deployed the targeted skills during the peer review process, which is also essential for facilitating the transfer of these skills to new contexts.

IMPLEMENTING HIGH-ROAD PEER REVIEW TRANSFER THROUGH BACKWARD- AND FORWARD-REACHING REFLECTION

In addition to transparent goals for peer review, reflection is a widely recognized transfer-oriented practice (Driscoll; Yancey et al.; Adler-Kassner et al.). Reflection on the tools and strategies used to navigate peer feedback and on specific skills and learning that students can transfer into future writing contexts is necessary because transfer in general does not automatically take place within or beyond curriculum settings. This need for reflection is compounded by historically-grounded perceived gaps between peer review as a "remedial" and "school" genre and as a workplace genre with opportunities for useful post-graduation "soft" skill development. We must also keep in mind that as we shift from a process-informed approach to peer review to one rooted in TFT, reflection must also be repositioned for transfer. Writing instructors who wish to extend peer review's impact to students' long-term writing, meta-cognitive, and interpersonal skills must actively build connections between peer feedback skills and other courses, workplaces, and community settings. Reflection highlights and amplifies the skills students utilize to observe, craft, and evaluate their own feedback and aids in transferring learning.

Process-era researchers considered reflection to be a central element in the recursiveness of the writing process. Since process pedagogies sought to push back against, as Sondra Perl explains, "the traditional notion that writing is a linear process with a strict plan-write-revise sequence," reflection assignments and studies created awareness of writers' uses of recursive strategies (364; Sommers). TFT takes a different orientation towards reflection. Kara Taczak states succinctly: "Systematic and intentional reflection prompts writers to transfer" (qtd. in Adler-Kassner et al. 29). She elaborates that systematic reflection "asks writers to look backward as a way to *recall* prior knowledge [. . .] to look forward as a way to frame and *reframe* writing situations, and to look outward as a way to *relocate* knowledge in effective and meaningful ways in different contexts" (29; emphasis in original). This echoes Perkins and Salomon's backward- and forward-reaching transfer, which I draw upon as a framework for this chapter's examination of peer review. Transfer researchers since the 1980s have distinguished between learning transfer required in "near" or similar versus "far" or seemingly unrelated contexts of practice. This distinction leads to different types of TFT interventions. Perkins and Salomon's influential distinctions between "high road" and "low road" transfer formulate these two approaches based on how similar or different students perceive two writing contexts to be. With low-road transfer, students recognize some commonalities between a new and a previous writing situation and utilize prior knowledge without much prompting or thinking. By contrast, high-road transfer presents students with the task of applying prior knowledge to a situation that does not appear to be similar to past writing experiences. Here, additional facilitation is necessary to help students develop connections. Perkins and Salomon suggest that both "forward-reaching" and "backward-reaching" transfer guide students to see connections to future or prior writing practice and identify strategies that apply in either direction from the present context. TFT reflection differs from a process approach to reflection in its focus on utilizing prior learning to not only foster self-awareness to inform writing decisions for the task at hand but also to stimulate thinking and strategizing for future skill applications.

Perkins and Salomon first proposed forward- and backward-reaching transfer as a response to the complications posed by high-road transfer situations or transfer between activities that students do not perceive as very related to one another. The authors view forward-reaching transfer as actively anticipating connections between a current learning activity and a future setting where it could be applied. They offer the scenario of "an enthusiastic economics major learning calculus" who considers how this course could apply to economics-oriented problem solving (Perkins and Salomon 26). In backward-reaching transfer, this same economics major might be faced with a challenging calculation and reflect back on knowledge from the calculus class to apply in the current situation. Importantly, both forward-reaching and backward-reaching transfer require conscious reflection or abstraction in identifying useful similarities between the current task and prior learning or future applications. By contrast, low-road transfer takes place subconsciously without awareness and reflection, such as, Perkins and Salomon suggest, when a student opens a chemistry textbook and automatically reads based on "reading habits acquired elsewhere" (25). Shepherd observes that forward-reaching transfer has held more scholarly focus, but both deserve our attention in writing studies:

> As a field, we have tended to be more concerned with what students have learned in the classroom and helping them project forward to new writing contexts than we have with learning what students already know and helping them connect that knowledge to the current classroom context. I would argue that both of these types of transfer are important, and students cannot successfully engage in one type of high-road transfer without the other. (110)

As we consider how peer review can reinforce connections between the classroom and future writing and exchange experiences, both backward- and forward-reaching transfer offer opportunities for peer review.

In order for learners to enter into peer review with both awareness of the rhetorical and interpersonal setting and meta-awareness of their own choices and skill development, instructors must ensure that they reflect back on prior experiences of peer review and forward to new applications. Many students will understand peer review as being unidirectional: They must provide feedback on a peer's draft so the writer can consider an outside perspective and make revisions. Peer reviewers can be more attuned to the complexities of this exchange by reflecting on their past encounters with peer review assignments. If we ask students to reflect out loud or individually on what types of feedback they typically receive and what they prefer or don't prefer to get from peer feedback, students will often begin by identifying the impacts (or lack thereof) peer review had on their revisions or grade. They often point out that their reviewers responded with more feeling than substance, such as not "liking" a draft without explaining why or being "too nice." Both of these backward-reaching reflections highlight typical, rather flat understandings of peer review as either simply for improving a grade on an assignment or too unpredictable and unhelpful because of the interpersonal dynamics between peers.

To facilitate backward-reaching reflection, students should engage in some form of written, oral, or activity-based recall and reconsideration of prior peer review experiences. In addition to sharing a transparent assignment prompt (Appendix), instructors can integrate a variety of low-stakes assignments into introducing a peer review assignment. These could include reflective writing prompts or mini-skits where students pretend they are providing feedback to a peer in a prior class (such as high school or first-year writing). For example, students could model effective or ineffective feedback, share (or perform) aloud, and then discuss how these feedback experiences impacted them as writers or learners. What was the purpose they perceived of engaging in peer feedback exchange? How did they react to and utilize the suggestions they received in response? Instructors could also provide examples of peer-written feedback and have students discuss in online forums or face-to-face small groups what types of comments are more and less helpful in the sample feedback. It is also worthwhile to address the issue of divergent or conflicting feedback: What do writers gain from having all reviewers state the same major points? What's missing? What do we gain from receiving multiple differing feedback points? What's challenging about this? Here again, a follow-up, full group discussion or instructor comments ought to highlight how certain types of feedback—generally more specific and carefully justified—are more beneficial to writers.

I aim to emphasize two key takeaway points from backward-reaching reflection with my own courses. First I want students to recognize that they have just put themselves in the place of the writer who is receiving feedback in order to evaluate which types of comments are most useful. Second, I underscore that they have just heard from their peers, to whom they will be giving feedback, that their questions and critiques are welcome. The first point is important to acknowledge as we consider the ways we can use our classroom-implemented approaches to peer review beyond the classroom through forward-reaching reflection. The second point helps push back on lingering perceptions that peer review is simply a "busy work" activity that is done for the instructor; I want them to realize that their peers are eager to hear their perspectives and experiences of the texts they are reviewing. The anecdotal evidence I see that this backward-reaching approach to peer review reflection works is that (1) students largely produce strong, detailed, and perceptive peer review comments—both written and in face-to-face conversation and (2) I have seen many semesters of anonymous course feedback that expresses how valuable peer feedback was for student writers during the semester.

Forward-reaching reflection helps make peer feedback's rhetorical challenge even more relevant because it encourages writers to navigate peer review with an understanding that they are developing precisely the types of useful, collaborative workplace skills that they will encounter with their colleagues after college. To facilitate forward-reaching reflection, I find that testimony about the uses of and skills learned from peer review gets students' attention. Even more valuable are opportunities for students to draft and rehearse ways of engaging in the transferable skills and practices using case study scenarios or imaginative prompts. We can help learners see that they have successfully articulated the rhetorical and interpersonal complexities that peer feedback poses to them as writers through this initial reflection. With this new awareness of their own reluctance or ambivalence towards peer review, they must consider not just how to "improve" someone else's draft but also how to help another writer be receptive to, understand, and be able to use the feedback that they provide. Instructors can help students consider how to map out and respond to social-emotional dynamics through their peer feedback by asking them to recall what kinds of feedback they had positive or negative reactions to about their past performances in writing or elsewhere. Hearing from other students in the class can reinforce shared experiences of frustration, appreciation, and confusion related to receiving feedback from a peer reader. We can invite students to draw upon these experiences as readers and receivers of peer feedback to cultivate "sensitivity, and the ability to interact respectfully with all people and understand individuals' differences" ("Career Readiness Defined") as well as to craft more rhetorically astute commentary on another's work. Backward-reaching transfer requires that learners consider and apply prior experiences to negotiate a new situation. With peer review, prior experiences can help writers empathize with their peers and adapt their responses to take their very real audience members' reception of feedback into account.

One example that I have begun to share with my students as part of forward-reaching reflection comes from an article about Jennifer Lee, who took over as Walt Disney Animation Studios' chief creative officer in 2018. According to a National Public Radio story, the workplace environment of Disney Studios involves "Teams of writers and directors not only work[ing] on their own movies, but also lend[ing] a fresh set of eyes and ears to the movies being made by other teams" (Blair). One of Lee's colleagues described her rise through the ranks as part of her contributions to this collaborative feedback environment:

> "She just accepted that the story team is in there trying to help build this story," he says. "You've got to keep that vision but listen to the ideas and figure out what is really behind

those ideas. 'How is that going to help propel the character forward?' and 'Where do I push back and where do I actually listen and figure out how I'm going to alter where I see the story at this point in time?'" Lee's immediate embrace of Disney Animation's collaborative process "made the entire studio just fall in love with her," Spencer says. (qtd. in Blair)

I have students read this part of the article and discuss why a creative executive might have been so appreciated for her skills in peer feedback. Students in the past two semesters offered their hunches about how Lee may have demonstrated sensitivity, provided astute and helpful contributions, understood group dynamics, or even showed the ability to "smooth over" interpersonal tensions to accomplish the task at hand. A helpful follow-up to this forward-reaching transfer discussion is to pair this article excerpt with the NACE descriptions of career competencies. "Leadership," in particular highlights deeply interpersonal and "soft" skills, which students might be able to connect to Lee's example and to their own future uses of peer review experience. "Leadership," according to NACE, involves the ability to "Leverage the strengths of others to achieve common goals, and use interpersonal skills to coach and develop others. The individual is able to assess and manage his/her emotions and those of others; use empathetic skills to guide and motivate; and organize, prioritize, and delegate work" ("Career Readiness Defined"). This explicit definition from NACE can help students better reflect on and frame the skills they used and even the challenges they faced during peer review with forward-reaching workplace applications in mind. For example, I often conclude a peer exchange assignment by asking students to use their peer review experience to draft responses to job interview questions such as "Tell me about a time when you had to give someone bad news" or "when you disagreed with a new direction for a project." By situating peer review as both informed by prior experiences and anticipating future experiences, students can often describe in much richer detail a multidimensional peer exchange involving drafts and feedback as well as person-to-person exchange, draft-to-draft comparisons, and feedback-to-feedback comparisons. Reflection activities that ask students how they approached their peer feedback, what considerations they used to decide what and how to communicate to a peer writer, and how they evaluated their own drafts and feedback compared to their peers prepare them to recognize and adapt these meta-awareness skills to workplace exchanges.

Rather than hope or assume that students are actively looking backward and forward at ways to inform and eventually utilize learning in our classrooms, we must build reflection and application into every peer review in order to teach for transfer. TFT once again offers a clear purpose for reflection, and facilitating peer review using reflection as well as transparency will more readily enable learners to transfer the skills they develop during peer feedback. Reflection and transparency are particularly critical for facilitating the transfer of writing, meta-awareness, and inter/intrapersonal skills in peer review because of added distance instilled by past iterations of peer review practice. Learners may be frustrated in assuming that peer review is asking students to perform the "teacher's" task of correcting someone else's draft. If instructors do not recognize and help learners reflect on these prior beliefs, there will be limited potential for applying peer review skills in subsequent professional settings. Backward- and forward-reaching reflection specifically scaffolds learning transfer between settings that appear to be dissimilar to student writers.

CONCLUSION

Peer review and process pedagogy continue to inform writing instruction today, but current pressures and exigencies necessitate a re-examination of peer review's purposes as well as assumptions. The 2020 coronavirus pandemic has disrupted and recalibrated many teaching and learning practices and priorities. Peer review itself offers much-needed interaction in online and hybrid courses, which are now a necessity in higher education. While a process-informed approach to peer review sought to distribute power, center students' writing and voices, and underscore the recursiveness of writing, such goals today overlook some of the pressing concerns students bring into twenty-first-century post-COVID classrooms. Teaching for transfer presents a way to connect with students regarding their lives as professionals and writers outside of the classroom during a time when the world beyond the college classroom shapes and disrupts much of our work with students.

CCCC and CWPA issued a statement in June 2020 that seeks to guide writing instructors' course design decisions and changes in response to COVID-19. The "Joint Statement in Response to the COVID-19 Pandemic" offers actionable items for instructors and their administrators to consider as programs weigh course design and delivery decisions that emphasize student-to-student interaction and reflection. It does not, however, present much in the way of student-oriented language about why a writing course would involve working with peers, "iterative" and "incremental" drafting assignments, and models of self-assessment of learning. As instructors continue to adapt pre-COVID-19 pedagogies and approaches to changing learning contexts, TFT would fill this gap and enable further transparency about the long-term learning objectives of preparing students for the types of writing and rhetorical savviness needed in professional and community writing workspaces. The statement encourages peer feedback specifically as a way to implement one of the six stated "core principles" of "writers need readers." This recommendation, along with utilizing discussion boards, drafts, and self-assessment activities, includes a brief justification that is practical rather than praxiological; all of these teaching suggestions are recommended because they facilitate learning habits such as "flexibility," "motivation," and "engagement." Though clearly informed by online writing instruction research, process pedagogy, writing about writing, and even transfer to some extent, the statement itself omits pedagogical justifications to succinctly present "core principles of effective writing instruction drawn from disciplinary research." What I take from this document is our field's ongoing general value of both peer review and reflection as ways to achieve participation and offer a variety of writing and learning opportunities in college writing courses even during this stressful pandemic period. While peer feedback and reflection are useful components to include in courses where learners may be working and interacting remotely, I believe that students want additional reasons to participate in peer-to-peer exchanges, reflection, and self-assessment with such tremendous health, political, and social justice movements and upheavals taking place around them. Peer review can support connectedness even without a teaching-for-transfer approach, but if we add TFT we extend these valuable experiences to connect with today's students and offer transparency and variety in the ways in which we assess student learning.

Integrating TFT with peer review means stating clearly what the transferable skills are for exchanging peer feedback and facilitating that transfer through, I argue, forward- and backward-reaching reflection along with transparent goals. This shift from process- to transfer-informed peer review may benefit our courses now more than ever because articulating long-term uses for assignments offers a chance to demonstrate that we are invested in creating courses and outcomes that apply to students' lives outside of the classroom. Even before coronavirus-related stresses of physical distancing, the loss of jobs and job prospects, and patchwork public health policies, studies indicated that students coming into college classrooms today, so-called "Generation Z" or "iGen," have been asking for workplace and community applicability in their coursework (Pappano). They are eager to see connections between their classroom efforts and the career and community-engaged lives they aim to lead after graduation. Jean M. Twenge argues in her book on Gen Z that this generation was already significantly impacted by witnessing the Great Recession as adolescents and are more motivated to obtain job security and acquire skills for career advancement. It seems all the more important that we make clear how students' investment of time and effort into activities such as peer review and individual or group reflections promotes writing habits that apply to places beyond writing classrooms. We must also keep in mind that we cannot assume that learners view peer review as similar to collaborative workplace writing settings. In fact, as I have cautioned in this chapter, learners and instructors may assume peer draft exchange is a remedial activity or simply a way to reduce how much feedback the instructor "needs" to give to each student based on historical trends and legacies of integrating peer review in over-crowded and lower-level courses. In short, we limit the impacts of our instruction and close off opportunities to dovetail our pedagogical interests with the goal-oriented spirit of many students in Gen Z if we do not discuss how the rhetorical and inter/intrapersonal skills they are learning can translate into other spheres of their professional and community lives. Amidst many distractions for learners today, it is all the more productive to articulate the purposes and future uses of assignments such as reflection and peer review through TFT.

WORKS CITED

Addison, Joanne, and Sharon James McGee "Writing in High School/Writing in College: Research Trends and Future Directions." *College Composition and Communication*, vol. 62, no. 1, JSTOR, 2010, pp. 147–79, https://www.jstor.org/stable/27917889.

Adler-Kassner, Linda, and Elizabeth Wardle, editors. *Naming What We Know: Threshold Concepts in Writing Studies*. Utah State UP, 2015.

Adler-Kassner, et al. "Assembling Knowledge: The Role of Threshold Concepts in Facilitating Transfer." *Critical Transitions: Writing and the Question of Transfer*, edited by Chris M. Anson and Jessie L. Moore, UP of Colorado, 2017, pp. 17–48.

Bacon, Nora. "The Trouble with Transfer: Lessons from a Study of Community Service Writing." *Michigan Journal of Community Service Learning*, vol. 6, ERIC, 1999, pp. 53–62, https://eric.ed.gov/?id=EJ618245.

Beaufort, Anne. *College Writing and Beyond: A New Framework for University Writing Instruction*. Utah State UP, 2007.

Blair, Elizabeth. "Disney Animation Chief Jennifer Lee Is the Queen Behind Elsa and Anna." *National Public Radio*, 21 Nov. 2019, https://www.npr.org/2019/11/21/780972977/disney-animation-chief-jennifer-lee-is-the-queen-behind-elsa-and-anna.

Brent, Doug. "Crossing Boundaries: Co-op Students Relearning to Write." *College Composition and Communication*, vol. 63, no. 4, 2012, pp. 558–92.

Bruffee, Kenneth A. "Collaborative Learning and the 'Conversation of Mankind.'" *Cross-Talk in Comp Theory: A Reader*, edited by Victor Villanueva, 2nd ed., National Council Teachers of English, 2003. pp. 415–36.

Conference on College Composition and Communication and Council of Writing Program Administrators. *CCCC and CWPA Joint Statement in Response to the COVID-19 Pandemic*. CCCC and CWPA, 2020, https://cccc.ncte.org/cccc/cccc-and-cwpa-joint-statement-in-response-to-the-covid-19-pandemic.

"Career Readiness Defined." National Association of Colleges and Employers, https://www.naceweb.org/career-readiness/competencies/career-readiness-defined/.

Ching, Kory Lawson. "Peer Response in the Composition Classroom: An Alternative Genealogy." *Rhetoric Review*, vol. 26, no. 3, 2007, pp. 303–19. *JSTOR*, https://www.jstor.org/stable/20176793.

Connors, Robert J. *Composition-Rhetoric: Backgrounds, Theory, and Pedagogy*. U of Pittsburgh P, 1997.

Dorman, Steve, and Kelli Brown. "The Liberal Arts: Preparing the Workforce of the Future." *Liberal Education*, vol. 104, no. 4, 2018, pp. 58–63.

Downs, Doug, and Elizabeth Wardle. "Teaching about Writing, Righting Misconceptions: (Re)Envisioning 'First-Year Composition' as 'Introduction to Writing Studies.'" *College Composition and Communication*, vol. 58, no. 4, Jun. 2007, pp. 552–84.

Driscoll, Dana Lynn. "Building Connections and Transferring Knowledge: The Benefits of a Peer Tutoring Course Beyond the Writing Center." *Writing Center Journal*, vol. 35, no. 1, fall/winter 2015, pp. 153–81.

Finley, Ashley, and Tia Finley McNair. "Assessing Underserved Students' Engagement in High-Impact Practices." *Association of American Colleges and Universities*, 2013, *ERIC*. Accessed 8 May 2023, https://files.eric.ed.gov/fulltext/ED582014.pdf.

Flower, Linda. "Cognition, Context, and Theory Building." *Cross-Talk in Comp Theory: A Reader*, edited by Victor Villanueva, 2nd ed., National Council Teachers of English, 2003. pp. 739–71.

Howard, Rebecca Moore. "Collaborative Pedagogy." *A Guide to Composition* Pedagogies, edited by Gary Tate et al., Oxford UP, 2001, pp. 54–70.

Gaillet, Lynée Lewis. "An Historical Perspective on Collaborative Learning." *Journal of Advanced Composition*, vol. 14, no. 1, winter 1994, pp. 93–111. *JSTOR*, https://www.jstor.org/stable/20865949.

Gere, Ann Ruggles. *Writing Groups: History, Theory, and Implications*. Southern Illinois UP, 1987.

Hart Research Associates. *Falling Short? College Learning and Career Success*. Association of American Colleges and Universities, 2015, https://www.aacu.org/sites/default/files/files/LEAP/2015employerstudentsurvey.pdf.

Jarratt, Susan C., et al. "Pedagogical Memory: Writing, Mapping, Translating." *Writing Program Administration*, vol. 33, no. 1–2, fall/winter 2009, pp. 46–73, http://associationdatabase.co/archives/33n1-2/33n1–2jarratt.pdf.

Kitzhaber, Albert R. *Rhetoric in American Colleges, 1850–1900*. Southern Methodist U, 1990.

Kuh, George D. *High-Impact Practices: What They Are, Who Has Access to Them, and Why They Matter*. Association of American Colleges and Universities, 2008.

Moore, Jessie. "Mapping the Questions: The State of Writing-Related Transfer Research." *Composition Forum*, vol. 26, fall, 2012, https://compositionforum.com/issue/26/map-questions-transfer-research.php.

Nowacek, Rebecca. *Agents of Integration: Understanding Transfer as a Rhetorical Act*. Southern Illinois UP, 2011.

Pappano, Laura. "The iGen Shift: Colleges Are Changing to Reach the Next Generation." *New York Times*, 2 Aug. 2018, www.nytimes.com/2018/08/02/education/learning/generationz-igen-students-colleges.html?WT.nav=top-news&action=click&clickSource=story-heading&hp&module=second-column-region&pgtype=Homepage&region=top-news.

Perkins, David N., and Gavriel Salomon. "Teaching for Transfer." *Educational Leadership*, vol. 46, no. 1, 1988, pp. 22–32, https://pdfs.semanticscholar.org/d1fe/324a-117c069b09cbc4ae8a82c5ac18ba3ac9.pdf.

Shepherd, Ryan P. "Digital Writing, Multimodality, and Learning Transfer: Crafting Connections between Composition and Online Composing." *Computers and Composition* vol. 48, 2018, pp. 103–14.

Sommers, Jeffrey. "Behind the Paper: Using the Student-Teacher Memo." *College Composition and Communication*, vol. 39, no. 1, Feb. 1988, pp. 77–80.

Tobin, Lad. "Process." *A Guide to Composition* Pedagogies, edited by Gary Tate et al., Oxford UP, 2001, pp. 1–18.

Topping, Keith. "Peer Assessment Between Students in Colleges and Universities," *Review of Educational Research*, vol. 68, no. 3, Fall 1998, pp. 249–76, https://doi.org/10.2307/1170598.

Twenge, Jean M. *iGen: Why Today's Super-Connected Kids Are Growing Up Less Rebellious, More Tolerant, Less Happy—and Completely Unprepared for Adulthood (and What This Means for the Rest of Us)*. Atria Books, 2017.

Van den Berg, Ineke, et al. "Design Principles and Outcomes of Peer Assessment in Higher Education." *Studies in Higher Education*, vol. 31, no. 3, June 2006, pp. 341–56. *EBSCOHost*, https://doi.org/10.1080/03075070600680836.

Wardle, Elizabeth. "'Mutt Genres' and the Goal of FYC: Can We Help Students Write the Genres of the University?" *College Composition and Communication*, vol. 60, no. 4, June 2009, pp. 765–89. *JSTOR*, https://www.jstor.org/stable/40593429.

Winkelmes, Mary-Ann. "Transparency in Teaching and Learning." Smart Talk Interview, no. 25 by Alison Head and Kirsten Hostetler. *Project Information Literacy*, 2 Sept. 2015, https://www.projectinfolit.org/mary-ann-winkelmes-smart-talk.html.

Winkelmes, Mary-Ann. "Transparent Assignment Template." 2013, https://www.unlv.edu/sites/default/files/page_files/27/Provost-Faculty-TransparentAssgntTemplate-2016.pdf.

Winkelmes, Mary-Ann, et al. "A Teaching Intervention that Increases Underserved College Students' Success." *Peer Review*, vol. 18, no. 1/2, winter/spring 2016, https://www.aacu.org/peerreview/2016/winter-spring/Winkelmes.

Yancey, Kathleen Blake, Liane Robertson, and Kara Taczak. *Writing across Contexts*. Utah State UP, 2014.

APPENDIX: SPRING 2020 "TRANSPARENT" PEER LETTERS ASSIGNMENT PROMPT

*I ran the first-year writing course from which this prompt is taken fully online in Spring 2020, but I added a peer letter template after COVID-19 hit my

Northeastern state hard in March prior to the peer review assignment. I share more on COVID-19's effects on peer review, transparency, and TFT in the conclusion.

Peer Letters (2 per assignment)
250–300 words per letter
Research Paper Peer Letters Due: **Sunday, April 5th**
Optional/Extra Credit Portfolio Peer Letters Due: Friday, May 1st

Purpose: Peer letters offer clear and targeted feedback on your classmates' drafts. They are actually a form of writing you will use in a workplace. Becoming comfortable stating how effectively or not another person's writing is—and explaining why—is a really important skill for working with your colleagues. In fact, the current chief creative officer of Walt Disney Animation Studio rose to her position because of how effectively she collaborated on peer feedback. Peer letters also develop your writing skills from the perspective of a reader.

Skills: The aim of this assignment is to help you practice the following skills that are essential to your success in this course and in your future careers:

- Identifying what stands out to you as an audience member/reader for another writer's work
- Describing what you took from someone's writing
- Explaining what effect a writer's choices had on you as a reader—both positive and negative effects
- Achieving an appropriate tone for real readers—your classmates—who needs to use your feedback to improve their drafts

Knowledge: This assignment will also help you to become familiar with the following important writing-related knowledge for use across disciplines:

4. Higher and lower-order concerns or issues in a draft
5. Letter structure

Task: You will find the first drafts of your peers' essays on the Blackboard Discussion Board. You will then write one letter to two writers in your peer group (ask me if you have questions about who you should write letters to).
Each letter should include:

- A summary of <u>what you understood the main argument to be as a reader</u> (this could be a couple of sentences)
- A discussion of the <u>paper's strengths</u> (*notice this is the paper's strengths, not the writer's strengths*), and point to <u>specific examples</u> from the paper and <u>explanations of why</u> they were effective
- An explanation of any <u>higher-order issues</u> you found as a reader, with <u>specific examples</u> and <u>suggestions for revising</u>

143

- A note about any lower-order issues the writer may want to consider
- Concluding remarks

\>\>You may use this letter template if you want:

Dear [name]:

I enjoyed reading your first draft of the Research Paper. What I understood your argument to be about was [*put their argument in your own words*].

I thought the major strengths of the draft were [*introduce higher-order strengths*]. For example, on page/in the __ paragraph, you discussed [*give specific examples of what was effective or strengths*]. I also found _____ to be effective because [*say why it was effective*]. Finally, _____ was a good choice because [*say why*].

I did have a little trouble understanding [*introduce what was not as effective or confusing from the draft—more higher-order issues*]. I thought this was [*explain what was confusing*]. Perhaps you could [*offer a suggestion for improving*]. Another part where I had difficulty was _____. Here I thought you could try. . . .

— OR — I didn't have difficulty understanding the organization or argument in your draft. One possible revision you could consider would be to [*offer a higher-order suggestion about paragraph order, introduction, thesis, topic sentences, sources, conclusion, etc.*]. This would make it so that [*explain what the alternative approach would achieve for the draft or its readers*].

There were some lower-order concerns in some sentences. For example, look at the __ paragraph's __ sentence. It's missing a word or two . . . [*Explain no more than 3 sentence-level or lower-order issues you noticed in the draft*].

Good luck with your second draft!

Sincerely,

[your name]

Criteria for Success:

- Did you write two 250–300-word letters to two different peers?
- Are your letters addressed to the writer and signed off by you?
- Do you cover:
  - What you thought the main argument was about?
  - Specific higher-order strengths?
  - Specific higher-order issues?
  - Why each example was effective or difficult to you as a reader?
  - How to revise each issue?
  - Any lower-order concerns you noticed?

PART THREE. PEER REVIEW: CULTIVATING INCLUSIVENESS

CHAPTER 7.

PEER REVIEW AND THE BENEFITS OF ANXIETY IN THE ACADEMIC WRITING CLASSROOM

Ellen Turner
Lund University

Peer review activities are now an integral part of the teaching of academic writing in most universities, and the benefits of such student-centered teaching methods are well-documented (Lundstrom and Baker). However, one of the most serious concerns regarding peer review is that it can potentially increase anxiety for learners. This anxiety is two-fold; both the giving of feedback and the reception of criticism can induce feelings of discomfort for students (Winer; Murau; Liu and Sadler). Moreover, in order for peer review activities to be successfully implemented, a desire amongst students to want to help each other as part of a learning community needs to be in place. This chapter aims to investigate the role that self-reflection on the peer review process can play in alleviating student anxiety, whilst simultaneously helping to foster empathy and community spirit within a group. The present study examines the way in which students articulate their emotional responses to peer review. One of the central assumptions that this current piece will challenge is whether anxiety is necessarily always negative. Clearly, too much anxiety can be detrimental and even paralyzing to students. However, a degree of anxiety can be beneficial in raising levels of student achievement and ensuring that all students get the most out of a learning situation.

Anxiety is usually understood to be a detrimental emotional response in a learning environment and there are a vast number of studies which explore the negative facets of learner anxiety (Zeidner; Wu and Lin; Demirel). According to Moshe Zeidner's contribution to the *International Handbook of Emotions in Education*, "[t]he core theme in anxiety is danger or threat to ego or self-esteem, especially when a person is facing an uncertain existential threat" (Zeidner 267). Zeidner explains that anxiety frequently occurs in educational settings particularly in social situations where there is "the prospect of personal evaluation," whether "real or imagined." This anxiety is at its most salient, according to Zeidner, "when a student perceives a low likelihood of obtaining satisfactory evaluations from others" (269). Peer review situations, in particular those which are classroom based, may be likely to cause anxiety as they normally involve appraisal by one's peers in situations which entail a high degree of social interaction. For this reason, understanding anxiety in relation to classroom-based peer review is crucial.

Challenging the conception that anxiety is unequivocally negative, Peter MacIntyre and Jean-Marc Devaele, ponder the suggestion that "a focus on anxiety's negative effects is dealing with only half of the issue" (240) and rather propose exploring positive as well as negative facets of the learner experience. In their study of the second language classroom, MacIntyre and Devaele discuss the complex "emotional dynamics" which mean that "anxiety and enjoyment" are not necessarily mutually exclusive (261); in other words, that it is possible for a learner to simultaneously experience positive emotions and anxiety at one and the same time. Along similar lines, it has been suggested that anxiety should not always be conceived as undesirable as it is a necessary part of grappling with complexity and uncertainty (Barnett 252). Learning is about coming to terms with the inevitable anxiety which accompanies sometimes bumpy and uncomfortable educational journeys across thresholds into new understandings and competencies. According to Ronald Barnett's manifesto, learning in an age of uncertainty is "a matter of learning to live with uncertainty." Barnett proposes "a form of learning that sets out not to dissolve anxiety—for it recognizes that that is not feasible—but that sets out to provide the human wherewithal to live with anxiety" (Barnett 252). Acknowledging that, for some students, a degree of anxiety is inevitable when it comes to peer review, we can look for ways to harness this anxiety so that it becomes constructive to learning rather than detrimental.

As with other forms of peer learning, it is of vital importance that educational facilitators recognize the emotional facets of implementing peer review activities in the classroom (Boud 4). The present chapter will consider findings from an academic writing course, originally developed by Fabian Beijer at the English Unit at Lund University, Sweden. This is a classroom-based course in which peer review was conducted face-to-face. Evidence of student perceptions of the peer review process has been taken from 95 learning journals, collected over eight semesters, in which students were asked to record their reactions to participating in such activities. Even though I explore the process of peer review from a particularly Swedish perspective, where collaborative practices are the norm and, to some extent, entrenched in the Swedish psyche, students nevertheless tend to express nervousness about both giving and receiving feedback. In addition to exploring how students articulate their emotional responses to peer review, I also make practical suggestions about how these reactions can be addressed. By encouraging self-reflection on the peer review process, I suggest that negative emotional responses can be reconceived in a more positive light. Not only do students benefit from the peer review in terms of developing the critical and analytic competencies in relation to their academic writing abilities, but they also develop crucial graduate competencies related to reflective practice. Reflecting on what makes the peer review process potentially anxiety-provoking leads students to better understand and use these usually negative responses.

PREVIOUS RESEARCH

Indebted to David Boud's recognition of the importance of the emotional aspects of peer review, there is now a nascent body of work exploring the role of feelings and perceptions in relation this kind of peer-to-peer activity. Sara Värlander, for instance, premises her research into students' emotional response to receiving feedback on the notion that "[e]motions are constitutive of the activity of learning and shape the learning experiences" (149); in other words, it is imperative to give due regard to emotions in learning environments not just because they are by-products of any given situation, but since they play an active role in shaping that situation. Furthermore, Värlander articulates the complexity inherent in the fact that emotions are not merely the "product of individual experiences" but are instead constituted through "social relationships in the classroom between peers, and between peers and tutors" (149). These complexities mean that the findings from research into student perceptions of peer review activities tend to be highly socially contingent.

In a recent review based on evidence from 103 articles, Carrie Yea-huey Chang points to the burgeoning research in peer review in both the L1 and L2 classroom which begun in the 1980s and is still very much alive today. Chang's synthesis of two decades of peer review research, with a particular focus on the L2 context, provides a valuable resource to those seeking an overview of current research. Research on student perceptions in peer review - defined by Chang as that which "refer[s] to learners' beliefs and attitudes toward peer review" (86)—forms one of the three central pillars in Chang's account. And one of the main conclusions drawn from this synthesis regarding this strand of peer review research is that "[m]ore studies are needed to understand student writers' and reviewers' respective attitudes toward/perceptions of the advantages and disadvantages of peer review" (107).

Recent research in the field of student perceptions has suggested that making use of peer review in the classroom can have a positive effect on combating writing anxiety, particularly amongst non-native speakers of English. Gülşah Çınar Yastıba and Ahmet Erdost Yastıbaş's findings suggest that Turkish students in the English as a foreign language classroom tend to perceive peer review as an encouraging and affirming activity which "reduces their writing anxiety" (537). Yastıba and Yastıba report that peer review enables students to recognize that "making mistakes is a part of learning and they can help each other in improving their writings by interacting and collaborating with each other" thus contributing to a "less anxious and stressful" learning environment (537). However, there may be some circularity in the argument that peer review can contribute to a more collaborative and thus less-anxiety provoking experience for students since alternative studies have shown that peer review activities are at their most effective when such a cooperative environment already exists. For instance, Gayle L. Nelson and John M. Murphy have found that "[w]hen writers interacted with their peers in a cooperative manner, they were more likely to use the peers' suggestions in revising. When writers interacted with their peers in a defensive manner or did not interact at all, the writer was less likely to use the peers' comments" (140). Whether peer review itself can help to produce this cooperative environment, or whether peer review only functions well if this environment is already in place, is a question which remains as yet unanswered.

One of the resounding arguments in favor of peer review is its role in enabling learners to develop autonomy in relation to the decision that students make in evaluating their own work. For instance, in having to grapple with receiving conflicting advice from their peers, learners must decide for themselves what action to take in their own writing based on feedback received. This is affirmed by David Nicol, Avril Thomson and Caroline Breslin in their recent study investigating the cognitive processes involved in peer review. Exploring students' perceptions of the benefits of both giving and receiving feedback, Nicol et al. report on the fact that students who engaged in peer review felt an increased sense of control over their own learning journey which was primarily a result of "the reflective process it [peer review] engenders." Nicol et al. conclude that "[t]his form of control goes well beyond students becoming better users of teacher feedback, as it puts feedback processes firmly in their hands" (118). Furthermore, previous research has suggested that peer review can facilitate the development of competencies that go beyond the classroom to benefit students in their chosen paths beyond the university walls. Nicol et al. note that in staging peer review in such a way that "feedback production is recognised as just as valuable for learning as feedback receipt" can empower students in cultivating skills which will form an important part in "professional life beyond university" (120).

However, despite its well-enumerated advantages in terms of tackling writer anxiety and in the development of cognitive competencies which extend to facets of life beyond the classroom, peer review in itself can often be a source of anxiety for students. Winer's 1992 diary study based on student-teachers' reflections on the peer review process concluded that the "feelings of insecurity, anxiety, and dread expressed" by students requires some form of intervention in order to circumvent obstacles to learning (76). Andrea Murau's investigation into student perceptions of peer review in the 1990s was, along with Winer's study, one of the earlier explorations on the "possible negative effect of peer review on writing anxiety" (72). Murau recognized that student often experienced feelings of embarrassment both in the giving and receiving of criticism. The results of Murau's study suggest that both first language (L1) and second language (L2) learners who participated in peer review tended to feel either anxious or embarrassed by the process, but where L1 learners perceived the overall positive effect of peer review to offset these negative emotions, L2 learners "noted more negative feelings about it than positive" (74). One recommendation made as a result of these findings was that teachers who are considering conducting peer review in their own classrooms should first of all inquire into how students feel about having their work reviewed by their peers and reviewing the work of others. By conducting such a pre-peer review evaluation teachers might be able to mediate some of the negative reactions to the process. Maria Amores suggests that the student perceptions of peer review are often overlooked by teachers who fail to see beyond the effects that peer review has on improving writing to the elements of social interaction with which students are most concerned. Amores writes that the students who formed the basis for her study "seemed to be more concerned with the personal, social, and emotional aspects of peer-editing (e.g., who has the "right" to impose views)." Accordingly, "they accommodated their speech to the 'threatening' situation so they would not hurt each other's feelings" (Amores 521). Amores found definitively that peer review "generates a sense of discomfort and uneasiness among the participants" (519).

Amongst more recent studies which support Amores' findings is that conducted by Raoul Mulder et al. in which approximately half of students in the sample group expressed anxiety towards peer review which stemmed from a variety of concerns. The most prominent of these concerns was in striking "the right tone and balance between positive and negative feedback" (Mulder et al.., 662). In addition to worries about abilities to communicate feedback in an appropriately constructive way without causing offense, students in the Mulder et al. study also raised concerns in relation to reviewers potentially being "too nice." A significant proportion of students in the study also had concerns over their authority as givers of feedback given their lack of experience in providing such feedback (Mulder et al. 662). Even though students reported an overall positive experience of peer review regarding the value to learning, concerns about the authority of feedback given remained. These findings relating to fears about peers being appropriately qualified to give feedback are ones that are substantiated by other similar studies (for instance Cheng and Warren).

Though the more recent studies cited above have begun to make headway in examining student perceptions of peer review, there is still a consensus that this research is still in its infancy. As Nicol et al. testify, "[t]here is no doubt that more research is required on peer review and its different components, including more studies of students' experiences, perceptions and responses to the different feedback arrangements that are possible during its implementation" (119). From the disparity of the results from studies on peer review and student perceptions, inferences can be drawn that outcomes vary greatly depending on the social context and individual group dynamics in any given situation. However, it seems reasonable to expect that in any given classroom and in any given context there will be individuals who respond negatively towards peer review for a variety of reasons.

Where the gap in previous research is at its broadest is in examining ways to mediate the negative emotional responses to peer review. One of the exceptions in this body of scholarship is a study conducted by Jun Liu and Randall W. Sadler in which they recognize that "the nature of responding to peers' drafts sometimes generates a sense of discomfort and uneasiness among the participants" which can generate a tendency for students to act "defensively" in the face of peer criticism (194). Liu and Sadler suggest that combining computer-mediated feedback with the traditional face-to-face peer-review format is one way to tackle this problem.

One study which, like the present paper, has also explored the role that learning journal reflection can play in charting student perception of peer review is that conducted by Daniel Boase-Jelinek, Jenni Parker and Jan Herrington. Here Boase-Jelinek et al. make use of blog entries made by students which charted their observations on peer assessment. Amongst the conclusions drawn from this study was the fact that although most students reported positive reactions to the peer-review activities, a significant proportion of students expressed anxiety particularly in relation to the giving of feedback. This anxiety often stemmed from "concern[s] about offending a peer with critical (corrective) comments" (Boase-Jelinek et al.125). Interestingly though, the authors of the study also note that students often reported a mixture of both positive and negative reactions. As an example, they cite a student who manages, through the process of reflection, to articulate how what initially felt like a "personal attack" was actually "designed to help you get better marks" and as such, in the words to the particular student in question, was able to "stop being upset" once the benefit was realized (126).

Winer reports that the mere fact of recording their reflections acted as a "powerful trigger to awareness and thus development" (64) and described progress in relation to self-awareness throughout the course as "stunning" (77). This present study builds on the existing body of research which has begun to explore peer review in terms of student perception but looks more deeply into the role that reflection can play in helping students to negotiate some of the perceived negative emotional reactions to both giving and receiving peer feedback. In *Reflection: Turning Experience into Learning* David Boud, Rosemary Keogh, David Walker state that despite the fact that "emotions and feelings are a significant source of learning, they can also at times become barriers" (29).

When these feelings and emotions form roadblocks in learning, they "need to be recognized as such and removed before the learning process can proceed" (29). Reflection is, according to Boud et al., an effective means with which to pass through potential obstructions which might be the result of negative feelings and emotions. Since the capacity for critical reflection "may be innately present in only a small proportion of students" (Coulson and Harvey 401), scaffolding to enable such reflection, particularly when it comes the emotional components of experiential learning, is important: "Supporting learners to develop their capacity for reflection and structuring opportunities for reflection before, during and after the experience will enable learners to navigate the inherent complexities of learning through experience" (Coulson and Harvey 403). My investigation is underpinned by this philosophy and is supported by Winer's still relevant findings related to the positive impact of scaffolding peer review with reflective activities.

THE PRESENT STUDY

Murau's study recommended that teachers consider assessing how each individual cohort of students feel about peer review *before* implementing such activities. Likewise, in offering recommendations for the effective implementation of peer review, Jette G. Hansen and Jun Liu suggest that facilitators should actively work to encourage classroom reflection and discussion in relation to students' prior experience of peer review activities and the cultural norms that shape these experiences (33). These recommendations underpinned the design of the reflective scaffolding around the peer review activities in this particular study. In what follows, a brief description of the peer review component of the course will be provided, along with a description of the reflective learning journal which supplemented the peer review activities. The course on which the analysis in this present paper has been based is an undergraduate level academic writing and written proficiency course provided by the English unit at a Swedish university.

The students who took this course came from a wide variety of disciplinary backgrounds. The course was worth 7.5 credits (equivalent to European Credit Transfer System points), equating to one-quarter of a full-time workload over one semester. This study spans eight semesters from between the spring of 2012 to the spring of 2016. The course ran during both the autumn and the spring semesters, and the reflections have been taken from those semesters in which I was course moderator. During the five-year span over which the reflections have been taken, the course has inevitably been subject to development and revision. Where the revisions have particular bearing on the present study, they have been duly noted. Here I focus specifically on student reflections in the learning journal component in which students were required to record their reflections on their journey through the course. The learning journal was a supplement to two other assessed components in the course: a grammar exam and an academic essay task.

The highest stakes assignment on the course was an academic essay (worth 50 percent of the overall grade). Students were asked to write an essay on a subject of their choice and took part in three in-class peer review sessions at various points in the writing process. Students were divided into small peer groups typically comprised of 3 to 5 students. Peer groups were randomly assigned and, where possible, were kept the same for all three peer review sessions to order to facilitate continuity and foster a sense of community spirit within each group. At each peer review session, students were asked to read and prepare comments on the draft prior to coming to class, and then to deliver feedback verbally in the classroom situation. Students were provided with a list of questions to consider in relation to each essay draft. As well as receiving peer-to-peer feedback, teacher feedback on essay drafts was also provided. Prior to the first peer feedback session, a presentation on effective feedback techniques was given alongside a class discussion on students' previous experience of peer review and the perceived benefits and drawbacks. After each peer review session, students were given the chance to share their thoughts on the process in an activity debriefing. In the autumn of 2013, I introduced structured reflection questions which students could use to scaffold their own reflections immediately after the activity took place.

Keeping a learning journal was an obligatory part of the course and allowed students to chart their progress in a dialogue with the teacher. Course participants submitted a total of five short reflective entries staggered at strategic timings throughout the semester. In these entries, participants were encouraged to reflect on the course and the learning material as well as their own learning journey. The purpose of the learning journals was multifaceted. As well as encouraging the development of higher order critical thinking skills, the learning journals offered an avenue for participants to overcome some of the challenges with writer's block, lack of confidence and the development of voice. It also allowed for a two-way conversation between teacher and student, and I was able to respond to concerns raised by students and address potential roadblocks to learning at an early stage. The final learning journal containing all five entries was submitted for assessment at the end of the course. One of the potential limitations of this study is that the recorded reflections that form the basis for the present analysis were part of the assessment for the course, and this may have had some bearing on the texts provided by students. However, the impact of this is potentially lessened by the fact that this was a low-stakes assignment for which the grading criteria emphasized the importance of critical reflection and personal exploration. In the autumn of 2013, the instructions of the learning journal were revised such that rather than submitting completely open journal entries, students were instead asked to reflect on specific topics and additional scaffolding, such as questions to consider, were provided. Inevitably, this shaped the contents of learning journal entries which became more directed. This may of course be interpreted either positively or negatively in terms of this study. On the one hand, providing more scaffolding for students to structure their reflections potentially allowed for more focused and ultimately fruitful reflections. On the other hand, such scaffolding might be conceived as leading and might subtly prompt the writer to respond in a certain way.

In interpreting the learning journal reflections in the following analysis, I have remained alert to this potential limitation. In this study students taking the course from the autumn of 2013 and onwards were asked to reflect specifically on the peer review process in one particular journal entry. Prior to composing the entry, students were encouraged to consider questions prompting reflection of their past experiences of peer review in learning environments. They were asked to consider what they perceived to be the most significant benefits and drawbacks of peer review in general and how they felt about the peer review activities on this particular course. They were asked to reflect on their experience as both giver and receiver of feedback and consider the impact of their feelings towards the process. Other entries in the journal were more open and discussing the peer review component of the course was just one of many options open to students. Many students chose to make use of the open entries to discuss their thoughts about the peer review activities throughout the course.

ANALYSIS

Allowing students the opportunity to express their opinions before, during and after feedback sessions was one way in which I was able to monitor student reactions throughout the course. What follows is a qualitative analysis of students' learning journal reflections. The majority of the participants reported positive feelings towards the peer review process. Students frequently described that they perceived the peer reviews to be "fun," "rewarding," "pleasurable," and one student went so far as to describe the process as "thrilling." It was also not uncommon for students to report that the peer review discussions enabled them to bridge threshold concepts, allowing them to experience a sense of breakthrough; as one student relates: "I am finally on to something! This essay seems terrific and the peer review sessions truly rewarding." Typically, students valued the generally friendly and cooperative atmosphere within groups. Other students remarked on the benefits of receiving multiple sets of eyes on their texts as well generally positive group dynamics that meant they were "not afraid" to deliver constructive comments.

Some of the students also wrote in their journal entries that the benefits of the peer review extended beyond the confines of the classroom, with peer groups forming support networks facilitated by additional student-arranged peer group meetings and social networking sites such as Facebook. The mainly positive responses to the peer review process could be part of the dangers inherent in requiring students to submit learning journal reflections as part of the assessment for the course; though this was a low-stakes assignment, it did contribute to the overall grade for the course and therefore there is a hazard that students were disinclined to emphasize the pitfalls. For this reason, I have chosen to treat such responses with caution and instead concentrate my analysis on the conventionally understood negative emotional reactions, particularly those that involve feelings of anxiety, that students express in their journal reflections. Where I explore what might be said to be positive reactions, they are usually those that are arrived at firstly by working through perceived negative responses. The tripartite structure for the analysis below is structured around three pillars: anxiety about giving feedback, anxiety about receiving feedback, and finally, using reflection to mediate anxiety.

ANXIETY ABOUT GIVING FEEDBACK

From the evidence from learning journal reflections, it was overwhelmingly clear that one of the main concerns of students who expressed negative feelings about reviewing their peers was anxiety about giving feedback. Many students reported a general sense of being outside of their comfort zone in delivering feedback, and much of this unease appeared to stem from a well-intentioned desire not to harm the feelings of others within the peer group as the following extracts demonstrate:

> "I found it quite hard to criticize others' work since I wanted to give constructive criticism without being mean."
>
> "I try to tone down my personality when doing so though, since I can come across as aggressive and I do not wish to make anyone upset because of something I have said."

More specifically, the analysis of the journal reflections identified a trend in those who reported anxiety related to the giving of feedback which connected the giving of feedback with a sense of the lack of authority to be providing such feedback. These findings accord with those of previous research (Cheng and Warren; Mulder et al.). Students found it disconcerting to be asked to undertake such a task when they felt they lacked adequate practice. The following extract illustrates such responses: "I *really* don't like to criticize the others. It would feel ok if I was an expert on the subject but I'm as new to this as the others and it just feels weird to tell somebody that their choice of word or structure is bad." Other students commented that only the teacher should have the authority to provide such feedback and remarked on anxieties about not being properly qualified to formulate and deliver comments in an appropriate and pedagogically sound way that did not risk offending other students. There was also a tendency to worry about how such feedback might be received by fellow students.

With the exception of just a few course participants, students' mother tongue was not English, and several students reflected on the fact that this served to increase anxiety when delivering feedback by increasingly this sense of absence of authority. Lack of confidence in one's ability to use the language with preciseness, subtlety, and in the desired tone was reported by more than one student, and is exemplified in the following extract:

My ability to express a balanced critique is limited and although I am sure my point becomes clear, it is sometimes expressed clumsily and sounds more rough and mean than I intend it to come across as, or all too soft. So it is a hard, but necessary practice. Therefore, it is good that the practice can take place within this group, since no one has English as his or her mother tongue and limitations are accepted."

Though this study was not comparative and does not intend to make conclusions about the differences between L1 and L2 learners (nor could it possibly be equipped to do so), findings from the set of learning journals analyzed in this study seem to accord with Murau's 1993 article which posits that L2 learners tend to experience a higher degree of negative feelings in the peer review process than their L1 counterparts.

ANXIETY ABOUT RECEIVING FEEDBACK

It is interesting to note that concerns about giving feedback were sometimes directly related to corresponding concerns about receiving feedback:

> Giving feedback was a bit difficult, but I still think it's a
> very good exercise. I'm always a bit concerned about hurting

> other people's feelings, probably because I'm not very good at receiving feedback myself. I often take it personally when someone criticizes something I've done, even though I know it isn't personal. So practicing [. . .] how to give and receive feedback has probably been good for me.

Though it did not feature in journal entries with such a high prevalence, the second most significant source of anxiety apparent was that associated with being on the receiving end of feedback. The very fact that students were more concerned about hurting the feelings of others, rather than being hurt themselves is in its own right worthy of discussion. I would agree with Cheryl Hogue Smith's suggestion that in classroom-based peer review "[s]tudents [. . .] tend to be anxious and distracted during the face-to-face peer review process because they often pay more attention to the peer marking their paper than they do to the paper they are supposed to be reviewing" (27). Smith's subsequent claim that this is particularly the case when students "perceive that peer to be a more effective and successful student," (27) appears perhaps not to apply so strongly from the evidence garnered in this project. Yes, students were sometimes more concerned with the person than the paper; however, this was largely out of empathy for their peer, rather than out of concern for their own perceived inadequacies.

Anxiety in respect to being the reviewee was sometimes seemingly the result of inexperience at being on the receiving end of feedback, but was, in the case of the extract below, part and parcel of concerns about whether peer reviewers were qualified to be providing feedback:

> I felt nervous before our first peer review session. Not only was it the first peer review session of this course but also the first in my life. I have never been judged and criticized in the process of writing an essay by a student before - this role has always fallen on my tutor. [. . .] I remember how nervous I was, especially before the first peer review session, but all the peer review seminaries went well.

Furthermore, several students reported feelings closely aligned with anxiety, such as confusion and frustration, when it came to receiving conflicting advice. Sometimes this sense of frustration was the result of receiving opposing advice from different peer group members, or advice which contradicted teacher feedback. However, sometimes, this frustration appeared to be the upshot of disparities between their own expectations of what a good essay consisted of, and the expectation of their peers. This was particularly the case in students who reported coming from non-Swedish educational backgrounds. One such student related that the cultural differences in expectations led to annoyance; in this particular instance, balancing a conviction that one's own approach was the "right" one with contradicting viewpoints became difficult for the author to reconcile. There were a wide range of opinions amongst students with regard to the potential advantages and drawbacks of a disciplinary and culturally diverse peer review with some students remarking particularly on the fruitful "cultural osmosis" between students and their ideas.

USING REFLECTION TO MEDIATE ANXIETY

Evaluation, be it "through examinations, appraisals, reviews, observations, student ratings or even just friendly critics," can, according to Greg Light et al., elicit anxious and defensive responses from students. Light et al. suggest that most academics are familiar with the feeling of anxiety as we ourselves are frequently evaluated in various guises, including self-evaluation, and oftentimes find that we are our own worst critics. However, the authors point to the idea that "anxiety can change to pleasure" given the appropriate measures of engagement with the evaluative comments. We should, accordingly, "link the critical process with a constructive one" (Light et al. 237–238).

In this particular study I was able to draw the general conclusion that when students were given the appropriate scaffolding with which to approach peer review and were provided with support on how to deal with the feedback received, they were more inclined to perceive the process as constructive and to experience a reduced degree of anxiety. What I tended to see was that students were able to use the reflective process facilitated by the learning journal to take criticism, reflect upon it, and thus flip previously negative reactions into essentially more positive ones; in the words of Light, "anxiety" was reconceived as "pleasure," at least to a certain degree.

Whilst a not insubstantial proportion of participants reported negative emotions akin to anxiety, I found that quite often they did so whilst concurrently contemplating the affirmative nature of the peer review process. For some students this change in attitude appeared early on in the learning journal, suggesting that even just brief reflection is sometimes enough to elicit positive results. For other students, the change manifested itself more gradually over time. It is important to recognize that the process of change is not always instantaneous and might require more prolonged reflection. A number of students reported that though they might have had prior concerns about the peer review activities, these fears were not realized. For other students, in the move from negative to positive emotional responses, it was the anxiety itself that became the driving force behind change. As one student articulates, anxiety can actually be perceived as helpful:

> I don't really like to criticize others but I very much liked to hear what the others had to say about my plan and I got a few good advices. [. . .] I'm still stressed and a bit worried but it's the helpful kind of stress that makes me more focused. Hopefully I won't get too fried at the peer review session.

However, the student's use of the word "fried" could potentially imply a more negative attitude toward the forthcoming peer review. Though "fried" might be used light-heartedly in this context, it could also be an indication that although they recognize the potential benefits of anxiety, continued reflection on the process may be necessary to ensure that productive anxiety does not transform into damaging anxiety.

Likewise, a further student communicates a similar attitude when they write of the importance of developing the higher order critical thinking and evaluation competencies that activities such as peer review nurture:

> By discussion of them in our group, we have learned how to formulate both critical and positive feedback in an academic way. I think that it is important to keep in mind that the conception "feedback" is more about giving proposals about how to improve the text rather than to try to find as many faults as possible—which really are not what constructive feedback is about. I prefer to see it as something positive, something that can help us to both give and receive assistance and support in our writings.

This student demonstrates a conceptual shift, interpreting an emotional response commonly understood as detrimental and instead reconceiving it more favorably. Within the collection of learning journals that I analyzed I found several other examples where students had used words like "thrilling," or "exciting" to describe similar feelings that others had articulated in less positive terms. In the extract below, the student describes actively looking forward to being, in their own words, "grilled" by their peers even though they feel uncertain about the quality of work they have submitted for evaluation:

> The essay plan has been submitted and I have signaled my continued commitment to the course. I am not entirely convinced by my plan nor of my ability to execute it. But it is now out there, ready to be scrutinized by my peers. I am looking forward to be grilled.

As already mentioned, the learning journals offered students the opportunity to work through some of their potentially negative initial responses. It was relatively common to witness in the journal entries the actualization of the transformative reflective process. One student reported that though they might be upset by criticism during the peer review process, this dissipated over the course of several days: "You might get upset when receiving a negative response, but after a few days you realize that it might actually be true, and you appreciate that somebody told you before handing in the final version to be graded." The learning journal allowed this student to view the event from a temporal distance from which they could appreciate the value of the criticism received. Often, the learning journal offered the participant the space to think about how defensive attitudes to receiving feedback might be potentially counterproductive and to reconceive their initial reactions with a more positive slant. For instance, one student's early journal entry expressed a rather negative attitude towards peer review:

> The peer-review sessions have not been very rewarding even though it is a good idea. It feels as if we all know each other so poorly that everyone is afraid of being rude. This has the consequence that everyone tries to be very nice and exaggerate the positive parts and just mentions the [weaker] parts incidentally.

However, a later entry demonstrates just how much this attitude had changed during the course:

> The final peer-review session was way better than the first one. It was really good that you were clear about how important it was and it got clear for me that I need to work extra on before I hand it in.

The student's reported altered attitude to peer review could be the result of various reasons, such as improved group dynamics and an increased sense of security within this group, as well as a greater familiarity with the course and increased writing confidence. However, the fact that the student specifically mentions the scaffolding ("you were clear about how important it was") adds weight to the claim that this contributed to the more favorable outcome in this case.

The very act of writing about the process appeared to be, in some instances, the catalyst to change. Interestingly, in one student reflection, it was possible to see meta-level reflection occurring in which the process of writing about the peer review experience is actively recognized as the stimulus for reframing negative perceptions. In the extract below, the student first reflects on their perfectionist tendencies and how these contributed to peer-review nerves:

> I'm a bit nervous because I always rewrite my essay a million times before I'm happy and I don't want anyone to think my essay isn't good enough before I'm done and happy with it myself. I wasn't sure if the peer review was good or bad for me. I came in to class with a subject and an essay plan that I was pleased with but I left feeling very unsure with my subject, thesis and if my essay could be argumentative enough. Everyone in my group gave me such good feedback and asked just the right questions that made me wonder if this was going to be a too difficult subject.

Despite the fact that the journal entry reports a sense of unease immediately following the peer review, on figuratively putting pen to paper, the author is able to concretize their thoughts and recognize previously unobserved positives:

> It took me until I sat down to write this to realize that the peer review session was actually really helpful. Much more than I thought [it] would be. It made me question the essay in a good way and it might have saved me from writing an essay around a subject that wouldn't have worked.

In line with one of the basic premises of the Writing Across the Curriculum movement, in this instance we can clearly witness an instance of *writing as thinking* (Bazeman et al.; Bean). It took the author of the above extract "until they sat down to write" the entry to make the discovery. Without this process of reflection, the student could well have been left with a lingering negative attitude towards the peer review session but was able to transform this into a more constructive attitude. Recognizing that it is the process of writing itself which has occasioned this change is in itself a valuable tool for future learning for the student.

In other learning journal entries, it was apparent that students were able to use the writing process to mediate and come to terms with some of the negative emotions involved in the peer review process. One such participant talks about "worries" and "fears" related to the receipt of feedback in a general sense but then gravitates the discussion to how the process can function as a "challenge" to precipitate development in both one's own work and in the work of others. Another student who reports having had experience of the peer review process beyond the current course, uses the writing and reflection process to articulate something of the journey that they have been through:

> I myself know that I have grown with my practice through the English courses I have taken these three semesters. I, like my current group, was unsure in the beginning about what I should focus my critique on and I was afraid I would hurt the recipient's feelings. The suggestions I gave a year ago were vague in an attempt to not step on anyone's toes, as were most of the ones I received during this peer review session. That kind of critique is usually not very helpful when writing your essay, as those things are usually things you are aware of. Good peer reviewing is when you step out of your comfort box, looking at the text with a critical eye, and give honest but constructive critique. Honest/blunt critique might momentarily make someone feel poorly about their text as it is someone pointing out a flaw in something they made, but as long as the critique is constructive it leads to a better essay in the end. However, it is not always easy to take that step towards honesty/bluntness in one's comments, especially not when you are addressing the author directly.

Here the participant recognizes their former self in other less experienced group members, reflecting on common fears about framing feedback in such a way as to avoid offense. Formulating feedback in an appropriate and constructive tone is in this particular instance, a bridge that the student has struggled to cross, but from the other side is able to see its value.

Even some of those students who initially had doubts (generally expressed in early entries) about the usefulness of the peer review process reported that their perceptions had changed having experienced the classroom sessions first-hand. For instance, one student who "confessed" to being "a little bit skeptical" about the peer review because of a reluctance "to criticize directly someone's work when the person concerned stands in front of them." The participant goes on to reveal that they imagined the peer review would be so "uncomfortable" that they would be unable to participate. Fortunately, in this case, the process "wasn't the traumatic experience" the student thought it would be and reports that:

> My overall impression about the experience of the peer review process is positive: it made me face a great number of issues that I was able to solve thanks to my group mates' help.

What is particularly noteworthy about this entry is not that the peer review process turned out to be easy, or even comfortable for the student, but that it forced a confrontation with difficult tasks which ultimately proved rewarding.

What the learning journal has allowed in this case, is a recognition that facing such situations can be meaningful.

It is worthwhile to quote at length from another course participant who, though initially uncomfortable (the experience is described as "very unpleasant"), came to realize the benefits of the process on reflection:

> Even if it was a very unpleasant experience at the time, I still felt (already when it happened) that it was a very valuable experience for me. I was quite surprised at my own strong reaction (I thought I was beyond taking comments on my written works personal since I have gone through such processes several times, during education, with my supervisors, when having articles peer-reviewed etc.). It made me think a lot about how the students I teach experience the peer-reviewing processes I let them go through. Hopefully, this has made me more careful when commenting on other people's works, trying to be a little more considerate. If I myself, who is used to peer-reviewing and consider myself quite an experienced student, could feel so miserable and powerless in a situation like that, I imagine that it must be ten times worse for someone who is not as experienced, perhaps taking his/her first course at the university and being in a group where everybody else might have more experience. This is something that I try to bear in mind when I teach.

In this instance, the participant reflects upon their role both as a student on this particular course, but also as a teacher elsewhere. Even though they consider themselves to be experienced at both giving and receiving feedback, this process remains uncomfortable, however effective it might be. This participant's dual perspective as both teacher and student is particularly noteworthy as it reminds as that however intimidating giving and receiving feedback might be for us as relatively experienced members of the academic community, it is important to place ourselves in the shoes of our students to recognize that such anxiety can be multiplied when there is a lack of experience. A similar reflection is made by another student who describes the process from the vantage point of experience:

> Unfortunately I felt that some of my peers seemed uneasy in the situation when they had to give feedback, as if they feared that the person getting his/her text reviewed would be hurt by the criticism. I think it is valuable and important to learn to take and give criticism, therefore it is important to start at this level.

Recognizing in their less experienced peers a greater degree of apprehension at the giving of feedback, this participant insightfully notes the importance of providing such learning opportunities at an early stage of university studies.

CONCLUSIONS

The purpose of this current study was to explore students' emotional responses to the peer review process as reported through the 95 learning journal entries. What I was particularly interested in was investigating what are commonly perceived as disadvantageous reactions to the process, especially responses clustered around a sense of anxiety. My findings suggest that although the majority of students reported positive responses to the peer review process on the course in question, there was still a significant number of potentially more negative responses, which made the exploration of these worthy of further attention. Most significantly, students reported anxiety related to the giving of feedback, and this was largely the result of concerns about legitimacy and about causing unintentional offense in the delivery of feedback. A not insignificant number of students also reported anxiety in relation to being on the receiving end of evaluation.

One of the most significant conclusions to be drawn from this study is that the perceived negative responses to peer review can potentially be mediated by careful scaffolding and reflection. In this study, the scaffolding functioned primarily by promoting discussion surrounding peer review and emphasizing its constructive potential. The reflective learning journal, and formative feedback accompanying this, allowed for a greater sense of ownership of the learning process as well as enabling students to maintain a line of communication with the teacher. Students were able to raise doubts in a safe environment and receive guidance from a source of perceived authority. When students have a safe space to reflect on their anxieties, they are better able to put in place coping strategies.

This study points to several student responses which suggest that anxiety, and associated emotions, can sometimes be beneficially reconceived in a more positive light. The study also suggests that in some cases, recording reflections in writing actually paved the way to a conceptual shift in attitudes towards dealing with evaluative judgements from others. This finding is consistent with MacIntyre and Devaele's assertion that "[p]ositive emotion can help dissipate the lingering effects of negative emotional arousal, helping to promote personal resiliency in the face of difficulties" (241). Using written reflections to grapple with negative responses can help students to articulate their concerns, and thus begin to institute changes in attitude. Recognizing the constructive benefits of peer review can also assist in enabling students to reconcile themselves to potential feelings of unease experienced.

It was also encouraging to see students actively reflecting on the transferable nature of skills developed during the peer review activities. As Keith Topping asserts, "[l]earning how to give and accept criticism, justify one's own position, and reject suggestions are all useful, transferable social skills" (24). Topping suggests that well-thought-out scaffolding to peer assessment activities mean that "potentially negative social issues can be ameliorated and students can develop social and communication skills, negotiation and diplomacy, and teamwork skills" (24). One way in which to "ameliorate" peer review anxiety is through the use of reflection. This study, though exploratory in nature, presents initial findings which suggest that the use of a learning journal might be one way in which students can use reflective practice overcome the anxiety often associated with peer review.

WORKS CITED

Amores, María J. "A New Perspective on Peer-Editing." *Foreign Language Annals,* vol. 30, no. 4, 1997, pp. 513–22.

Barnett, Ronald. "Learning for an Unknown Future." *Higher Education Research & Development,* vol. 23, no. 3, 2004, pp. 247–60.

Bazerman, Charles et al. *Reference Guide to Writing Across the Curriculum.* Parlor Press and The WAC Clearinghouse, 2005, https://wac.colostate.edu/books/reference guides/bazerman-wac/.

Bean, John. *Engaging Ideas: The Professor's Guide to Integrating Writing, Critical Thinking, and Active Learning in the Classroom.* John Wiley and Sons, 2011.

Boase-Jelinek, Daniel, et al. "Student Reflection and Learning Through Peer Reviews." *Issues in Educational Research,* vol 23, no. 2, 2013, pp.119–31.

Boud, David. "Introduction: Making the Move to Peer Learning." *Peer Learning in Higher Education: Learning from and With Each Other,* edited by David Boud et al., Routledge, 2014, pp. 1–20.

Boud, David, et al. *Reflection: Turning Experience into Learning.* Routledge, 1994.

Chang, Yea-huey. "Two Decades of Research in L2 Peer Review." *Journal of Writing Research,* vol. 8, no. 1, 2016, pp. 81–117.

Cheng, Winnie, and Martin Warren. "Having Second Thoughts: Student Perceptions Before and After a Peer Assessment Exercise." *Studies in Higher Education,* vol. 22, no. 2, 1997, pp. 233–39.

Coulson, Debra, and Marina Harvey. "Scaffolding Student Reflection for Experience-Based Learning: A Framework." *Teaching in Higher Education,* vol. 18, no. 4, 2013, pp. 401–13.

Demirel, Elif. "Take It Step by Step: Following a Process Approach to Academic Writing to Overcome Student Anxiety." *Journal of Academic Writing,* vol.1, no. 1, 2011, pp. 222–27.

Hansen, Jette G., and Jun Liu. "Guiding Principles for Effective Peer Response." *ELT Journal*, vol. 59, no. 1, 2005, pp. 31–38.

Light, Greg, et al. *Learning and Teaching in Higher Education: The Reflective Professional*. Sage, 2009.

Liu, Jun, and Randall W. Sadler. "The Effect and Affect of Peer Review in Electronic Versus Traditional Modes on L2 Writing." *Journal of English for Academic Purposes*, vol. 2, no. 3, 2003, pp. 193–227.

Lundstrom, Kristi, and Wendy Baker. "To Give is Better Than to Receive: The Benefits of Peer Review to the Reviewer's Own Writing." *Journal of Second Language Writing*, vol., 18, no. 1, 2009, pp. 30–43.

MacIntyre, Peter, and Jean-Marc Devaele. "The Two Faces of Janys? Anxiety and Enjoyment in the Foreign Language Classroom." *Studies in Second Language Learning and Teaching*, vol. 4, no. 2, 2014, pp. 237–74.

Moon, Jennifer. *Learning Journals: A Handbook for Reflective Practice and Professional Development*. Routledge, 2006.

Mulder, Raoul, et al. "How Does Student Peer Review Influence Perceptions, Engagement and Academic Outcomes? A Case Study." *Assessment & Evaluation in Higher Education*, vol. 39, no. 6, 2014, pp. 657–77.

Murau, Andrea M. "Shared Writing: Students' Perceptions and Attitudes of Peer Review." *Working Papers in Educational Linguistics*, vol. 9, no. 2, 1993, pp. 71–79.

Nelson, Gayle L., and John M. Murphy. "Peer Response Groups: Do L2 Writers Use Peer Comments in Revising their Drafts?" *TESOL Quarterly*, vol. 27, no. 1, 1993, pp. 135–41.

Nicol, David, et al. "Rethinking Feedback Practices in Higher Education: A Peer Review Perspective." *Assessment & Evaluation in Higher Education*, vol. 39, no. 1, 2014, pp. 102–22.

Smith, Cheryl Hogue. "Basic Writers as Critical Readers: The Art of Online Peer Review." *Journal of Teaching Writing*, vol. 30, no. 2, 2016, pp. 21–46.

Topping, Keith J. "Peer assessment." *Theory into Practice*, vol. 48, no. 1, 2009, pp. 20–27.

Värlander, Sara. "The Role of Students' Emotions in Formal Feedback Situations." *Teaching in Higher Education*, vol. 13, no. 2, 2008, pp.145–56.

Winer, Lise. "'Spinach to Chocolate': Changing Awareness and Attitudes in ESL Writing Teachers." *TESOL Quarterly*, vol. 26, no. 1, 1992, pp. 57–80.

Wu, Chia-Pei, and Huey-Ju Lin. "Learning Strategies in Alleviating English Writing Anxiety for English Language Learners (ELLs) with Limited English Proficiency (LEP)." *English Language Teaching*, vol. 9, no. 9, 2016, pp. 52–63.

Yastıbaş, Gülşah Çınar, and Ahmet Erdost Yastıbaş. "The Effect of Peer Feedback on Writing Anxiety in Turkish EFL (English as a foreign language) students." *Procedia-Social and Behavioral Sciences*, vol.199, 2015, pp. 530–38.

Zeidner, Moshe. "Anxiety in Education." *International Handbook of Emotions in Education*, edited by Reinhard Pekrun and Lisa Linnenbrink-Garcia, Routledge, 2014, pp. 265–88.

CHAPTER 8.

MULTIMODAL PEER REVIEW: FOSTERING INCLUSION IN MIXED LEVEL COLLEGE CLASSROOMS WITH ELL LEARNERS

Beth Kramer
Boston University

The advantages of peer review have been well documented, making it a "mainstay" of the traditional composition classroom. Lindsey Jesnek, in her article for the *Journal of College Teaching and Learning*, notes that peer review "provides for an alternate means of instruction and important social construction of learning that teachers simply can't provide in their role of authority" (18). Ngar-Fun Liu and David Carless, in their impressive study of peer review and peer assessment, also stress the engagement aspect of peer review as it allows for students to take "an active role in the management of their own learning" (280). The active nature of the process is part of its appeal for these scholars—by participating in a shared mutual project, the editing, collaboration, and teamwork skills attained through peer review may transfer into a student's writing process in a way that teacher-driven feedback cannot. Another benefit of peer review is that students can often work with others at a higher or lower "skill" level and benefit either by learning new techniques and viewing stronger work, or by learning how to teach and edit.

However, in recent years the influx of English Language Learners (ELLs) into the college classroom has complicated this assumed model. ELLs are the fastest growing subgroup of students in the public education system in the United States (Pyle 103). At Boston University, where I have taught rhetoric for the last eight years, the percentage of international students has risen steadily over the last decade to reach 24% of the 2022 student body representing 87 countries (*BU Today*). As a result, many composition classrooms become a mix of quite fluent native speakers and writers, with other students who struggle and are much less skilled writing in English. The assumed model in traditional peer review is that the ELL students, even if paired with an adept native speaker, will benefit from viewing fluent work, and the native speakers will benefit by providing guidance and insight to the ELL students. Nevertheless, the disparity in writing ability when complicated by communication difficulties often undercuts those benefits, leaving students at each end of the spectrum frustrated. Despite this frustration, there remains much less study on peer review and its benefit and use to ELL students (Sukumaran and Dass 27).

This chapter hopes to fill this gap by confronting the complexities of peer review in the mixed level composition class. After exploring some critiques of peer review in relation to ELL needs and trends, I will detail what I have developed as multimodal peer review to address the challenges faced by this student population, problems such as anxiety about their performance and skill levels and assistance in oral and grammatical skills not needed by native speakers. While forgoing peer review or turning to anonymous online platforms to lessen anxiety may seem viable options, such responses deprive ELL students of precisely the social interaction that they need to develop core social and collaborative skills. By using multimodal tools which emphasize more frequent opportunities for oral reflection and interaction in lower-stakes assignments, educators can preserve the social and community aspects of peer review for both ELL and native speakers in these mixed classes where both groups can encounter problems. The goal is to modify peer review so that it has the flexibility to challenge and engage a diverse range of learning styles and skill levels.

PEER REVIEW, DISTRUST, AND DISPARITY

Peer review has a long history in composition, both with its supporters and its critics. On one hand, peer review is one moment of "flipping" the classroom or providing an alternate classroom model where students must take on the role of educator and showcase their active mastery in a collaborative setting. Long before it was trendy to "flip" the classroom, composition instructors were using peer review workshops as just one way to rethink the confines of the traditional professor-student dichotomy. Liu and Carless articulate the advantages of this model:

> A further important reason for engaging learners with peer feedback is that learning is likely to be extended from the private and individual domain, to a more public (i.e., to one or more peers) domain. One important way we learn is through expressing and articulating to others what we know or understand. In this process of self-expression, we construct an evolving understanding of increasing complexity. (281)

Liu and Carless capture both the engagement/social function of peer review, along with its educational mission of allowing students to showcase and present knowledge. Peer review works against the misconception that writing is a solitary action by bringing it into the realm of public discussion and debate. They also discuss the "practical" aspect of peer review, that it allows for quicker turnaround time for comments and feedback than often a single teacher can provide (281). As Lindsey Jesnek succinctly explains, "Although peer editing has never posed as a simple or flawless process, it has been well-received by the vast majority of composition professors in recent years" (18). Its ability to engage and model a type of public discourse is one reason it has thrived in composition classrooms for decades.

On the other hand, Jesnek hesitates in her praise, following up with the concern: "but it [peer review] is perhaps too applauded" (18). Jesnek, while appreciative of the positive benefits that peer review provides, expresses apprehension that peer review does not meet the needs of "lower level composition students" (18). While recognizing the immense benefits in upper-level writing courses where skill levels and interest are more uniform, she anecdotally bemoans the dissatisfaction she sees surfacing in classrooms filled with less adept and committed writers. Jesnek turns to Charlotte Brammer and Mary Rees' 2007 study to search for quantitative data to address the general unease she feels about peer review in her introductory courses. This study showcases how the majority of first year composition students expressed distrust of both peer review and the merits of their reviewer (80). "This attitude of distrust toward the peer reviewer is not uncommon" Brammer and Rees explain, stressing that in many cases students are looking for answers and solutions rather than realizing the collaborative potential of the peer review process. "Correction" rather than "collaboration" is the way that they view the problem, bemoaning that many students have unrealistic or misguided expectations of the process (80–81). Both Jesnek and Brammer and Rees struggle with how to shift the student mindset about peer review and move students toward more global feedback rather than local or grammatical suggestions in beginner courses.

Jesnek further expresses the difficulty in pairing students as part of the peer review process. While she sees less disparity in upper-level composition classes, lower-level ones "contain a wide range of student writing abilities, which makes effective peer editing sessions all the more difficult to facilitate" (21). Going into great detail on the complications of different types of pairings (from similar levels to immense gaps in skills), she ends her piece finding no appropriate grouping that satisfies her course objectives. She asks educators to take a long look at peer review and to examine its "effectiveness;" she challenges her audience to rethink peer review and its merits from the student satisfaction perspective, taking into account student outcomes and perceptions (23). While Jesnek does not specifically address ELL students in her article, her focus on the particular plight of the lower-level composition student would only become magnified when addressing the mixed-level classroom with non-native speakers.

In addition to disparity and pairing issues, peer review can also raise anxiety for ELL students about their speaking and writing ability. In their study of peer review in the ELL classroom, Kavitha Sukumaran and Rozita Dass explain that although studies have noted unease felt by ELL students serving as peer reviewers, these "are not based on empirical evidence about the origins of students' anxiety and negativity about peer feedback" (28). Through a comprehensive review of past research on ELL students and peer review, they attempt to improve the research by tracing and addressing the source of this negativity. They find that ELL students are often at odds with peer review because they approach it with a completely different mindset and set of assumptions (including anxiety about their language skills being judged by others); they find that involving ELL students in the modeling and criteria process, and moving the review online for anonymity, are some useful techniques to increase their comfort with the process (31). Sukumaran and Dass cite one student who responded that "Being online helps me to be more critical and generally not partial to my peers' feelings" (37). Therefore, moving peer review online could seem like a clear way to improve the process for ELL students. Nevertheless, this type of move, while helpful in addressing some bias and sensitivity issues that may especially impact ELL students, undercuts one of the core tenets of peer review. Making the process anonymous in a sense erases the collaborative engagement aspect that is particularly impactful in person. Sukumaran and Dass note this very detriment in their conclusion, explaining that students often view online peer review "as a technical tool rather than a tool for interaction among classmates and teacher" (38). Thus, while Sukumaran and Dass take on the important task of examining the root cause of ELL struggle with peer review, they do not offer us completely viable solutions.

Another critique of peer review made by Liu and Carless is that peer review is often assessment-focused with "students frequently being reported as driven by a natural desire for high grades . . . even when such instrumental motivations may lead to adverse impacts, such as surface learning" (279). Weak students become demoralized that they cannot produce the type of polished work they see in their partner, and strong students believe they are not getting the "help" or "correction" they need from their classmates to achieve the desired grade. Gavin Heron, in his recent study of different assessment practices, finds that strong concentration on the graded aspect of high-stakes assignments "can lead to students jumping through the assessment hoops and jettisoning efforts to engage in deeper approaches to learning" (277). Heron emphasizes that there is a risk to focusing too much on the final product over the system and process that leads to it. Peer review that only occurs late in the writing stage without opportunities for instructors to guide and intervene, might be especially problematic for ELL students who would feel anxiety about their skill level and their ability to achieve a desired grade.

Therefore, if peer review were to be redesigned with student satisfaction and outcomes in mind, simply taking it online would not be going far enough. While it might address some of the vulnerability that ELL students face, it would leave out the important discussion, listening, and collaborative thinking that is embedded in peer review. In addition, peer review would ideally need to become distanced from the grading process and would function best with emphasis on the thinking and analytical processes that lead to better writing. With this difficulty, is it even possible to modify peer review in a way that would satisfy so many different objectives?

ELL TRENDS AND CHALLENGES

Better understanding the needs and challenges for ELL students will help to answer this difficult question. Peer review is a complicated process for ELL students because of the academic and social pressures they may face in college classrooms. As Guogang Li and Patricia A. Edwards reveal in their comprehensive overview of best practices for teaching ELL students, the requirements for ELL students include being able to "understand and produce Academic English, both orally and in writing. If [they] don't, there is a real chance of falling behind [their] classmates, making poorer grades, getting discouraged, falling further behind, and having fewer educational and occupational choices" (Li and Edwards 16). What Li and Edwards are emphasizing is the way that language learning and composition are tied to broader social and emotional success for ELL students. These scholars highlight that this type of perceived failure can translate into real-world obstacles that can affect later career choices and prospects (16).

At the college level, the issue is compounded as the number of international students studying at US universities has skyrocketed. According to the 2017 Executive Summary produced by the Bureau of Educational and Cultural Affairs, the number of international students has risen for eleven consecutive years to reach over one million students. The study reveals: "In 2016/17, there were 85 percent more international students studying at U.S. colleges and universities than were reported a decade ago" (*Open Doors*). The 85% increase in only a decade is an impressive figure, and one celebrated by many media outlets like *USNews* for the improvements to campus diversity (Haynie). But what these celebratory figures often elide are the resulting social and academic consequences that occur for ELL students in college classrooms with a large disparity in writing and language ability.

The social and academic consequences for ELL student were recently raised in a report published by Yale University on Mental Health and Chinese International students. The researchers reveal: "In addition to adjusting to a new educational system and a new social environment, international students face unique sources of stress such as homesickness, culture shock, language barrier, financial difficulties, immigration requirements, racial discrimination, and strenuous academics" (1). The last comment, "strenuous academics," most certainly relates to the daunting task of producing academic work in a non-native language; it helps explain the subsequent statistic that "45% had depression symptoms and 29% had anxiety symptoms" (5). Ketevan Mamiseishvili, in her study of retention among ELL students at US universities, also notes that resources are often spent on the recruitment of international students, but much less on their retention and care (2). But she falls short of outlining ways that educators can adjust classroom practices to assist this student population.

Helen Gao, a graduate student at Harvard University writes honestly of these struggles both academically and emotionally in her *NY Times* piece. Gao reveals:

> The Chinese students acknowledge the usual challenges of living abroad—like the language barrier and cultural differences—but cite academic pressure as the most likely cause of stress. Despite all they have heard about a liberal arts education, they are often surprised by the rigor needed to succeed. The results-oriented mind-set with which many Chinese tackle their studies doesn't fit well in a system that emphasizes the analytical process and critical thinking. (Gao)

Gao is addressing an important component of working with international students in the composition classroom. While they do bring a wonderful diversity to the student dynamic, part of that diversity may include conflicting ideas of collaboration, critical thinking and "results-oriented" methods. Gao's comments reflect a reality that ELL students strongly benefit emotionally and academically from peer engagement in the classroom which prevents isolation and allows for peer modeling and improved literacy. Socially, peer discussion over shared projects and collaborative tasks would also prevent disconnection between ELL students and native speakers. Yet, at the same time, traditional views of peer review and group work may not fit this student body; simply pairing students with disparity in skills and asking them to "comment" on a paper could lead to frustration and additional disconnection. ELL students might find themselves looking for direct, methods-oriented feedback that is purely quantifiable, and native speakers might not be able to look past the grammatical mistakes of less fluent work.

Therefore, Gao's article highlights the vulnerabilities that ELL students may face socially and academically in a composition class if the process and goals of peer review are "assumed" rather than taught. The question then shifts: can peer review be implemented in the mixed-level composition class so that listening, oral skills, and critical thinking are still emphasized, while making adjustments for ELL vulnerabilities such as anxiety about writing ability and diverse understanding of analytical methods? And can peer review still be a challenging and productive exercise for native speakers, who are also looking to grow and develop their own critical thinking and writing skills?

ELL LEARNERS AND THE POSITIVE POTENTIAL OF PEER REVIEW

Given the vulnerability of ELL students and the difficulty of implementing peer review in the mixed level classroom, an obvious response might be to forgo peer review altogether. Anecdotally, I have heard colleagues voice this concern and suggest that in classrooms with extreme disparity in skill, only teacher-centered feedback is meaningful. However, despite the concerns surrounding peer review, scholars keep revisiting the benefits of collaboration and engagement that peer review provides at the same time that it can improve oral and literacy outcomes. Considerable research emphasizes how peer engagement allows ELL students to thrive socially and academically. On one hand, students exposed to collaborative opportunities tend to have stronger performance in the classroom. Peer review, with its built-in cooperative framework, has the potential to improve language outcomes, literacy, speaking and listening skills. On the other hand, it also is a way to introduce students to the type of deep thinking and meta-processes that higher education relies upon. And perhaps most importantly, peer review has the potential to break barriers and create new communities in the classroom, especially for ELL learners. Examining the research behind these benefits points against forgoing peer review and rather towards modification and adaptation.

In "Academic Effects of Peer-Mediated Interventions with English Language Learners: A Research Synthesis," researchers discover that: "Students who had access to cooperative and collaborative interventions had significantly higher literacy achievement scores than students who did not have access to cooperative and collaborative interventions" (Pyle 107). Yingling Chen, in his study of ELL student perceptions toward collaborative work, builds on this idea expressing that "collaboration means to practice in a safe environment which is made up of an accepting and diverse group of people who have a common interest . . . When students work collaboratively, second language learners have chances to enhance their oral skills and experience conflict on goals and tasks" (2). It is this ability to reflect on and confront ideas that he feels is central to ELL student growth; he goes on to suggest that "through collaborative learning, the results show that students quickly realize that they are able to solve problems as a group that they would not be able to solve as individuals" (3). Both sets of scholars emphasize that with a supportive environment, peer review provides an opportunity not just to receive feedback but also to practice important oral and teamwork skills. Peer review is part of community building and social connection and also has strong ties to higher literacy and writing outcomes. Even though educators risk their classrooms becoming distracted by too much socialization, these scholars highlight the importance of the collaborative process even more than the written product itself.

Along these lines, Liu and Carless suggest that peer review methods "develop skills such as critical reflection, listening to and acting on feedback, [and] sensitively assessing and providing feedback on the work of others. Students can learn not only from the peer feedback itself, but through meta-processes such as reflecting on and justifying what they have done" (289). ELL students would most certainly benefit from increasing these collaborative opportunities and strengthening moments when they could more fruitfully understand "meta-processes" crucial for social and academic success in the US university classroom. If, as Gao suggests, ELL students are often confused by the discussion-oriented and exploratory aspects of liberal arts study, then it seems vital that they experience these processes in the classroom in ways that show how these types of methodologies lead to stronger written and spoken work. Peer review could be such a mechanism that allows students to discuss ideas, brainstorm, evaluate, critique, and ask questions in a classroom setting open to instructor guidance and intervention.

Mikel Cole addresses this collaborative need for ELL students in his 2013 study: "In contrast to teacher-centered models of instruction, instructional approaches that employ peer-mediated learning offer tremendous promise to improve language outcomes and interrupt the pervasive messages of silence that ELLs face" (148). While Cole does not address composition peer review directly, he does emphasize the importance of having ELL students interact, question, and assist native speakers in a variety of projects or "mediated" work. Cole finds that classrooms must employ opportunities to allow peer-to-peer feedback, and that resisting these models because of disparity can have "dire" consequences for the progress of ELL student learners who become withdrawn and "silenced" (163). Although he is focusing on all types of collaborative learning beyond peer review, he finds "ELLs performed much better in settings where they were not segregated from their non-ELL peers" (163). There is an obvious benefit in exposing less fluent writers and speakers to those at a stronger level for literacy and language fluency. ELL students should not feel, in his view, that their ideas are not important or that they do not have the capacity or means to make worthy reflections on peer work. Therefore, Cole's research discourages moving away from peer review because of its difficulties, and points towards modifications that take into account the particular requirements of ELL students.

Thus, these scholars overwhelmingly highlight that we would be doing ELL students and our classrooms a disservice to forgo peer review altogether. However, the research informing ELL trends simultaneously argues for changes and adaptations to be made to the practice. Based on the theory informing of ELL best teaching practices, I will outline in the following sections how I have modified peer review into a multimodal practice in my rhetoric courses to adapt to the influx of ELL learners. By integrating peer review into more frequent, lower-stakes guided workshops, and integrating podcast technology in meaningful ways, I have worked to preserve key writing, community building, and critical thinking skills in the process while acknowledging the social, oral, and literacy needs of ELL students.

FREQUENT, LOW-STAKES PEER REVIEW

One key way to transform peer review is to make it a practice that occurs throughout a course at all stages of the writing process. Some traditional ways of implementing peer review in the composition classroom occur at the draft stage of the writing process, usually for a high-stakes assignment that will soon receive a summative graded assessment by the professor. According to Dante Dixson and Frank Worrell in their analysis comparing assessment methods, summative assessments usually occur at the end of "learning segments" and are less frequent and almost always graded (156). Quite often, peer review mirrors this process and occurs close to an assignment due date. Students are paired off, exchange papers, and provide written and/or oral feedback throughout the draft. Although students do not provide grades, much weight is placed on how they evaluate a product close to the period in which it will be evaluated by the instructor.

However, this type of review process adds to the misconception that peer review is solely for the purpose of eventually achieving a higher grade, and it makes pairings of weak students with strong students that much more discouraging. Shifting the focus of peer review to frequent smaller stakes assignments can serve multiple purposes in the mixed level composition classroom. By moving peer review to a more frequent "peer *feedback*," over "peer *assessment*" as Liu and Carless suggest, instructors can model the peer review process at much earlier periods throughout the semester, in ways that are less intimidating and overwhelming to non-native speakers (279). The idea is to make students more aware that their goal is to guide and collaborate with their peers, rather than critique and judge in a top-down way. It is not about students deciding if writing is "strong" or "weak," but working together throughout the writing process to make the product as thoughtful and rich as it can be.

For example, I have had success in pairing students with differences in skill level to provide peer feedback on paper proposals at the start of a research unit. This type of in-class engagement facilitates a classroom atmosphere of open discussion and cultivates a climate of scholarship crucial to the ultimate written product. It also places the emphasis on global feedback compared to local suggestions, as the ungraded proposal is the first stage in having students conceptualize larger issues and questions at stake with their topic. Since the proposal is ungraded, feedback is not about perfecting the grammar but rather thinking deeply about argument and idea. Instructors can also easily model what a short peer review of a proposal might include, so that ELL students unfamiliar with peer review have clear expectations and understanding of the process itself early in a writing project.

Before I implemented frequent, low-stakes peer review, students would display reluctance or frustration if they were not paired with a friend or were placed with someone at a weaker level. However, when I adjusted peer review to occur consistently in most classes during the semester, native speakers and ELL students became much less resistant to the process. While ELL students might be more hesitant with the first experience, conversations flowed more easily as the semester went on, and they had many opportunities to practice listening and discussion skills, leading to richer and more nuanced feedback each time. All students had the opportunity to work with almost everyone in the class by the end of the semester, lessening the tension and anxiety of a few high-stakes interactions. Also, by reviewing the comments made between students, I had indications about how students were understanding the topic and conceptualizing ideas at a stage when I could easily intervene or shift my own teaching methods.

In addition to using peer review earlier in the course outside of formal drafts and papers, I have also broken down peer review so that students are rarely assessing an entire draft at once. To accomplish this task, I modify peer review so that it becomes integrated into a series of lessons leading up to a high-stakes assignment. Frequent, low-stakes peer review is a version of the popular "scaffolding" teaching strategy. As Pedro Silva explains, scaffolding "consists of providing a temporary structure which will allow the learner to identify each of the components of any specific topic, while creating a provisional structure which will allow the development of a specific skill" (89). In his analysis of scaffolding in relation to first year writing assignments, Silva discusses the way in which scaffolding gradually introduces the necessary parts of an assignment to allow for the learner to reach their ultimate success level. This technique is particularly important for beginner students, as Gareth Green and his research team similarly convey, because often "they ha[ve] not yet developed the procedural schemata" for the given task (146). Similar to ELL students who might lack familiarity with the process and/or mindset of peer review, Green sees scaffolding as designing assignments and workshops so that the sequence of assignments builds the framework of thinking for the later tasks (146). In this model, the instructor takes a strong role in breaking down lessons into component parts and giving their students tools that they become less dependent upon as the final products emerge.

I utilize this directed workshop concept in creating a "scaffolded" peer review series; for example, in one class I may divide students into pairs and have them workshop a much smaller segment of their draft, such as only the introduction or only the conclusion. By combining this peer review with an instructor-led lesson on introductions or conclusions, it allows me to add much more structure and direction into the workshop, and to move away from an assessment to a more collaborative learning paradigm. Providing templates and models, such as introductions written by former students, can offer some of the necessary framework to give both strong and weaker students varying goals/objectives for their later peer review session. This modification shifts students from thinking about peer review as providing all the "correction" or grammatical help they need for this one large assignment, to thinking more about the ideas and parts that come together to make an argument into a larger whole. For instance, my ELL students often realize through a workshop series where they receive three different views of their introduction that there are multiple ways of beginning of an essay, and after a subsequent workshop on conclusions, they start to understand how choices they make about their introductions inform their endings. It also breaks down the process so that weaker writers are gradually introduced to longer assignments and papers.

There are also opportunities for students to work with more than one partner over this type of series, helping to expose students to a range of writers at multiple skill levels. This benefits ELL students as well as native speakers, who grow by guiding others but also benefit from reading the work of other strong writers. Further, I have the ability to see a range of student papers across these sessions, helping me guide certain papers and modify my own approach when needed. Therefore, rethinking peer review as a continuous, frequent, and low-stakes practice can be crucial to providing structure to ELL students while also having multiple check-in moments from the instructor's perspective. It also helps cultivate a community of writers who learn how important discussion and collaboration are to their final written project.

PODCASTS AND AURAL ARGUMENT AS PART OF PEER REVIEW

In addition to making peer review more frequent and integrated with teacher-led workshops, technology can also be an important modification to make peer review more inclusive for ELL students. Yi Xu, when looking at the effects of electronic peer review in the classroom, has some findings that may prove useful when addressing the challenges for students at varying skill levels. He explains that while first year students "do not necessarily benefit more (nor less) from e-editing itself, they do benefit from new experiences in the classroom. They tend to treat assignments more seriously when the assignment appears to be "new" and "interesting" (13). Xu finds that electronic peer editing in itself did not cause as much increase in learning as did the packaging of peer review in a novel and modern way. While this might seem intuitive on one level, he also builds upon prior research which finds that with "students' different preferences, it seems most advisable to use a combination of the technological method as well as the traditional method in a language or writing classroom" (13). Xu offers the perspective that we need to be flexible in our approach to peer review, experimenting with different vehicles and technologies to keep it fresh and exciting for all students.

Building upon his ideas, I have found the podcast form can serve as an excellent vehicle in this process, allowing me to transform frustrating parts of the peer review process while preserving key aspects. The strong relationship between podcasts and listener engagement has been well researched, and many recent scholars have noted the connection between ELL learning outcomes and opportunities to listen and hear texts as well as read them (Cole and Kramer 9). As Linda Flanagan reveals in her study of skills gained by ELL teens using podcasts, "An unfamiliar word that might stop them on the page doesn't compel them to tune out from a story told aloud. Also, kids for whom English is a second language benefit from hearing spoken English and following along with an accompanying transcript" (Flanagan). Flanagan highlights that fluency and comprehension increase for students when aural texts are utilized in the classroom, and that it can lead to increased engagement and literacy.

To integrate podcasts into a research composition unit, for example, I often have students listen to a few episodes of Sarah Koenig's *Serial* podcast, to both model an inductive method of research exploration and to acquaint students with modes of aural argument. *Serial,* produced by WBEZ and *This American Life,* is Sarah Koenig's research-based podcast that traces the murder of Hae Min Lee and the subsequent incarceration of her ex-boyfriend, Adnan Syed. The audio narrative explores multiple possibilities for the murder without being reductive and does an excellent job introducing and analyzing evidence from diverse viewpoints. I use the podcast as a model for the students' own research assignments, where they are asked to study a complex ethical issue and to integrate evidence from varying perspectives. When my students are then closer to draft stages of their own research, I will often play moments from the podcast before students look at portions of their classmates' drafts. This podcast prelude evolves into a modified peer review that gives them targeted direction for how to discuss written moves and techniques such as balancing multiple points of view or reflecting on evidence. Students listen to how the narrator in the podcast introduces a key point and provides analysis, and then look for similar sophisticated moves in their classmates' work. While students of all levels enjoy the multimodal aspect and the variation it provides to traditional peer review, ELL students in particular benefit from this type of direction. Comments between students tend to be more specific and focused on analytical processes like integrating quotes, leading to better substantiated written products. Many students respond on their end-of-year reflection that this podcast peer review was integral to how they understand research writing and critical thinking.

In addition, the podcast form itself can be integrated into the peer feedback process. I often have students record their comments to their classmates on written work and create a "podcast" of peer feedback to their classmate. Like the *Serial* podcast that they listen to, creating an exploratory peer-feedback podcast highlights writing as an act of exploration and discovery and prevents approaches that try to sum or wrap it all up with one large comment. Students realize that the paper itself doesn't need to be "solved;" a recorded podcast of suggestions mirrors Koenig's strategy of each voice adding feedback to the argument, moving it towards not perfection but fluidity. For example, if is a student is leaving audio comments on the first half of their classmate's draft, they do not need to fix every grammatical mistake or give one comment that encapsulates a singular point of view. Rather, they can move through the essay and discuss areas that resonate with them, places which are confusing, and perhaps end with questions like Koenig does, rather than a reductive comment. This is a way in which ELL students can strengthen oral, listening as well as written skills, and it moves discussion into more global rather than local feedback. This multimodal transformation of peer review provides necessary guidance for ELL students, while strengthening oral presentation and listening skills for all students.

In fact, multimodal peer review has incredible possibilities beyond aural argument, and instructors can institute variations to teach visual as well as aural analysis. While in my courses I have been focusing on aural texts, movies and digital texts can be used as similar vehicles in peer review; students can have a choice to make a digital photo gallery of comments or a movie representing their suggestions. This approach poses a challenge to strong writers but can also give ELL learners a range of flexible options to participate in the peer review process. Overall, I have found both ELL students and native speakers are more engaged in these multimodal projects, and that not only do the final papers have more depth and structure, but students leave better enjoying and understanding a scholarly writing approach. While extreme disparity in communication cannot be erased, these types of collaborative, multimodal projects build skills that are crucial to composition classes and increase the kinds of bonds between learners that we hope to cultivate in our courses. Overall, using technology strategically in peer review will engage students at all levels and will provide moments for learning and collaboration that are particularly suited to the ELL student population.

INCLUSION IN THE MIXED LEVEL CLASSROOM

Preserving the strengths of the peer review process, while adjusting for challenges presented by mixed level composition classrooms, will inevitably require compromise in the coming years. By utilizing frequent, low-stakes multimodal peer review, we can find new ways to engage and support ELL students as well as writers at all skill levels. Part of the solution must rest in acknowledging the immense task faced by ELL students who approach writing and critical thinking from diverse perspectives, and being adaptable to a host of flexible, multimodal techniques to create an atmosphere of inclusion and growth. Mamiseishvili's study reveals what keeps ELL students enrolled and successful in college beyond their first year:

> If international students successfully integrate in the academic system of campus, they will more likely stay enrolled in the institution. Specifically, the findings highlight the importance of study groups and peer interactions [. . .] about coursework, assignments, or other academic matters. (13)

Taking Mamiseishvili's view that peer review in fact models most of the factors necessary for ELL students to learn successful study and social skills, the impetus for revisiting and revising peer review becomes that much more pressing. Constructing the right models inside of class, for ELL students as well as adept writers, will energize our classrooms and build the type of globally inclusive communities that we hope to foster in higher education. By using multimodal tools which emphasize more frequent opportunities for oral reflection and interaction in lower-stakes assignments, educators can preserve the social and community aspects of peer review for both ELL and native speakers. This will involve rethinking traditional pairing and comment methods and adding instructor-guided workshops that break down essays into more manageable parts. In addition, we can work to use technology like podcasts in innovative ways to both model and teach listening and speaking skills. Rather than simply taking the process online or forgoing it altogether, implementing multimodal peer review will allow us to preserve its strengths while transforming it for the 21st century.

WORKS CITED

Brammer, Charlotte, and Mary Rees. "Peer Review from the Students' Perspective: Invaluable or Invalid?" *Composition Studies*, vol. 35, no. 2, 2007, pp. 71–85.

BU Today, "Here's Who BU Invited to Join the Class of 2026." http://www.bu.edu/articles/2022/class-of-2026-admitted-students/.

Cole, Mikel W. "Rompiendo El Silencio: Meta-Analysis of the Effectiveness of Peer-Mediated Learning at Improving Language Outcomes for ELLs." *Bilingual Research Journal*, vol. 36, no. 2, 2013, pp. 146–66.

Cole, Rick, and Beth Kramer. "Podcasts and the Twenty-first Century College Classroom." *IMPACT: The Journal of the Center for Interdisciplinary Teaching and Learning*, vol. 6, no. 2, Summer 2017, pp. 8–12.

Chen, Yingling. "Perceptions of EFL College Students Toward Collaborative Learning." *English Language Teaching*, vol. 11, no. 2, 2018, pp. 1–4.

Dixson, Dante D., and Frank C. Worrell. "Formative and Summative Assessment in the Classroom." *Theory into Practice*, vol. 55, no. 2, 2016, pp. 153–159.

Ferlazzo, Larry. *Peer Review, Common Core, and ELLs*, March 30, 2016, https://www.edutopia.org/blog/collaborative-peer-review-core-ells-larry-ferlazzo-katie-hull-sypnieski.

Flanagan, Linda. "What Teens are Learning From Serial and Other Podcasts." KQED.org, March 11, 2015, https://www.kqed.org/mindshift/39461/.

Gao, Helen. "Chinese, Studying in America, and Struggling," *NY Times*, 12 Dec. 2017, https://www.nytimes.com/2017/12/12/opinion/chinese-students-mental-health.html.

Green, Gareth P., et al. "Deep Learning in Intermediate Microeconomics: Using Scaffolding Assignments to Teach Theory and Promote Transfer." *The Journal of Economic Education*, vol. 44, no. 2, 2013, pp. 142–57.

Han, Xuesong, et al. "Report of a Mental Health Survey Among Chinese International Students at Yale University." *Journal of American College Health*, 2013, pp. 1–8.

Haynie, Devon. "Number of International College Students Continues to Climb," *USNEWS.com*, November 17, 2014. https://finance.yahoo.com/news/number-international-college-students-continues-climb-120000668.html.

Heron, Gavin. "Examining Principles of Formative and Summative Feedback Source," *The British Journal of Social Work*, vol. 41, no. 2, Mar. 2011, pp. 276–95.

Jesnek, Lindsey M. "Peer Editing in the 21st Century College Classroom: Do Beginning Composition Students Truly Reap the Benefits?" *Journal of College Teaching and Learning*, vol. 8, no. 5, 2011, pp. 17–24.

Koenig, Sarah. *Serial.* WBEZ Chicago, 2015–2016. https://www.serialpodcast.org.

Li, Guofang, and Patricia A. Edwards. *Best Practices in ELL Instruction.* Guilford Press, 2010.

Liu, Ngar-Fun, and David Carless. "Peer Feedback: The Learning Element of Peer Assessment." *Teaching in Higher Education,* vol. 11, no. 3, 2006, pp. 279–90.

Mamiseishvili, Ketevan. "International Student Persistence in U.S. Postsecondary Institutions." *Higher Education,* vol. 64, no. 1, 2012, pp. 1–17. *JSTOR,* https://www.jstor.org/stable/41477916.

Pyle, Daniel, et al. "Academic Effects of Peer-Mediated Interventions with English Language Learners: A Research Synthesis." *Review of Educational Research,* vol. 87, no. 1, 2017, pp. 103–33.

Silva, Pedro. "Scaffolding Assignments: Analysis of AssignMentor as a Tool to Support First Year Students' Academic Writing Skills." *E-Learning and Digital Media,* vol. 14, no. 1–2, 2017, pp. 86–97.

Sukumaran, Kavitha, and Rozita Dass. "Students' Perspectives on the Use of Peer Feedback in an English as a Second Language Writing Class." *Journal for Interdisciplinary Research in Education (JIRE),* vol. 4, no. 1, 2014, pp. 1–14.

Xu, Yi. "Re-Examining the Effects and Affects of Electronic Peer Reviews in a First-Year Composition Class." *Reading Matrix: An International Online Journal,* vol. 7, no. 2, 2007, pp. 1–21.

Witherell, Sharon. *Open Doors 2017 Executive Summary.* US Department of State, https://www.iie.org/news/2017-11-13-open-doors-2017-executive-summary/.

PART FOUR. PEER REVIEW: THE PROMISE OF TECHNOLOGY

CHAPTER 9.

LEVELING THE PLAYING FIELD FOR ELL STUDENTS: THE CASE FOR MOVING PEER REVIEW TO AN ONLINE ENVIRONMENT

Vicki Pallo
Virginia Commonwealth University

As a pedagogical practice, peer review has garnered an abundance of attention for scholars of composition as well as second language acquisition. Over the years, both the positives and negatives of this teaching practice have been much explored, although the consensus to date is that it can be a beneficial practice for the composition classroom—under the right circumstances (DiGiovanni and Nagaswami 264–265; Hyland 176). This topic has been especially debated in relation to English Language Learner (ELL) writers; research confirms that this population learns to write differently, especially when learning through the filter of cultural background, reading comprehension and vocabulary acquisition (Ortmeier-Hooper, *Writing Across* 6–12; Show 238). In addition, due to language-specific challenges, ELL students often contend with a host of insecurities regarding communication in oral and written forms, which can become an issue in and out of the classroom and can impede their progress in a composition course if left unchecked. However, with the right instruction and learning environment, peer review can be an important writing tool for ELL students. The challenge for instructors is to find ways to make this activity a positive learning experience for these students. Both research and experience suggest that asynchronous online peer review can be an effective method of overcoming potential obstacles and encouraging success for ELLs. While no class activity is without its challenges, the overall benefits of moving peer review to an online environment for non-native speakers make it worth considering. If properly employed, writing instructors can use technology to make peer review activities an egalitarian and successful experience for the ELL student.

THE CHALLENGES OF PEER REVIEW FOR ELLS

As with any student-driven activity, there is always the risk that the expected outcomes and benefits of the peer review process will not be achieved. When you add in the additional challenges created by learning and using another language, the potential for pedagogical failure becomes even more pronounced. There are many factors that can impede success of the peer review process for ELL students (e.g., Andrade and Evans 115; Ferris 149; Kim 600; Ortmeier-Hooper, *Writing Across* 109; Show 240–242). Some of the most significant are a general lack of experience in both the peer review process and language acquisition, the influence of culture, increased anxiety, low risk tolerance, and the need for additional time to process ideas and complete tasks. However, while these factors can present barriers to learning, the potential benefits ultimately make overcoming them a worthwhile goal.

Lack of experience. Peer review is one aspect of the writing process that can feel very unfamiliar to international students in particular. The process approach to writing, with its emphasis on the practices of collaboration, authorial voice, and revision, is often a new experience for students who received their writing instruction abroad (Hyland 20). Added to this, ELL students understandably have varying levels of facility with the English language, presenting a number of challenges to completing writing assignments. As Soo Hyon Kim observes,

Having English learners (ELs) from diverse backgrounds who are in the process of developing their language skills can make it even more challenging for teachers to facilitate peer review . . . [they] may have little prior experience with peer review and a lack of confidence in their English proficiency, which are factors that can hinder them from fully enjoying the benefits of peer review. (599)

This can lead to false expectations and "a lack of confidence in the credibility of feedback they give and receive" (Kim 600). Matsuda and Silva similarly point to a mistrust of the peer review process on the part of ELL writers (17). Low self-confidence can also extend to the ELL students' own abilities; feelings of inexperience in the language or the peer review process can lead to self-doubt and insecurity in their ability to offer meaningful feedback (Show 238, 242; Costino and Hyon 75; Carson and Nelson 11, 14). In addition, many ELL students claim to have "difficulty in articulating problems and suggestions" to their peers (Kim 600). In some cases, inexperience with peer review and concern for improving English speaking skills can cause ELL students to place an unnecessarily strong emphasis on language and "local" or sentence-level issues (Leki and Carson 90), thus missing the purpose of many peer review activities.

Cultural differences. For many ELL students, cultural backgrounds also heavily influence their receptiveness to and success with the peer review process. Many are more comfortable with the authority of the teacher voice in response to their work and may not see any value in the feedback of their peers (Andrade and Evans 115; Fordham 20; Kim 600; Zhang 211). In some cases, ELLs can have a tendency to be uncomfortable with the collaborative or critiquing process due to cultural factors such as a desire to "save face" by not giving negative or incorrect feedback, or avoidance of asserting ideas that might be perceived as negative in order to maintain group harmony (Carson and Nelson 9; Costino and Hyon 75). Some ELLs, especially those that are not considered "international" students, often desire to blend in with the dominant language and culture and may fear the potential stigma that comes with identification as an ELL student. Avoiding the risk of exposure can impede their participation in peer review activities (Costino and Hyon 76; Miller-Cochran 21; Ortmeier-Hooper, "English May Be" 393).

In addition, students coming from less "mainstream" cultural backgrounds may not have received explicit instruction in the genres used in the typical composition classroom. As Ken Hyland observes, this makes successful peer response to these genres a challenge, as ELL students "commonly do not have access to this cultural resource and so lack knowledge of the typical patterns and possibilities of variation within the texts that possess cultural capital" (19). In this way, "Students outside the mainstream [. . .] find themselves in an invisible curriculum, denied access to the sources of understanding they need to succeed" (Hyland 20).

Increased anxiety. All of the above factors can contribute to poor ELL engagement with peer review activities and lead to a great deal of anxiety on the part of the student. This anxiety can also be developed in response to the perceived or real sense of impatience that the ELL student may feel from their peer review partners. In George Braine's comparative study of ELL and "mainstream" composition courses, many of his subjects noted that "NS [native speaking] students were impatient with them, and one student said that he overheard a NS student complain to the teacher about her inability to correct the numerous grammatical errors in his paper" during the peer review process (Braine 98). The participants in this study often shared their fears and embarrassment at speaking up in class, noting that they did not perceive teacher support when they did so (Braine 100). Matsuda and Silva also point to the anxiety that ELLs are likely to experience in the writing classroom, explaining that "Some ESL students tend not to do well in mainstream courses partly because many of them feel intimidated by their NES peers who are obviously more proficient in English and comfortable with the U.S. classroom culture" (17). In a survey conducted by Show, she ranked the top concerns and challenges of ELL students in the college writing classroom; anxiety appeared as the fourth most common difficulty on her list (Show 241).

Anxiety can lead to a number of difficulties for students trying to learn or improve academic writing skills and can derail the peer review process. Braine points to the association between anxiety and "feelings of uneasiness, self-doubt, and worry" (101) which can hinder a writer's ability to think and communicate effectively. Additionally, research done by Mike Rose demonstrates how anxiety can lead to a limitation in "the development of mechanical, grammatical, and rhetorical competence" along with "confusion, frustration, and anger, resulting in writer's block" (Rose, qtd. in Braine 101).

Low risk tolerance. These challenges can promote a negative attitude towards the peer review process and academic writing in general and undermine any potential benefits of the collaborative learning experience that an instructor is trying to foster. Writing is difficult under the best of circumstances and involves a certain level of vulnerability in order to engage in the process. Language learning also comes with its own share of discomfort; when both learning challenges are combined, fear of the risks may outweigh the desire for any of the benefits on the part of the ELL student. As Evans and Andrade observe,

> Language learning . . . involves risk-taking, making mistakes, trial and error, and a willingness to show a lack of knowledge or ability. NNESs [non-native English speakers] in higher education may mask their linguistic incompetence or lack of confidence by not participating, avoiding challenging courses or majors, not asking questions, or not seeking help. (8)

Smith echoes this concern, noting that it is particularly prevalent among first-year students, who are often the ones sitting in the composition classroom. As she explains, "a common response to such feelings of uncertainty is for students to eschew risk and error and take what they see as the safest route to meet the demands, both real and perceived, of their new environment, even though risk and error are often the best routes to learning" (Smith 36). And Braine takes it a step further, suggesting that the fear of mistakes can lead to "apathy, silence, or flight—a quick withdrawal from the class" (Braine 101). Lack of participation—and in some cases the complete absence from the peer review activity—is concerning; in composition courses focused on writing as a process, students need to be able to engage in each stage of this process in order to obtain the maximum benefit.

Need for time. In reflecting on the various challenges and emotions that an ELL writer can experience in the college writing classroom, one factor which seems to offer the most potential for either a strongly negative impact or a positive influence on student success is *time*. The impatience experienced by the ELL students in the discussion above, for example, can often be the result of the common desire for many students to rush through their work; any impediment to rapid and successful outcomes on an assignment can be viewed negatively. ELLs often need more processing time in order to formulate ideas in a manner that they deem acceptable for sharing (Leki and Carson 90; Raimes 247; Show

240). Show's study illustrates the significance of the time factor: "Writing fluency . . . was the third ranked writing difficulty. Students stated that they stop many times to think about what to write when they write English essays. They often think for extended periods of time but find only a few words to express a quite complicated idea; therefore, they have serious problems with fluency" (240). While this points specifically to writing essays, it is easy to see that this concern would apply equally to written or oral feedback on peer essays. Leki and Carson also analyze the desire many ELL students express for more time when it comes to language acquisition and writing efficiency, noting that their focus on sentence-level concerns such as grammar and vocabulary might not be misplaced, but rather demonstrate "an interest in efficiency and [. . .] a desire to cut down on their workload and their work time" (92).

When one is communicating in their native language, it is easy to forget—or fail to comprehend—the incredible amount of time required for the various cognitive shifts that need to happen in order to communicate in a second or third language (Evans and Andrade 7; Ferris 149). And of course, time is a beneficial ingredient in writing instruction for *all* students—native and non-native speakers alike. Ann Raimes sums up this need for time effectively:

> To take advantage of this extraordinary generative power of language, we need to give our students what is always in short supply in the writing classroom—time. The time they need to write has to take precedence over the time we need to complete a syllabus or cover the course material. That time is needed, too, for attention to vocabulary. To generate, develop, and present ideas, our students need an adequate vocabulary. This is also true of native speakers. (248)

If students (both native and non-native speakers) are to receive the most benefit from peer review and make strides in improving their academic writing, adequate time for reflection, processing language, and formulating effective critiques is not a luxury; it is one of the most essential ingredients in the process.

A PEDAGOGICAL SHIFT: USING ONLINE TECHNOLOGY TO ENHANCE THE PEER REVIEW PROCESS

If peer review proves to be such a struggle for ELL students, perhaps the logical choice would be to omit it from the writing process altogether. Yet while this might be an understandable temptation for some educators, research shows that peer review has the potential to provide a positive impact on student writing, even when English is not the students' first language. Through peer review, students obtain a variety of perspectives in response to their ideas, creating a more authentic sense of audience (Caulk 184; Kim 600; Sommers 148; Tsui and Ng 166). It also increases autonomy in the student writer (Sommers 149–150; Tsui and Ng 164) and heightens the ELL students' understanding of the assignment goals. It can provide them with model essays, as well as examples of what they should avoid in their own writing. As they see the errors of others and discover that they too find writing a challenging process, they can gain confidence in their own abilities and suggestions (Ferris, 2003b; Fordham 48; Mittan, 1989; Tsui and Ng 166), which in turn leads to more self-corrections (Miao et al. 191).

Further, Miao et al. note that while teacher feedback may be more heavily used by ELL writers, the impact peer comments have on student writing is significant. They found that the latter form of feedback often led to more revisions focused on clarity and variety of ideas, rather than the sentence-level changes that often resulted from teacher feedback (Miao et al. 193). When participating in peer review, students are engaged in active learning and critical thinking, as well as the exercise of communication and negotiation of ideas (Mendonca and Johnson 765–66; Miao et al. 193). Lundstrom and Baker found that in some cases, the benefits of peer review are even *greater* for the ELL writer than for the native speaker. They note that ELL students not only benefit more from giving peer feedback than receiving it (31), but that the increased learning curve they often have with writing and communicating in English allows for more recognizable growth in ELL writing over the duration of a course (38–39).

This is not to suggest that peer review is a one-size-fits-all approach to teaching writing; as acknowledged earlier, there are potential difficulties to using peer review in the classroom. Instruction in best practices for peer review is certainly a necessary precursor, as many scholars have shown (e.g., Hoogeveen and van Gelderen 497; Lundstrom and Baker 31; Miao et al. 183; Rollinson 24; Tsui and Ng 168). Yet given all of the evidence that this can be a beneficial activity for ELL students in particular, it is imperative that we find an effective way to help these students overcome their challenges with the process and provide them with every opportunity for success. Shifting peer review to an online platform is one method that has the potential to accomplish this goal.

While the idea of moving peer review online might at first seem unconventional, in reality, most teachers of composition already embrace technology in many aspects of our teaching practice. Much of what we do in and out of the classroom is multimodal, a point which Kathleen Blake Yancey insightfully observes:

> . . . when reviewed, our own practices [as teachers of composition] suggest that we have already committed to a theory of

communication that is both/and: print and digital. Given the way we *produce* print—sooner or later inside a word processor—we are digital already, at least in process. Given the course management systems like Blackboard and WebCT, we have committed to the screen for administrative purposes at least. Given the oral communication context of peer review, our teaching requires that students participate in mixed communicative modes. ("Made Not Only" 307)

In light of this fact, it seems contradictory to expect our students to stick solely with the more "traditional" learning experiences. Yet all too often, when we create writing assignments and activities for our students, we are not able to see beyond the walls of the physical classroom. However, as Cheryl Smith puts it, "[e]volutions in writing demand evolutions in pedagogy" (57)—and it's time that our approach to peer review in the writing classroom evolved right along with the rest it.

Some might voice the concern that not all students are "digital natives," and that implementing more technology tools simply creates another stumbling block for the already challenged ELL student in the writing classroom (see Nakamaru 382). It may be true that many students in higher education are not as well versed in some of the online technology tools that we employ in our courses as we would hope. However, the fact is that we live in a world where we are all continually engaged in the act of composing—often doing so in an online, collaborative way, as Yancey notes:

> [S]een historically this 21st century writing marks the beginning of a new era in literacy, a period we might call the Age of Composition, a period where composers become composers not through direct and formal instruction alone (if at all), but rather through what we might call an extracurricular social co-apprenticeship . . . In the case of the web, though, writers compose authentic texts in informal digitally networked contexts, but there isn't a hierarchy of expert-apprentice, but rather a peer co-apprenticeship in which communicative knowledge is freely exchanged. ("Writing in the 21st Century" 5)

As teachers of composition, our task is to instruct students in how to apply these skills to the more academic and professional uses they will encounter during their time in higher education and beyond (Pennington 287).

Clark also urges educators to use tools that "[engage] students in the interactivity, collaboration, ownership, authority, and malleability of texts" (28). She invokes Richard Lanham's claim that "the computer is a rhetorical tool" (28), sharing that her goal is to use this tool "to re-create the contemporary worlds of writing that our students encounter everyday" (29). Further, Fiona Hyland asserts that "[c]omputer-mediated feedback and computer tools offer opportunities for new modes of feedback and open up new avenues for communication between teachers and students and between students themselves" (177), and encourages ELL educators to "recognize that many of the new generation of second language writers may be totally at ease with computer-mediated communication and may in fact prefer this form of feedback to the face-to-face mode, as it is a relaxed, flexible and routine means of communication between themselves and their peers" (178). Sousa reminds us that "[m]any ELLs get their first exposure to the English language through media rather than through formal schooling" (218) and asserts that the appropriate use of technology can have a positive impact on the ELL student, often increasing the speed and accuracy of language acquisition, as well as leading to improvements in critical thinking, writing and analysis (219). And in Warschauer's view, ELL students "[tend] to see English and computers as a natural combination" and view electronic literacy as an important life skill that they need to develop (45–46).

In many ways, then, computer-mediated communication (CMC) is ideally suited as a rhetorical tool for ELL students. Kessler highlights this potential: "CMC practices can benefit language learners in numerous ways, particularly due to the collaborative and constructive manner in which netspeak is created" (210). He goes on to cite scholars who confirm many additional benefits of CMC, including "increased motivation and opportunities for out-of-class practice . . . increased authenticity and self-regulation . . . and student autonomy" (Kessler 217). Pennington also encourages the use of computer-related tools for ELL students, noting that "[m]any studies have shown that beyond their facilitating effects, word processors have an impact on student writers' attitudes, the characteristics of their texts, their revising behavior and the attention they pay to form and mechanics, and the order and the type of writing activities in which they engage" (288). Additionally, she notes that CMC can relieve the anxiety of writing for the ELL student (288–89) and increase the quantity and quality of revisions (290).

Inevitably, there will be a learning curve for some ELL students; however, the potential benefits and relevance for our students outweigh any resistance we might encounter in the process. Incorporating various technology tools more intentionally into the writing process affords opportunities for increased facility with language, self-confidence, more useful/usable feedback, better collaboration and participation, and perhaps most significantly, it levels the playing field of communication for both native and non-native speakers alike.

The time factor. Of all the ways in which we might best empower ELL students, by far one of the most impactful is the luxury of time. Earlier I noted the potentially negative impact a lack of time can have on ELL students during in-class peer review activities. It perhaps goes without saying, then, that affording more time to complete activities, to process ideas, to think through the language and word choice, to simply *read* the writing of their peers more thoroughly and with greater comprehension, can only be beneficial for the ELL writer. Shannon Sauro, in her discussion of computer-mediated corrective feedback, explains that "one factor affecting what elements of input learners notice is time pressure" and notes that the delays caused between responses in online peer-to-peer communications can create more processing and planning time for the ELL student, which contrasts with the on-demand responses in a face-to-face peer response activity (101). Belcher also suggests that the additional time afforded by CMC can act as an antidote to anxiety:

> CMC, with its hybrid written conversation, not only affords additional and possibly less anxiety-provoking (than face-to-face interaction) means of learner-to-learner communication within language classrooms but extends the interaction possibilities beyond the classroom walls, hence beyond its time constraints and the usual limited circle of interlocutors of classroom pair and group work. (255)

While online written communication of ideas can perhaps be viewed as more formal or perhaps even artificial in some cases, it *is* authentic communication, conducted in a way that favors the ELL writer: "current research indicates that 'computer conversations' are a form of hybrid communication,' which allows students to respond spontaneously, yet offers them the opportunity to reflect on their ideas, rehearse their responses, and work at their own pace" (Janet Swaffar, qtd. in DiGiovanni and Nagaswami 269). However, there is one important caveat to this mode of communication. If online peer review is implemented, it is important that it be conducted asynchronously. As Liu and Sadler demonstrated in their comparison of electronic and traditional modes of communication between students, creating a synchronous peer exchange not only reproduces the anxiety-inducing time constraints of the face-to-face peer review activity; it may in fact worsen the impact, due to the lack of non-verbal cues and risk of misunderstanding spontaneous and informal language (219). Kessler supports this view, suggesting that "[asynchronous computer-mediated communication] provides participants with time to reflect before responding, perhaps contributing to more thoughtful and in-depth engagement" (211). Creating a gap of time between sharing and responding to the writing will produce the best results, allowing for the exchange of ideas to be more meaningful and positive for all students involved.

Increased participation. One thing I often used to struggle with when implementing peer review in my writing courses was the balance between overseeing the activity to keep students accountable, and not wanting to hover over students during the session or ask them to turn in their feedback (which would seem to defeat the purpose, since I wanted them to have the notes for their own reference). Usually, I would resort to walking around the room, quickly scanning notes or checking off that they were completing work and trusting that somehow the feedback would be useful for each of the students participating in the exercise. If I'm being honest, I know that was not always the case, and students would often allude to this fact as well. So one of the most surprising benefits of moving peer review online was that there was a clear opportunity for my presence to be felt, without having to directly interject my comments or have students formally turn in an assignment. I typically use online LMS discussion boards to complete the activity, and provide a set of parameters including suggested topics for feedback, number of essays to review, and a timeline in which to complete the assignment. Because students know that I can easily view their comments, I have seen a higher number of participants overall, and better quality in the responses (far fewer of the "it looks ok" type responses, for example).

My experience confirms ideas put forth by DiGiovanni and Nagaswami, who described several advantages of online peer review (OLPR) related to teacher presence. They observed that in OLPR, students "remained on-task and focused," that "teachers can monitor students' interaction much more closely than in face-to-face situations," which will enable them to offer more training in peer review to specific groups as needed, and that teachers can "assess the impact of peer review on [students'] revised drafts" (268). While Rollinson is not specifically talking about OLPR, he also notes the potential benefit of instructor oversight provided by written feedback: "Written feedback also gives the teacher a better chance of closely following the progress of individuals and groups, both in terms of feedback offered and revisions made" (27).

In addition to (or perhaps influenced by) the accountability provided by teacher presence, I have observed that as a rule, *more* students participate in the peer review process overall when it takes place in an online environment. Less vocal students who would normally stay silent during a face-to-face peer review session (and this certainly includes ELL students in many cases) are often more comfortable responding online, where the fears and anxieties of verbal communication have been removed. Liu posits that "lack of face-to-face interaction seem[s] to be beneficial for some students whose cultural backgrounds do not encourage such interactions in a classroom environment" (qtd. in Liu and Sadler

218). Kessler considers a different explanation, sharing research from Bloch suggesting that "the act of writing for a public audience can increase motivation and, therefore, the quantity and quality of writing" (210). Whether or not it is due to cultural differences, audience awareness, accountability, or some other reason, the fact that some students seem more comfortable and vocal online is confirmed by research from Warschauer, who found that there were "much more equitable conversations in the CMC mode than in face-to-face interactions as the less vocal students seemed to participate more" (qtd. in Liu and Sadler 196). Liu and Sadler also point to Sullivan and Pratt's study, which "showed full student participation in electronic discourse as compared with 50% participation in face-to-face interaction" (196). Although working with a (perhaps) more highly motivated graduate student population, Belcher observes a similar trend: "The most significant outcome . . . was that voices—not anonymous, but clearly, and, to all appearances, confidently self-identified voices—which were never or seldom heard in class, were heard online" (264). From this evidence, it is clear that one way we can ensure that our ELL students show up for and fully engage in peer review is to shift the activity—at least to a degree—to an online environment.

Quality of feedback. When you combine more time with increased accountability, an interesting thing happens to the peer review comments: simply stated, *they get better.* This is certainly true for both native and non-native students, but it seems clear that OLPR is one way in which ELL students are able to truly show what they are capable of in the writing process. First, they are given more time to read their peers' essays critically, and reread if necessary in order to ascertain meaning and identify potential areas for comment. Thus, they are able to provide more thoughtful and thorough comments on their peers' writing, a point that Rollinson makes in connection with written comments as well: "[written feedback] gives both readers and writers more time for collaboration, consideration, and reflection than is normally possible in the cut and thrust of oral negotiation and debate" (Rollinson 27). Liu and Sadler also noted this phenomenon in their research: "One of the major findings of the study reveals that the overall number of comments made by the technology-enhanced peer review group was larger, and the percentage of revision-oriented comments was larger for this group as well, thus resulting in a larger number of revisions overall" (218). They further observed that using an online medium afforded the peer reviewers more space for sharing their ideas, as they were no longer constrained by a question-and-answer format on a piece of paper. Thus, although the students understandably said that the OLPR process was more time-consuming, their comments were more in-depth, and appeared to be more beneficial for their peers' writing overall (Liu and Sadler 219).

Given the additional time typically allotted in OLPR, ELL students also have the opportunity to "polish up" any language difficulties they struggle with, which is quite the opposite of what they might experience if they had to create comments on the fly during an in-class activity. Warschauer noted this potential for improvements in the language and syntax of online comments: "the electronic exchanges were longer and more lexically and syntactically sophisticated, suggesting . . . that the online environment encourages use of complex language" (qtd. in Belcher 256). And Liu and Sadler, citing the work of others, noted that OLPR has the potential to "enhance opportunities and motivation for authentic interaction and meaningful negotiation; reduce anxiety and produce more talk; and improve linguistic proficiency and increase self-confidence" (195). The ability to present a more clear and thorough set of comments sets up the ELL student for success, and undoubtedly increases their self-confidence as writers.

A further improvement in the quality of feedback pertains to the unfortunate but true experience that some students have during a face-to-face peer review session: negative feedback. To be clear, not all feedback needs to be glowing; I am referring to the tendency of some students (whether due to perceived superiority, impatience, or for some other reason), to be unduly harsh in their critique of another's work. Liu and Sadler summarize many of the concerns shared by other scholars over this type of peer review experience:

> . . . students sometimes can be hostile, sarcastic, overly critical, or unkind in their criticisms of their classmates' writing. Interactions of the group are at times unpleasant, with students being overly critical of each other's writings. In fact, the nature of responding to peers' drafts sometimes generates a sense of discomfort and uneasiness among the participants. Generally speaking, the students can become rather defensive when their work is criticized, especially by their peers. (194)

However, as noted earlier, the fact that peer comments are in a more "public" space creates a measure of accountability, which means that those who review the essays of ELL writers will usually be more judicious in their comments, avoiding any temptation they might have to respond negatively to what a native speaker might view as "clumsy" English construction. Rollinson confirms this, asserting that written feedback "reduces possible friction, defensiveness, or negative interactions" (27).

Ultimately, better quality and quantity in the feedback provided by and given to ELL writers will lead to an increase in revisions on student writing, a point that Frank Tuzi demonstrates in his study of the impact of e-comments on the revision process: "e-feedback resulted in more revisions than feedback from the writing center or oral feedback. E-feedback may be a viable avenue for receiving comments for L2 writers. Another interesting observation is that although the L2 writers stated that they preferred oral feedback, they made more e-feedback-based changes than oral-based changes" (Tuzi 229). As educators, we not only want our students engaged in the process; our goal is to provide opportunities for the most positive and effective learning possible to take place.

Written records. One final benefit of OLPR worth noting is the record-keeping quality of this format. In an oral peer review exchange, even with the encouragement to write notes during the exercise, the feedback students offer each other is for the most part ephemeral. Any notes written during the process tend to be brief, either due to space constraints as Liu and Sadler noted (219) or due to the brevity of the exercise. And, as mentioned earlier, there will simply be fewer comments overall due to the limited processing and response time of an in-class peer review. We all know that memory is not entirely trustworthy, and even if a student is recording notes during or at the end of the peer review activity, some ideas will be lost forever. Or perhaps the basic notes will be written, and then later the student will not be able to recall what the suggestion meant. Added to this fact is that ELL students often need time to translate phrasing or vocabulary and may simply not be able to fully comprehend a suggestion before it is lost forever. Williams discusses the gaps that occur for ELL students in face-to-face conversations, arguing that "noticing the gap may be a challenging process for language learners because they must compare interlanguage forms with memory traces that may have already degraded" (qtd. in Sauro 101). Thus, having a way to slow this process down and have a clear and thorough record of the peer feedback is ideal.

Several scholars have commented on the record-keeping factor of OLPR. Rollinson observes that "written feedback . . . provides the reader with a written record for later consideration" (27), and Digiovanni and Nagaswami also found the fact that "students do not have to rely on memory to recall feedback" a key advantage of the process (268). Sauro, citing the work of others in a discussion of text-chat feedback, notes that it creates an "enduring visual record . . . that may mirror the benefits of repetition and redundancy by allowing chatters to continually refresh memory traces" (101). In addition, Tuzi discusses the positive impact written records of peer feedback can have on subsequent revisions (229–230).

Another way in which the written form of feedback can be beneficial to students is by providing a diversity of models for the writing assignment. In a traditional peer review activity, students are typically placed in groups of two or perhaps three at most. This is quite practical, as time constraints and student interest would prohibit groups of any larger size. In fact, even in an OLPR situation, I would not ask students to review more than two other essays, unless perhaps I was offering extra credit for doing more. However, the mere fact that students can "browse" through the openly shared materials of all of the participating writers provides them with a wealth of examples from which to consider and contrast their own approaches to the writing assignment. I continually see evidence of this occurring in my course OLPR activities through comments made by students. Tuzi concurs, commenting that "An added benefit of the expanded audience is the ability to read other writers' drafts thereby providing opportunities for L2 writers to learn from the writing styles of others and incorporate them into their own writing" (232). As composition instructors, we may already provide models for our students, and perhaps even work through a critique of them in our class sessions. However, the additional repository of both good (and sometimes less effective) examples of student writing can be quite beneficial for the ELL student in particular, as it gives them more opportunity to see a diversity of styles, vocabulary, and interpretations of the writing assignment.

CONCLUSION

Given the positive impact that peer review can have on writing for both non-native and native students alike, it would be unfortunate to avoid using it in the composition or ELL classroom due to the struggles that some students face. While teacher feedback still serves a crucial role, student feedback equips emerging writers with the skills they need to succeed in their coursework and even beyond the classroom. At the same time, it is important to acknowledge that some methods of implementing peer review are not as well-suited for the ELL student, and can actually lead to an unsuccessful experience, or even encourage absence or disengagement from the process. Shifting to an online format for peer review provides a promising alternative and sets the ELL student up for a successful and rewarding experience. It also opens up opportunities for helping students gain more facility with the increasingly online and collaborative nature of communication that they will encounter in years to come.

For writing instructors who might be uncomfortable with the thought of completely abandoning face-to-face peer review activities, consider a two-step approach to the peer review process recommended by some scholars: begin in the classroom with some initial activities, training and discussion, and then move the reading and commenting stage to an asynchronous online format (DiGiovanni and Nagaswami 268; Liu and Sadler 221). If you do opt for a completely online approach, it is important to remember that the process will be more successful if conducted asynchronously.

We encourage our students regularly to take risks, knowing full well that doing so promotes more and deeper learning. As educators, it is imperative that we adopt the same philosophy for our own teaching practice. At times it may feel as though incorporating technology is simply buying in to the latest fad in education. However, evidence has shown that in some cases, it not only opens up new opportunities for learning, but it also serves as an equalizing factor—especially for the ELL student.

WORKS CITED

Andrade, Maureen Snow, and Norman W. Evans. "Developing Self-Regulate Learners: Helping Students Meet Challenges." *ESL Readers and Writers in Higher Education: Understanding Challenges, Providing Support,* edited by Norman W. Evans et al., Routledge, 2015, pp. 113–29.

Belcher, Diane D. "Authentic Interaction in a Virtual Classroom: Leveling the Playing Field in a Graduate Seminar." *Computers and Composition*, vol. 16, 1999, pp. 253–67.

Braine, George. "ESL Students in First-Year Writing Courses: ESL Versus Mainstream Classes." *Journal of Second Language Writing,* vol. 5, no. 2, 1996, pp. 91–107.

Carson, Joan G., and Gayle L. Nelson. "Chinese Students' Perceptions of ESL Peer Response Group Interaction." *Journal of Second Language Writing,* vol. 5, no. 1, 1996, pp. 1–19.

Caulk, Nat. "Comparing Teacher and Student Responses to Written Work." *TESOL Quarterly*, vol. 28, no. 1, Spring 1994, pp. 181–88.

Clark, J. Elizabeth. "The Digital Imperative: Making the Case for a 21st-Century Pedagogy." *Computers and Composition,* vol. 27, 2010, pp. 27–35.

Costino, Kimberly A., and Sunny Hyon. "'A Class for Students Like Me': Reconsidering Relationships among Identity Labels, Residency Status, and Students' Preferences for Mainstream or Multilingual Composition." *Journal of Second Language Writing,* vol. 16, 2007, pp. 63–81.

DiGiovanni, Elaine, and Girija Nagaswami. "Online Peer Review: An Alternative to Face-To-Face?" *English Language Teaching Journal,* vol. 55, no. 3, 2001, pp. 263–72.

Evans, Norman W., and Maureen Snow Andrade. "Understanding Challenges, Providing Support: ESL Readers and Writers in Higher Education." *ESL Readers and Writers in Higher Education: Understanding Challenges, Providing Support,* edited by Norman W. Evans et al., 2015, pp. 3–17.

Ferris, Dana. "Supporting Multilingual Writers through the Challenges of Academic Literacy: Principles of English for Academic Purposes and Composition Instruction." *ESL Readers and Writers in Higher Education: Understanding Challenges, Providing Support,* edited by Norman W. Evans et al., pp. 147–63.

Fordham, Sonja K. *Teacher and Peer Written Feedback in the ESL Composition Classroom: Appropriation, Stance, and Authorship.* Dissertation. U of AZ, 2015.

Hoogeveen, Mariëtte, and Amos van Gelderen. "What Works in Writing with Peer Response? A Review of Intervention Studies with Children and Adolescents." *Educational Psychology Review,* vol. 25, 2013, pp. 473–502.

Hyland, Fiona. "Future Directions in Feedback on Second Language Writing: Overview and Research Agenda." *International Journal of English Studies*, vol.10, no. 2, 2010, pp. 171–82.

Hyland, Ken. "Genre-based Pedagogies: A Social Response to Process." *Journal of Second Language Writing*, vol. 12, 2003, pp. 17–29.

Kessler, Greg. "Using Technology to Teach ESL Readers and Writers." *ESL Readers and Writers in Higher Education: Understanding Challenges, Providing Support*, edited by Norman W. Evans et al., 2015, pp. 209–22.

Kim, Soo Hyon. "Preparing English Learners for Effective Peer Review in the Writers' Workshop." *The Reading Teacher*, vol. 68 no. 8, 2015, pp. 599–603.

Leki, Ilona, and Joan G. Carson. "Students' Perceptions of EAP Writing Instruction and Writing Needs across the Disciplines." *TESOL Quarterly*, vol. 28, no. 1, Spring 1994, pp. 81–101.

Liu, Jun, and Randall W. Sadler. "The Effect and Affect of Peer Review in Electronic Versus Traditional Modes on L2 Writing." *Journal of English for Academic Purposes*, vol. 2, 2003, pp.193–227.

Lundstrom, Kristi, and Wendy Baker. "To Give is Better Than to Receive: The Benefits of Peer Review to the Reviewer's Own Writing." *Journal of Second Language Writing*, vol. 18, 2009, pp. 30–43.

Matsuda, Paul Kei, and Tony Silva. "Cross-Cultural Composition: Mediated Integration of US and International Students." *Composition Studies*, vol. 27, no. 1, Spring 1999, pp. 15–30.

Mendonca, Cassia O., and Karen E. Johnson. "Peer Review Negotiations: Revision Activities in ESL Writing Instruction." *TESOL Quarterly*, vol. 28, no. 4, 1994, pp. 745–68.

Miao, Yang, et al. "A Comparative Study of Peer and Teacher Feedback in a Chinese EFL Writing Class." *Journal of Second Language Writing*, vol. 15, 2006, pp. 179–200.

Miller-Cochran, Susan. "Beyond 'ESL Writing': Teaching Cross-Cultural Composition at a Community College." *TETYC*, Sept. 2012, pp. 20–30.

Nakamaru, Sarah. "Making (and Not Making) Connections with Web 2.0 Technology in the ESL Composition Classroom." *TETYC*, May 2011, pp. 377–90.

Ortmeier-Hooper, Christina. "English May Be My Second Language, but I'm Not 'ESL'." *College Composition and Communication*, vol. 59, no. 3, Feb. 2008, pp. 389–419.

———. *Writing Across Culture and Language: Inclusive Strategies for Working with ELL Writers in the ELA Classroom*, NCTE, 2017.

Pennington, Martha C. "The Impact of the Computer in Second Language Writing," *Exploring the Dynamics of Second Language Writing*, edited by Barbara Kroll, Cambridge, 2003, 287–310.

Raimes, Ann. "What Unskilled ESL Students Do as They Write: A Classroom Study of Composing." *TESOL Quarterly*, vol. 19, no. 2, Jun. 1985, pp. 229–58.

Rollinson, Paul. "Using Peer Feedback in the ESL Writing Class." *ELT Journal*, vol. 59, no. 1, Jan. 2005, pp. 23–30.

Sauro, Shannon. "Computer-Mediated Corrective Feedback and the Development of L2 Grammar." *Language Learning & Technology*, vol. 13, no. 1, Feb. 2009, pp. 96–120.

Show, Mei Lin. "A Study of ELL Students' Writing Difficulties: A Call for Culturally, Linguistically, and Psychologically Responses Teaching." *College Student Journal*, vol. 49, no. 2, 2015, pp. 237–50.

Sommers, Nancy. "Responding to Student Writing." *College Composition and Communication*, vol. 33, no. 2, May 1982, pp. 148–56.

Sousa, David A. *How the ELL Brain Learns,* Corwin, 2011.

Smith, Cheryl C. "Technologies for Transcending a Focus on Error: Blogs and Democratic Aspirations in First-Year Composition." *Journal of Basic Writing*, vol. 27, no. 1, 2008, pp. 35–60, https://doi.org/10.37514/JBW-J.2008.27.1.03.

Tsui, Amy B.M., and Maria Ng. "Do Secondary L2 Writers Benefit from Peer Comments?" *Journal of Second Language Writing*, vol. 9, no. 2, 2000, pp. 147–70.

Tuzi, Frank. "The Impact of E-feedback on the Revisions of L2 Writers in an Academic Writing Course. *Computers and Composition*, vol. 21, no. 2, 2005, pp. 217–35.

Warschauer, Mark. "On-line Learning in Second Language Classrooms: An Ethnographic Study." *Network-based Language Teaching,* edited by Mark Warschauer and Richard Kern, Cambridge, 2000, pp. 41–58.

Yancey, Kathleen Blake. "Made Not Only in Words: Composition in a New Key." *College Composition and Communication*, vol. 56, no. 2, 2004, pp. 297–328.

Yancey, Kathleen Blake. "Writing in the 21st Century." *NCTE*, Feb. 2009, https://www.ncte.org/library/NCTEFiles/Press/Yancey_final.pdf.

Zhang, Shuqiang. "Reexamining the Affective Advantage of Peer Feedback in the ESL Writing Class." *Journal of Second Language Writing*, vol. 4, no. 3, 1995, pp. 209–22.

CHAPTER 10.
LEARNING FROM PEER REVIEW ONLINE: CHANGING THE PEDAGOGICAL EMPHASIS

Phoebe Jackson
William Paterson University

Peer review has been a foundational practice in writing studies for decades, beginning with those teacher/scholars (Elbow; Murray; Moffett; Bruffee) in the process movement, who early on encouraged its use. To date, it is a practice that can be found in almost all first-year college writing classes and increasingly in upper-level writing courses. Though a widely accepted practice, it nonetheless has its detractors who question the validity of the practice overall and who specifically question the ability of students to write an effective peer review that would help a peer to revise an essay (Jesnek; Flynn).

Many teacher/instructors in writing studies too often tend to view peer review as an activity primarily focused on outcomes, one focused on the peer reviewer's ability to provide sound advice in a revision of a peer's essay. In a typical peer review workshop, instructors set up group sessions charging students to review the final drafts of an essay. Unfortunately, when instructors see the comments that peer reviewers have given, they are often dismayed with the results as the comments rarely live up to their expectations of what is needed in the revision process. In effect, they view student comments based on the response that an instructor would have given and when the peer review does not live up to that standard, they think that peer review workshop has not achieved its intended goal—the ability of a peer review to analyze and comment effectively on a paper draft. Acting as a proxy to the teacher, we hope our students will create a similar model of response that might mirror what we had to say about a given paper, even though most of us have spent years responding to student papers. When students are unable to replicate this response model, we throw up our hands in despair and disparage the peer review process.

This chapter proposes to reframe the practice of peer review to think about it in terms of what students can *learn* from the process of peer review rather than a focus on the outcomes. Too often, instructors judge a student's peer review comments solely on their effectiveness to communicate ways to improve a peer's essay. What goes unexamined is the learning that occurs for the peer reviewer in providing comments. In the following discussion, I examine the ongoing debate about peer review in writing studies, looking at perspectives from both instructors and students. Then, I review research in the field of education that studies what students *learn* by providing comments to their peers. This research offers writing studies instructors an alternative way to think about peer review, what I call a change in pedagogical emphasis. Finally, I provide an example of online peer review that enacts this change in pedagogical emphasis: one that shifts the focus from the student acting as a proxy for the instructor to one that examines how a student can learn about the writing process when engaging in peer review. Such a reorientation helps to reduce the expectations that instructors tend to have about a student's ability to write a substantive peer review and refocuses it on the learning that can take place for students.

THE ONGOING DEBATE ABOUT PEER REVIEW

Peer review is an accepted practice in most composition classrooms and has been since the 1960s and 1970s. Early practitioners like composition scholars Kenneth Bruffee and Peter Elbow saw great potential for students in the adoption of peer review practices. For both, the importance of peer review was a de-emphasis of the role of the instructor and a move toward an emphasis on a student audience for their work. During this time, the sharing of writing with peers accordingly gained traction for both its ability to place students in a "communicative transaction" (Elbow 24) and for its possibilities toward a practice in "collaborative learning" (Bruffee).

In his book *Writing Without Teachers* published in 1973, Peter Elbow recognized the significance of expanding one's audience beyond the instructor to include other students in the class. As such, Elbow had a specific goal in mind: "that it would be better if the student could get the experience of more than one reader. He would get a wider range of reactions to offset the one sidedness of a single reaction" (121). Addressing students, Elbow pointed out that feedback from classmates ultimately works to help them to achieve what they want in their writing and not necessarily the goals of the instructor. The intention of peer review in its early incarnation was not about accomplishing specific quantifiable outcomes, i.e., how substantial was the written peer review comment helping the writer to improve the text. Instead, it was meant for the writer to get the reader's honest reactions to the text.

Early practitioners of peer-response groups did see appreciable benefits to peer review. In her article "Writing Center Tutorials vs. Peer-Response Groups (1992), Muriel Harris elucidates the important attributes of peer response that process-oriented pedagogues noted in their classes: for Ann Ruggles Gere and Robert Abbott this amounted to "improving critical thinking, organization, and appropriateness of writing; improving usage; increasing the amount of revision; and reducing apprehension" (371–372). For Carol Berkenkotter peer response assured "the experience of writing and revising for less threatening audiences than the teacher, of learning to discriminate between useful and non-useful feedback, and of learning to use awareness of anticipated audience responses as writers revise" and finally for Karen Spear peer response meant "contribut[ing] to the evolution of ideas, mak[ing] the audience real, and sharing drafts to help share and test thought" (371–372). In those early decades of peer review, as Harris makes clear, practitioners viewed the practice in favorable terms focusing on larger educational outcomes.

Though peer review continues to be practiced in most composition writing courses and increasingly in literature courses, there are those instructors who question the effectiveness of the practice. Too often, in a first-year writing course, peer review tends to be done as a rote exercise whereby instructors put students into small groups and hand out a rubric or a document of pre-assigned questions to be filled in and answered by the peer reviewer. Sometimes there is time left over for questions and answers among the group participants, but too often students see the activity as an assignment to be done quickly to allow for some social networking before the class ends. Not surprisingly, instructors and students alike wonder about the effectiveness of such an exercise where the emphasis primarily is on the product and not the process. Both groups see peer review as a way to offer specific advice to revise an essay draft. When peer review falls short of both teacher and student expectations (the advice from the peer reviewer proves not helpful to revising), then both are apt to question its usefulness.

In an early article, "Students as Readers of their Classmates' Writing: Some Implications for Peer Critiquing" (1984), critic Elizabeth Flynn started to question the value of the peer review workshop. She found that the enthusiasm for peer review that Bruffee, Elbow, Moffett and others espoused was "often not backed up by empirical evidence" (qtd in "Re-viewing Peer Review"). Using her own first-year students as an example, Flynn noted that they weren't giving "very useful feedback" to their peers but tended to focus on surface-level issues rather than on larger order issues like organization, etc. From her anecdotal evidence, Flynn thus recommended that students needed more guidance from teachers in order to produce an "effective" peer review, one that would give more substantive advice. Her suggestion was to use "critique sheets," with the charge "to point out gaps, inconsistencies, and irrelevancies."

In a follow-up article, "Re-viewing Peer Review" (2011), Flynn explains that not much has changed in the ensuing years since the publication of her initial article. Though she continues to use critique sheets in her writing classes, Flynn remains doubtful of the effectiveness of peer review for students and notes that only occasionally do students remark that peer comments have helped them with their writing. Not ready to give up on peer critique entirely, Flynn concludes that it appears to be more beneficial for upper-level students who in her estimation are more capable of offering solutions and of making the necessary revisions from a peer's comments.

Similarly, in another 2011 article, "Peer Editing in the 21st Century College Classroom: Do Beginning Composition Students Truly Reap the Benefits?" critic Lindsey M. Jesnek comes right out to suggest "that peer editing may, in fact, be more detrimental than previously imagined" (17). In surveying quantitative and qualitative research on the topic, she found a great deal of dissatisfaction among both first-year composition students and faculty with peer editing. As she makes clear, both students and teachers assume that the purpose of peer editing is "to help with the revision of student drafts" (20). Students expected that peer editing would help them to find errors in their drafts with the eventual purpose of improving their grades (20). When the peer editing session falls short of its goal to offer advice to improve the essay draft, then its benefits are called into question. Ultimately, like Flynn, Jesnek concludes that peer editing is probably better suited for upper-level students.

Instructors are not the only ones to question the usefulness of peer review. In their article, "Peer Review from the Students' Perspective: Invaluable or Invalid," Charlotte Brammer and Mary Rees examine how students perceive the practice. From their study, they noted that most students find peer review" not very helpful" (75). Brammer and Rees found that students thought the primary function of peer review should be to help them catch proofreading errors (79). Coming from different writing backgrounds, some students expressed concern about the quality of feedback given to them if they perceived the writer to have weak writing skills (80). In their concluding remarks, the authors noted that more work needed to be done to address a student's understanding of the importance of peer review. Too often students tend to see peer review merely as an exercise in proofreading and fail to grasp what they can learn when working collaboratively.

In the examples above, the failure of peer review to achieve the desired goal of improving students' essays is reason for both instructors and students to question its usefulness. The main issue at stake for faculty is the perceived inability of students to provide substantive comments on drafts of student essays—a question of outcomes. Whereas, for many students the value of peer review resides in noting proofreading errors. At first glance, the goals of the students and the faculty would appear to be at odds with one another. However, students and instructors do seem to share a common concern: how to improve an essay draft.

In both cases, instructors and students fall victim to what Timothy Oleksiak in a 2020 article evocatively calls the "the improvement imperative" (306). Accordingly, when different peer review techniques fail to produce the desired outcomes, whereby a student's essay draft does *not* improve because of a peer's comments, writing instructors are quick to question the value of the practice. Nonetheless, since peer review is considered a foundational part of almost all writing classes, instructors carry on, hoping to find alternative techniques that will eventually achieve better results. Doing so, Oleksiak argues persuasively, just takes instructors down a rabbit hole seeking an unattainable goal. To continue to think of peer review exclusively in terms of the improvement imperative will not bring about the desired results of improved student writing.

In this chapter, I argue that instructors in writing studies typically have been too focused on the improvement imperative—a student's ability to write a concise peer review that improves a peer's revision—to the exclusion of what students can learn from the process of providing a peer review. Writing instructors need to rethink their pedagogical emphasis from one focused on the improvement imperative to one that recognizes the learning that can take place for a student providing a peer review. The real value of peer review is not in its outcomes, i.e., the comments to improve a peer's essay but what students learn by engaging in the process of peer review itself. The online environment, I will demonstrate, further augments this pedagogical shift from product to process.

EDUCATIONAL RESEARCH ON PROVIDING PEER REVIEW FEEDBACK

In her 2011 article, "Re-viewing Peer Review," Elizabeth Flynn noted a decline of published research about peer review in the field of writing studies—a trend beginning in the 1990s. Recent research about peer review, Flynn discovered has moved into a new direction, primarily concerned with L2 learners and with the use of computer-assisted peer review. It is difficult to speculate the reason for the decline in publications that Flynn mentions. It could be that new pedagogies in writing studies, for example, writing about writing and teaching for transfer, consider peer review a minor subset of the writing process and thus of a lesser concern. Nonetheless, peer review remains a mainstay in most writing courses, one that continues to offer challenges to many writing instructors and thus worthy of attention.

To that end in this section, I will re-direct attention to some of the scholarship on peer review that has come out of the education field. Interestingly, though teacher/scholars in composition studies often question the benefit of peer review, those working in the field of education tend toward a more positive view of the practice. These researchers begin with the premise that peer review in general is worthwhile to advance student learning about writing. While they acknowledge that the "research evidence on the impact of peer groups on writing quality is mixed," education researchers nonetheless agree that peer review/peer response/peer groups perform an important role in the teaching of writing (Pritchard & Morrow 89). They note the practice of peer review provides students with specific benefits including a sense of audience awareness; the ability to see "their own strengths and weaknesses" as a writer; and an enhanced understanding of the importance of collaborative learning; and the development of a sense of ownership of their writing (Tsui and Ng 147).

The premise that students can learn from providing a peer review is an important one (Zhang 698). To continue to look at peer review in terms of its improvement imperative will, as Oleksiak explains, only lead instructors in a never-ending search for other techniques that ultimately result in the same conclusion—dissatisfaction with student commenting to improve an essay draft. Looking at peer review from the perspective of what a student can learn offers teachers and students a productive way to reaffirm its importance as a meaningful part of the writing process.

In the following brief review, I highlight some of the research that has been done in the education field. While other writing studies scholars also mention the benefits that can accrue for students from providing a peer review (Reid) or what Melissa Meeks evocatively calls "giver's gain, research scholars in the education field including those doing L2 research have conducted quantitative and qualitative studies that specifically examine what students can learn from doing so.

In an early article (2006) Ngar-Fun Liu and David Carless examine both peer assessment and peer feedback. What is notable, for my purposes, is their research on peer feedback. Liu and Carless highlight the importance of peer feedback and its "potential for enhanced student learning" (279). According to the authors, one way students learn is through their ability to express and articulate what they understand to other students (281). Peer feedback, they suggest, provides the opportunity to practice a student's self-expression, moving their learning from the "private domain" into the "public domain" with their peers (281). The results of their study suggest that through the practice of peer feedback, students develop specific skills, including "critical reflection, listening to and acting on feedback, sensitively assessing and providing feedback on the work of others" (289). In their final assessment of peer feedback, the authors underscore the importance of cultivating peer feedback as an essential part of the learning process, a point, I would argue, that too often gets overlooked by compositionists (288).

Similarly, Kristi Lundstrom and Wendy Baker, in their article (2009), "To Give is Better Than to Receive: The Benefits of Peer Review to the Reviewers' Own Writing," looked specifically at L2 students in their research on peer review. The authors found that those students giving peer reviews "made more significant gains in their own writing over the course of the semester than [those students] who focused on how to use feedback" (30). At the end of their study, they observed two significant results: peer reviewers who were less proficient writers actually "made more gains than those at higher proficiency levels," and were better able to focus more on global issues in their writing than previously observed (30).

From their findings, Lundstrom and Baker contend that "L2 writer students can improve their own writing by transferring abilities they learn when reviewing peer texts" (38). In effect, engaging in the cognitive processes necessary to give a peer review, student reviewers "learn from these activities to critically self-evaluate their own writing in order to make appropriate revisions" (38). As a result, the authors observed that a student's capability to give a peer review positively corresponded to their own writing improvement. Their research suggests that for L2 students, and frankly for all students learning to write, they are engaged in more active individual learning about the process of writing through giving peer feedback.

The goal for researchers Young Hoan Cho and Kwangsu Cho in their 2010 article, "Peer Reviewers Learn from Giving Comments," was to look at how giving comments could improve a reviewer's own writing skills (630). Beginning with "the learning-writing-by-reviewing hypothesis," (630) they looked at both the reviewer's comments and the reception of the comments. In their findings, their study supported their initial hypothesis. They found that student reviewers in general did improve their writing by providing comments especially those comments that focused "at the meaning-level rather than the surface-level" (640). Most important their study revealed that students benefitted more from providing comments and less so from getting peer feedback (640).

Using the same "learning-writing-by-reviewing hypothesis" in a study conducted in 2011, researchers Kwangsu Cho and Charles MacArthur examine the ways that peer review can function as a learning activity and in turn help with the development of the peer reviewer's own writing (74). Their research identified a number of important takeaways for the practice of peer review. First, students came away with a better understanding of audience and audience awareness. Of greater significance, students had the opportunity "to practice problem-solving strategies important for writing improvement" (75) to include "detecting problems, diagnosing them, and generating solutions" (75, 78). These problem-solving strategies relate directly to a higher level of cognitive processes. Practice of these strategies, the authors conclude, can help students with their own writing. By providing commentary to writers, the peer reviewers have had to figure out problems in an essay and then have had to effectively explain to the writer how to go about solving those problems—all skills connected to cognition. At the conclusion of their study, the authors found that the active engagement of giving a peer review showed "considerable promise as an effective and efficient way to help college students develop their writing skills" (79).

David Nicol, Avril Thomson, and Caroline Breslin's study "Rethinking Feedback Practices in Higher Education: A Peer Review Perspective" replicates much of the findings of previous research. For their study, the researchers were interested in how students can learn from receiving peer feedback, feedback production, and "the cognitive processes that are activated when students construct feedback reviews" (102). For the purposes of this literature review, I want to focus on what the students in the study had to say about producing peer reviews. In their comments, half of the students in the study's survey remarked that they "learned how to think critically or how to make critical judgements" (111) and a majority noted that providing a peer review enabled them to rethink their own work. This study concluded that providing peer reviews "engages students actively in critical thinking, in applying criteria, in reflection, and through this, in learning transfer" (116).

In a 2015 *Instructional Science* article, "Understanding the Benefits of Providing Peer Feedback: How Students Respond to Peers' Texts of Varying Quality" cognitive psychology researchers Melissa M. Patchen and Christian D. Schunn (2015) reached similar conclusions. From their literature review of articles pertaining to peer feedback, they concluded that "constructing comments appears to be the most effective evaluation activity" (593) in peer review and that "the construction of criticism comments was positively related to student performance" (595). Their study began with the premise that in doing peer review, students necessarily had to engage a certain skill set: the ability to identify problems, troubleshoot them, and offer solutions (607). With practice they noted that students could strengthen those skills suggesting that they were learning in the process. Patchen and Schunn's research confirms the cognitive benefit for students who practice peer reviewing.

Looking at the research of peer feedback from an online perspective, Esther van Popta et al. (2017) in "Exploring the Value of Peer Feedback in Online Learning," undertook an extensive meta-analysis literature review analyzing studies that pertain specifically to research related to online peer feedback. Popta et al. argue that too much emphasis in the research on peer review revolves around an examination of the feedback that students receive rather than what students gain from giving feedback. Their study aims to flip that equation to understand what "learning benefits" accrue to the provider.

Focusing on how online peer feedback functions "as a learning activity", the researchers ended up with a much smaller sampling of journal articles—eight in total. In their analysis, they considered two factors: (1) the learning benefits that accrue from providing online feedback and (2) the cognitive processes involved in the activity of providing online feedback. Their research on peer review showed a distinct benefit specifically related to cognition. As they explain, by providing a peer review online, students engage in a number of cognitive processes: "[they] compare and question ideas; evaluate; suggest modifications; and reflect, plan, and regulate their own thinking. They think critically, connect to new knowledge, explain, and take different perspectives" (29). Their conclusions for online peer review support the claim that students benefit cognitively when providing peer feedback.

As research in the field of education demonstrates, students can learn from the process of analyzing a peer's essay and from providing comments. Their research comments directly on the numerous benefits that accrue for students who give peer reviews to include practicing self-expression (Liu and Carless); learning to self-evaluate their own writing (Lundstrom and Baker); and engaging in problem-solving strategies (Cho and MacArthur). By providing feedback to others, students are involved in more active learning. Too often the recipient of peer feedback does not understand the information given since it is another person's reading or misreading of a draft essay or it is helpful information that they are not yet ready to receive. Students learning through a process of their own discovery, I would argue, have a greater chance of adding and possibly transferring such information to their own writing.

These educational studies on peer review suggest that perhaps we as writing instructors have been too focused on peer review outcomes, specifically to the quality of feedback. Instead, they signal an important shift, one that values the learning that takes place for students when providing a peer review. It is a move away from an emphasis on the effectiveness of a student's comments for revision purposes that frequently leaves both teachers and students dissatisfied to one that proffers an alternative way for writing instructors to think about the goal of peer review—the learning that takes place in providing a comment. In so doing, it offers an opportunity to revitalize practice that is central to writing courses.

Critical to rethinking a change in pedagogical emphasis entails moving peer review online, even for those courses that are taught face to face. Such a move lends itself to engaging students in a manner that more effectively promotes their own critical thinking as they suddenly have more time to read and write at their own pace. It encourages them to reflect on their own ideas and thoughts and to gain practice articulating their ideas—in writing—to their peer group. Moreover, the online environment offers students more of an opportunity to collaborate and correspond with each other over a period extending the work on peer review that is typically relegated to one class period. As a result of reading, writing, and responding to each other's work online, students are in effect building spontaneous discourse communities and learning how to work together. For these reasons, I have found that doing peer review online moves students productively from a practice that too often is viewed as busy work and done in a hasty manner to one that allows the student more time to think and to process their thoughts away from the distractions that are inherent in a classroom environment. As a result, their commenting and responding to each other tends to be more thoughtful and shows a distinct level of engagement.

In this next section, I will explain how I have developed my writing-intensive course over time to embrace this shift in pedagogical emphasis that attempts to move the goal post from a focus on product to one on process—a consideration of what students can learn by doing peer review. For my purposes, peer review is a practice that necessarily takes place throughout the entire semester. It begins by scaffolding low-stakes writing assignments that eventually lead up to three different sessions of the peer review workshop. In these low-stakes writing assignments, students read, analyze, and comment on each other's responses. By doing so the entire semester, students learn to feel at ease communicating and collaborating in a community of other writers.

SCAFFOLDING WRITING ASSIGNMENTS

To frame this discussion, I want to talk about what students do in preparation leading up to the online peer review workshop. I begin by scaffolding shorter writing assignments to enable students to become more comfortable with reading and responding. The initial scaffolding assignment consists of two distinct steps: students write and post to the discussion board (DB). My classes use Blackboard as the Course Management System. Afterwards, they respond to at least two DB posts. These two steps are important because they begin to initiate students into a conversation online with others, thereby helping to develop a writing community where students read and share information.

Let me begin by describing the online class that I teach regularly. It is a portal class, Methods of Literary Criticism, for the English major, typically taken when a student is a sophomore. Because it fulfills a writing intensive requirement at my university and because it is offered online, appealing to those students who work, this course also attracts students from other majors, running the gamut from early childhood education to finance and marketing. Most of these students have had limited experience in writing courses other than the required first-year writing courses. To prepare this diverse group of students to participate as a community of writers, I begin with low-stakes writing assignments that eventually lead up to the peer review writing workshop.

STEP ONE: POSTING ON THE DISCUSSION BOARD

Students are required to write a 250-word post to one of the writing prompts that I have posted on Discussion Board (DB) about the reading for that week. Twice a week, I post writing prompt questions. I typically post three to four questions so that students get to choose whatever topic might be of interest them. These twice-weekly discussion board posts serve to get them to think more concretely about the course readings for that week.

STEP TWO: RESPONDING TO THE DISCUSSION BOARD POST

After they have posted their posts, students are responsible to go back into the DB to comment on two other student posts in the DB thread. They have the option of responding to others in the thread the day they post their responses, or they can go back the next day and write a response. Having students respond to each other on the discussion board begins the process of engaging them in a conversation with the group. It enables them to see how others have written to a prompt. In addition, it gives them the opportunity to reflect not only on *what* the student had to say about the topic but also *how* the person drafted the response to a topic with which they are familiar. Such an exercise begins to move them toward an engagement with the peer review process. They have had to read carefully, think about what they have read, and then consider how they will respond to their audience. As researchers and students have noted, the online environment in particular gives students the added advantage of spending more time thinking and reflecting before they undertake writing and responding to their peers (Pritchard and Morrow; Jensen).

In reading the DB posts, students can see how others in the class have responded to the questions I have posted for the DB thread. For many, these DB posts allow students to see different interpretations to the assigned reading, ones they had not considered. In that way, the DB post opens a door to new ideas. For others, the posts clarify issues in the readings that they missed or did not understand. Finally, reading the DB posts enables students to see how others have written up their response and what they have learned about writing from doing so. It can be as simple as noting that a student has used quotes or added examples to support a point.

I am going to quote from just a few student examples to show the ways that students respond to each other's posts even before they are asked to write a peer review. These responses show they are already reading and thinking critically in their communication with each other. The original writing prompt asked students to respond to Junot Díaz's short story, "Edison, New Jersey," focusing on issues of social class.

Example 1: I was surprised to read the "sex slave" and "mail order bride" angle so explicitly stated here, but I can see where your argument is coming from. Being that Yunior is a complete stranger to the maid, besides them both being from the Dominican Republic, it shows her desperation to leave Pruitt when she tells him "I want to get out of here . . . I'll pay you for a ride" (Diaz 133). The quotations you present about her amount of clothing versus the amount of Pruitt's belongings also demonstrate the possibility of her being abused. Yunior gets the urge to "ask her if she loves her boss" but refrains from doing so (Diaz 137). The balance of power in a boss-employee relationship would certainly be complicated if the maid was being "held" to work for Pruitt because of her lack of other options, as you suggest.

In this first example, the reader seems surprised to encounter a different way of thinking about the maid in Díaz's story—that she might be a "sex slave" and "mail order bride." The reader also goes on to remark on the writing strategies that the writer has deployed: an awareness that the writer is making an argument and that the writer used direct quotations to support points. Finally, the reader also takes the information they read in the response and draws their own conclusion—"the balance of power in a boss-employee relationship would certainly be complicated"—basically underscoring the writer's comments. This response shows the student critically engaged through analyzing and thinking through the writer's DB post—an important preparatory step for the practice of peer review.

Example 2: I enjoyed reading your thoughts on this discussion board post and thought you came up with some good examples from the text to help support your ideas. I liked how you wrote "Yunior enjoys being able to buy his girlfriend items but, this is a luxury that he cannot completely afford; stealing makes Yunior feel as if he is rich though." Yunior wants more for himself but I kind of got the sense that he feels that this is the life that's laid out for him and it was going to stay like that forever. I liked that he took out the calculator to work towards his own pool table, it shows that it is a luxury he really wants and is working towards.

For this second example, the reader clearly is impressed with what they have read from the DB post. They also note the importance of using "good examples" when trying to support an argument. It is interesting that the student goes back to the DB post to cite a direct quote, a point that they thought important to consider about the character. But even more important, the student adds to the writer's interpretation and conclusion by adding "but I kind of got the sense that he feels that this is the life that's laid out for him." In providing this commentary to the student's response, the reader demonstrates their ability to push their own thinking forward—to take what another person says, consider it, and to draw their own conclusion.

As these two examples demonstrate, very often the writer of the DB post has given the reader a different perspective to consider with regards to Díaz's story, in other words generating new knowledge about the text under review. Both students also comment on writing strategies that they found helpful or that have at least caught the reader's attention (making an argument and using direct quotes/and or examples to support a writer's conclusions). Finally, both readers demonstrate an active engagement with the writer's comments, one that evinces a "conversation" between the reader and the writer. This conversation acts as a form of brainstorming for the reader and possibly for the writer helping each to explore and to expand the ideas that began with the initial post. In that respect, students (reader and writer) can see how this back and forth can help them in their thinking process about how to develop and flesh out an argument.

In this low-stakes assignment, students need to go back into the DB thread and read through what others have written and then decide which two posts they want to respond to. Interestingly, almost everyone in the class receives at least one to three responses for their DB posts. It is a very rare occasion that a post does not receive a response. Sometimes a student will receive five responses making it clear that the writer's comments have grabbed the attention of numerous people. In that scenario, students usually begin by stating: "I agree with your point of view," "interesting point," "I like how you pointed out," "You make great points." But in all cases, the student responders address the point brought up by the writer and then add their thoughts to the writer's comments. This type of back-and-forth response illustrates how students can participate in learning new knowledge from each other.

When everyone has posted to the DB and then responded to the posts of two peers, I go back into Blackboard to collect all the writing from that discussion board thread (both posts and responses to posts) to read. Then I write my own response and general comments to the whole class rather than responding individually to each student. I see my participation as contributing to the conversation already underway. I am just another part of the larger audience. For my response, I usually ask follow-up questions to get students to think further about the topics that they have brought up. To do so, I typically choose a quote from a student's DB post, and then pose a question or comment to get students to see how their ideas could lead to further thinking and expansion. This activity models for students the importance of asking follow-up questions, allowing them to see that their ideas can always be examined further.

By the time I assign the first essay, typically the fourth week of class, the students have already written eight 250-word posts and have responded to 16 posts, writing an average of 100–150 words. While I tell them that the responses need to be at least 100 words in length, students typically write 150 words or more. That they write more than expected, I would argue, demonstrates an important level of engagement with the writer's text. For the most part, students read their peer's post with interest and respond in a thoughtful manner. They are developing a writing relationship with others in the class with me in absentia. Because I do not come in with my general response until all that work has taken place, their responsibility resides with each other.

Step Three: Rereading a DB Thread

Before beginning to write the first essay, I assign one more low-stakes writing exercise. In this assignment, I ask students to choose a previous discussion board thread (DB), one that discusses a story or topic that they think they would possibly like to examine further for their first essay assignment. Typically, they have four to five different DB threads from which to choose. For that assignment, I pose the following questions: (a) read through the entire thread and write a summary of the points that your peers discuss; (b) what conclusions can you draw from your peer's comments; (c) what point (s) do your peers bring up that you consider important to a discussion and understanding of the story? Explain why.

To cite two examples:

> **Student A:** In order to analyze the chapter "Aguantando" in *Drown* by Junto Diaz (sic), we can look to our peers and expand our opinions. It helps to read what others opinion is as well as their viewpoint and what they believe to be important for a story. What I believe to be important for the story its best if we can look back to who Mami is . . . both [students] point out great statements that emphasize that Mami has been left alone to tend for her two boy and being in a poor country leads to counting pennies . . . these two statements show how much Mami had to struggle alone in the Dominican Republic, but I think it shows how much of a fighter she was . . . money was just not easy to obtain so through everything Mami was still able to find a way to provide.

Student B: A majority of my peers focused on the theme of money and the impact it had on Yunior's life as relatively poor young Hispanic man who delivers pool tables to rich people. Some people mentioned that Yunior's view of money seems obsessive at times . . . because he never grew up with it and having it in his possession gave him a sense of worth and empowerment. However, a few others had a differing view of money in Yunior's life saying that he did not care about it at all and just lives day to day with the money he has . . . All of these differing views from the chapter were beneficial for me to read because they gave me more analyses of certain passages and scenes that I had not thought of before on my own.

These two examples demonstrate the reader's critical engagement with responses from other students after reading through one of the threads. In the first example, student A acknowledges that it is important to see what their peers have said about the short story, "Aguantando" and that in doing so, one can also learn to "expand our opinions." The student makes it clear that they are most interested in exploring a topic related to Mami, the narrator's mother, and summarizes what the other students have had to say about Mami. However, she sees their comments only go so far and don't focus on the specifics of Mami's personality: "I think it shows how much of a fighter she was." In that respect, engaging with the student responses, student A takes advantage of the opportunity not only to expand her initial thoughts about Mami but also to help her articulate and concretize her argument.

In the second example, student B ably summarizes what others have to say about the main character and his relationship to money. The summary demonstrates an ability to draw conclusions from a peer's comments and put them into two competing categories: for some, Yunior appears obsessive about money and for others, he doesn't seem to care about it. As such, student B uses their critical reading skills to understand the different ways to analyze a character. The student concludes by stating that this assignment has helped them to see "certain passages and scenes" that had been not previously considered. Such a statement also suggests that the student B possibly realizes the importance of "certain passages and scenes" that make a person's argument much more persuasive. Like the previous DB exercise, this low-stakes assignment allows the students in each example to enter a "conversation" with peers, reflect on their own thinking, draw conclusions, and explain their points—all of which are related to cognitive processes of learning.

Step Four: Peer Review Workshop

For the peer review workshop, I put students into groups of three on Blackboard where they post their rough drafts to the file exchange for others in their group to read. I also post an assignment that they are meant to follow: (a) briefly summarize the student's paper; (b) what point does the student appear to be making? Evaluate if the writer has been able to accomplish their intention for the essay; (c) identify area (s) of improvement that could help the writer accomplish what they have set out to do and offer a solution.

The first two questions of the assignment basically seek to get the reader to explain and then to articulate what they have read. Only the third one asks them to suggest an area of improvement. Putting more emphasis on reading and summarizing an essay's content gives them more time to think through and analyze what they are reading. In their actual peer reviews, the focus is more on their ability to articulate what they have understood and read. After answering the first two questions, students are then in a better position to address the third point of suggesting an area of improvement and possibly a solution. Summarizing the essay also helps them to see the paper from a more global perspective and not get bogged down in surface-level commentary—the default mode for many students giving a peer review.

For their first essay, the students were asked to choose one of Díaz's short stories from the collection *Drown* and to write a New Critical analysis deploying one literary term in their discussion. As I mentioned earlier, most of the students in this course are not English majors so this type of analysis is quite new to them. The following excerpts demonstrate a few ways that students have learned through reading a peer's essay and then responding to it.

> **Example One:** Reading your introduction lets me see the story from another point of view I had not thought of. Themes of physical and mental violence are evident in "Ysrael". I appreciate you setting the stage for what type of violence you plan on connecting to your points . . . In the next paragraph the connection of the boys being mentally beaten down by life "violently" is a cool connection . . . Drawing the connection of even Ysrael being attacked by an animal is another nod to your thesis . . . I like your conclusion as it draws everything back to the original thesis of how violence affects the future actions of Yunior, Rafa and even Ysrael being a sole victim of physical and mental violence.

Here, the student from example one demonstrates why it is important to have responders start off by summarizing a peer's essay to ensure that they have read it carefully. In so doing, the student has had the opportunity to observe a few important writing strategies from the peer's paper. First, the student has learned to see the story from a different perspective, one not previously considered. Then they comment on a few writing strategies gleaned from reading and analyzing the essay: commenting that the student writer has effectively "set the stage" for the reader to explain the type of violence that occurs in the story and observing the importance of the connections that the writer has made that refer to the original thesis. In noting this second writing strategy, the peer reviewer has become aware of possible ways to structure one's essay, strategies that might be useful in future writing assignments.

> **Example Two:** I really enjoy [sic] reading your essay . . . This is the first time I ever had to critique a classmate work online and in writing, so just bear with me. On the second, third, and fourth paragraphs you talked about motif as a literary device, explained what it is and provided a quote from the story in order to establish the relationship. On the fifth and six paragraph you talked about the point of view as a literary device, explained what it is and provide a quote from the story in order to establish the relationship. On the seventh, eight and nine paragraph you talked about diction. Maybe it would be wise to pick just one literary device to analyze and expand upon it. You developed a strong conclusion, perhaps you could just expand upon it.

Though the peer reviewer disavows any expertise about their ability to give effective feedback, the student then goes on to effectively analyze the person's essay breaking it down into paragraphs. By briefly outlining the essay, the peer reviewer has come to see that the writer is developing too many topics. The peer reviewer then offers the writer two solutions to the problems—"pick just one literary device to analyze and expand on it" and advises the student to expand on the strong conclusion. Although initially apologizing for never having done a peer review, the student is able to see where a writer can go astray when dealing with too many topics in an essay. While it is difficult to say if this information will successfully transfer to the peer reviewer's own writing, through analyzing the writer's paper, the peer reviewer does demonstrate new knowledge about the writing process—the problem with trying to discuss too many topics in one paper.

> **Example Three:** As a reader, I, without question find the discussion convincing. I wrote my essay on the same exact topic and I saw a lot of information and ideas that [the student]

used that I could have easily added to my own to make it better but instead felt like I repeated myself often and didn't add all the examples that I possible could have. Occasionally I find myself blanking and at a loss even when the answers are right in front of me. I felt like [the student] provided us with endless examples and evidence to back up their thoughts towards this chapter showing a lot of repetition.

In this third example, the student has not attended to the specific directions of the assignment, specifically to summarize the writer's essay. Not surprisingly, in a required intensive-writing course, the student responses for peer review run the gamut from those who are really invested in the course to those students who are less inclined to do so. Nonetheless, in reading through the essay and in writing a response, the peer reviewer has had the opportunity to reflect on their own writing and realize what might be missing in their paper. In their own essay on the same topic, the reviewer explains, "I repeated myself often and didn't add all of the examples I possible could have." By providing a peer review, the student seems to have thought about and considered the importance of citing what they call "endless examples and evidence." In suggesting as much, we can deduce that these "endless examples and evidence" have made the essay a more persuasive one for this student.

In the above examples, we can see these students thinking about writing and thinking about how others go about the practice of writing, thus enhancing their metacognition skills. Through writing a peer review, they have gained in some cases a better understanding of audience and an awareness possibly of the information readers need from a writer. Reading and providing a peer review has helped to generate new knowledge allowing these peer reviewers to observe and to learn new writing strategies that might prove helpful in future writing assignments. Ultimately, for me as an instructor, I place more weight on what the student reviewer has learned in the process of writing and in providing a peer review than on the quality of the feedback for the receiver. Writing, as we all know, is a process, and if a student can learn even one new idea about writing on their own, I would venture to say that information will take them a lot further in developing their writing skills than received advice. It is an example of active learning.

Because reading and responding to each other is an explicit expectation in the course, one that they have continuously participated in with the previous low-stakes assignments, I would argue that students develop a sense of themselves as a community of writers, collaborating and communicating with each other. Thus, the move to do peer review is not the typical one-off assignment. Instead, students participate in giving feedback—reading, analyzing, and composing their thoughts in much of the same manner they have been doing with previous low-stakes writing assignments. Finally, reading each other's essays affords another opportunity to learn about the writing process to see how others in the class have developed and constructed their essays.

STEP FIVE: REFLECTING ON PEER REVIEW

To get students to reflect on what they have learned by writing a peer review, I ask them to write a reflection piece after they have posted their final draft. In that assignment students respond to the following points: (1) What did you want others to understand from your essay? (2) How did your paper evolve through the process of writing it? (3) What did you learn by giving feedback to others in your group? (4) How did the comments from your peers help you to rework/rethink your paper?

Questions one, two, and four ask students to reflect on what specifically they want to communicate to their audience, the ways in which their essay changed in the process of writing it, and how student comments helped them to rethink their essay. Through all three of these questions, the goal is to get students to think and to reflect on their process of writing their essay and what they have learned in that process.

As compositionists like Kara Taczak have noted, reflection is central to the writing process. An active engagement with reflection as part of the writing process can help a student in their development as a writer (Taczak 78). In her book, *Reflection in the Writing Classroom*, Kathleen Blake Yancey details some of the key features of reflection: that it "is dialectical, putting multiple perspectives into play with each other in order to produce insight" (6) and that "[it] entails a looking forward to goals we might attain, as well as casting backward to see where we have been" (6). Yancey concludes that the ability of a student to "articulate" what they have learned in the process of reflection constitutes learning on their part (7).

For the purposes of this essay, I want to focus on question number three: what did you learn by giving feedback to others in your group? The following are a few comments students have written in their reflective pieces (emphasis added):

- Giving feedback to others in my group allowed me to realize what I lacked in my own paper. *I saw that many of my peers had amazing introductions* and that was something I lacked.
- Giving feedback to others definitely helped me answer some questions in my own paper after going back to read the first initial draft. *It*

- *helped me to understand what details were essential to my topic and what details sort of just went on a rant.*
- By giving feedback to others, I realized that others were struggling as much as I did, and I was happy to help as much as I could because then I could learn a thing or two as well. *I read a couple of very well written essays and it really gave me something to think about.*
- *What I learned from providing feedback to the others in my group is the necessary elements that my own paper lacked . . .* Even after I revised my first draft, it still lacked organization. I learned this by reading my peers' papers because I realized how organized and easy to read their papers were, versus my own paper. I tended to avoid using transitional words but realized they were important in guiding my readers through my paper.
- By giving feedback to others *I learned that it was helpful to provide them my opinion for another person's point of view.* As I was reading my peers essays [sic] I also noticed how strong and detailed they were which made me realize, I should go back to my own essay and re read it.
- When I was giving feedback to the one's in my group, *it helped me analyze a paper and really decipher what to be looking for within the essay.* By proofreading my classmate's work, it gave me a chance to reevaluate how well I need to look at my own work. I also enjoyed reading about people's arguments and the way *they provided their examples toward their essay topic.*

In their comments, students allude to the dialectical aspects of reflection—to a sense of "looking forward" and "casting backward." Through the interplay between reading a peer's essay and providing comments, students can identify aspects of the writing they thought noteworthy ("amazing introductions," "details," "organization," etc.). At the same time, their comments gesture to this idea of "casting backward" (what was missing in their essays) and of "looking forward" (to revise accordingly). Their ability to critically engage ideas in this manner and to remark upon them, I would argue, points to the learning that has taken place for them in their development as a writer. Moreover, their acknowledgement of what they have learned in the process of providing a peer review distinguishes it from its usual characterization as busy work to one that demonstrates a real engagement with their peers.

Throughout the semester, the scaffolding and peer review process occurs for three different essay assignments. This repetition of reading, writing, and responding in the discussion board, of providing peer reviews, and of reflecting on the writing process demonstrates the importance of the collaborative nature of writing for students. By repeating this scaffolding of writing activities, students get a better understanding of how peer review operates as an integral part of the writing process and of their development as writers. Finally, as their reflection comments suggest, they also develop a sense of agency as writers through an articulation of what they have learned and what could be valuable to them going forward.

CONCLUDING REMARKS

Research in the education field offers composition instructors a different way to think about the practice of peer review. Too often, instructors tie peer review primarily to the improvement imperative. In so doing, the learning that can accompany the practice of peer review gets discounted. Research in the field of education suggests that more attention should be paid to what students learn by providing comments. It offers writing studies instructors a way to rethink peer review extricated from a focus on outcomes in peer review that too frequently results in instructor and student dissatisfaction. Redirecting attention to what a student learns through giving comments can better enable them to see their own possible development in writing.

By scaffolding writing activities leading up to peer review, students come to see it as an integral part of the writing process. The repetition of reading, writing, and responding to each other through the discussion board, of providing peer reviews, and of reflecting on the writing process underscores the importance and the totality of each component and how all the various components support each other. Engaged in this semester-long process, students tend to develop a better sense of agency of themselves as writers that is further enhanced through the continual collaboration and support of their peers.

Over the years, peer review has been a constant evolving learning experience for me—of rethinking and of rearticulating a practice that I consider to be a central to the teaching of writing. No doubt, it will continue to engage and challenge all of us as practitioners. Ultimately, as E. Shelley Reid counsels, our goal should be "to teach students to *become reviewers* rather than to *complete successful reviews*" (229). If we keep that goal in mind, this shift in pedagogical emphasis will enable peer review to be a more positive experience for our students and for ourselves as educators—one where we all have the potential to learn.

WORKS CITED

Berkenkotter, Carol. "Student Writers and Their Sense of Authority over Texts." *College Composition and Communication* 35, Oct. 1984, pp. 312–19.

Brammer, Charlotte, and Mary Rees. "Peer Review from the Students' Perspective: Invaluable or Invalid?" *Composition Studies*, vol.35, no. 2, 2007, pp. 71–85.

Bruffee, Kenneth A. "Collaborative Learning and the 'Conversation of Mankind.'" *College English*, vol.46, no. 7, Nov 1984, pp. 635–652.

Cho, Young Hoan, and Kwangsu Cho. "Peer Reviewers Learn from Giving Comments." *Instructional Science*, 39, 2011, pp. 629–43, https://doi.org/10.1007/s112 51-010-9146-1.

Cho, Kwangsu and Charles MacArthur. "Learning by Reviewing." *Journal of Educational Psychology*, vol. 103, no. 1, 2011, pp. 73–84.

Díaz, Junot. *Drown*. Riverhead Books: Penguin, 1996.

Elbow, Peter. *Writing Without Teachers*. Oxford UP, 1998.

Flynn, Elizabeth A. "Re-viewing Peer Review." *The Writing Instructor*, Dec. 2011, *ERIC*. Accessed 6 May 2023, https://files.eric.ed.gov/fulltext/EJ959705.pdf.

Gere, Ann Ruggles. *Writing Groups History, Theory, and Implications*. Southern Illinois UP, 1987.

Gere, Ann Ruggles, and Robert Abbott. "Talking about Writing: The Language of Writing Groups." *Research in the Teaching of English*, 19, Dec. 1985, pp. 362–85.

Harris, Muriel. "Writing Center Tutorials vs. Peer-Response Groups." *College Composition and Communication*, vol. 43, no. 3, Oct. 1992, pp. 369–383.

Jesnek, Lindsey M. "Peer Editing in the 21st Century College Classroom: Do Beginning Composition Students Truly Reap the Benefits?" *Journal of College Teaching and Learning*, vol. 8, no. 5, 2011, pp. 17–24.

Jensen, Erin B. "Peer-Review Writing Workshops in College Courses: Students' Perspectives about Online and Classroom Based Workshops." *Social Sciences*. Basel, vol. 5, no. 4, 2016, https://doi.org/10.3390/socsci5040072.

Liu, Ngar-Fun, and David Carless. "Peer feedback: The Learning Element of Peer Assessment." *Teaching in Higher Education*, vol. 11, no. 3, July 2006, pp. 279–90.

Lundstrom, Kristi, and Wendy Baker. "To Give is Better Than to Receive: The Benefits of Peer Review to the Reviewer's Own Writing. *Journal of Second Language Writing*, vol. 18, no. 1, 2009, pp. 30–43.

Meeks Graham, Melissa. "Giver's Gain in Peer Learning." *Eli Review Blog*, 28 Mar. 2017. Eli Review Blog, https://elireview.com/2017/03/28/givers-gain.

Nicol, David, et al. "Rethinking Feedback Practices in Higher Education: A Peer Review Perspective." *Assessment and Evaluation in Higher Education*, vol. 39, no.1, pp.102-22.

Oleksiak, Timothy. "A Queer Praxis for Peer Review." *College Composition and Communication*, vol. 72, no. 2, Dec. 2020, pp. 306–332.

Patchan, Melissa M., and Christian D. Schunn. "Understanding the Benefits of Providing Peer Feedback: How Students Respond to Peers' Texts of Varying Quality. *Instructional Science*, vol. 43, issue 5, Sept 2015, pp. 591–614, https://doi.org/10 .1007/s11251-015-9353-x.

Popta, Esther van, et al. "Exploring the Value of Peer Feedback in Online Learning for the Provider." *Educational Research Review* vol. 20, 2017, pp. 24–34.

Pritchard, Jane Ruie, and Donna Morrow. "Comparison of Online and Face-to Face Peer Review of Writing." *Computers and Composition*, vol. 46, 2017, pp. 87–103.

Reid, E. Shelley. "Peer Review for Peer Review's Sake: Resituating Peer Review Pedagogy." *Peer Pressure, Peer Power: Theory and Practice in Peer Review and Response for the Writing Classroom*, edited by Steven J. Corbett et al., Fountain Head Press, 2014, pp. 217–31.

Spear, Karen. *Sharing Writing: Peer Response Groups in English Classes*. Portsmouth: Boynton/Cook, 1988.

Taczak, Kara. "Reflection Is Critical for Writers' Development." *Naming What We Know: Threshold Concepts of Writing Studies*, edited by Linda Adler-Kassner and Elizabeth Wardle, Utah State UP, 2015, pp. 78–79.

Tsui, Amy, and Maria Ng. "Do Secondary L2 Writers Benefit from Peer Comments?" *Journal of Second Language Writing*, vol. 9, no. 2, 2000, pp. 147–70.

Yancey, Kathleen Blake. *Reflection in the Writing Classroom*. Utah State UP, 1998.

Yancey, Kathleen Blake, Liane Robertson, and Kara Taczak. *Writing Across Contexts: Transfer, Composition, and Sites of Writing*. Utah State UP, 2014.

Zhang, Fuhui, et al. "Charting the Routes to Revision: An Interplay of Writing Goals, Peer Comments, and Self-Reflections from Peer Reviews." *Instructional Science*, vol. 45, pp. 679–707, https://doi.org/10.1007/s11251-017-9420-6.

CHAPTER 11.

THE POTENTIAL OF PEER REVIEW SOFTWARE THAT FOCUSES ON THE REVIEW, NOT THE DRAFT

Nick Carbone

Aptara

New software designed specifically for teaching students to give, to receive, to use, and to reflect on peer feedback offers writing instructors powerful new ways for making workshop pedagogies central in any course across the curriculum where writing is taught. The software can invigorate student-to-student workshops and help move peer review from an infrequently used pedagogy on the margins of a course to a regularly used pedagogy closer to the center of the course. When I say "margins of a course," I have in mind those courses that might do one peer review assignment per essay assigned. I consider that relatively infrequent. By "regularly used pedagogy," I mean peer review happens once or twice a week, at a minimum, becoming a central and constant course activity. Or put another way, writing workshops happen once or twice a week.

New peer review software makes it possible to shift peer review to a more central role in a course by making the work of peer review more visible—and thus more teachable—than prior technologies. The software treats the work of peer review—the writing of comments, the reading of comments, the decisions about which comments to apply during revision—as essential, even more essential to learning to write than the final draft of the paper under review.

The software, by making the work of review more visible, helps both teachers and students. For teachers, it makes it easier to see peer review as it is happening, thus making it easier to coach reviewers and writers. For students, as writers, they have tools for choosing comments to use, ranking their usefulness, and making choices about applying the feedback. As reviewers, students can see how their feedback is used and how it compares to feedback given by other reviewers. By being designed for teaching peer review first and foremost, the new software instantiates a belief in writing as process, in writing classrooms as sites of writers and reviewers workshopping their writing.

This essay will touch on four examples of this software. These examples were chosen for two reasons. First, they are currently available as I draft. And second,

I've had experience either working in them or reviewing their features in my work developing educational technology and as writing across the curriculum consultant. The four products used in this essay to illustrate the benefits of using peer review software are Eli Review, Peerceptiv, My Reviewer, and Calibrated Peer Review.

Before looking at this software, however, I want to take a brief look at past peer review technology. The past will help show the promise of the present. Early electronic tools allowed students and teachers to more easily access documents and freed them from the space and time restraints of the classroom. More importantly, though, they sowed the seeds that have made more recent technologies so effective—they began the process of aggregating peer reviews apart from the document under review and thus uncovering insights into what kind of comments are most likely to lead to revision.

THE TECHNOLOGY OF HARDCOPY AND WRITING WORKSHOPS

Student to student feedback on writing has always required technology. In the work of Murray, Elbow and Belanoff, Bruffee, Gere and even much of Ede and Lunsford, an assumed and underlying technology was simple proximity—writers in the same room, working in pairs or small groups.

In its classic form, after proximity, the second central peer review technology was, and may still be in many classrooms, paper and pen: writers come to class with one or more hard copies of their drafts. They sit in groups and read (or hear being read by the author) each other's drafts. If reviewers are not writing on their peers' drafts, then often the writer makes notes on feedback received. This is a workshop model.

As writers and their readers work through the peer review assignment, the instructor moves around the room, checking in with each group one a time. This helps keep writers on task as the instructor listens in, advises, and helps reviewers give better comments, and helps writers learn how to weigh the feedback.

With the advent of photocopiers and then printers, peer review was better able to become homework. Instead of discussing drafts during a class workshop, writers would come to imitate more the kind of solo review scholars do when they peer review an article for an academic journal. At the next class meeting, writers would receive their reviews, written by reviewers who worked in isolation. Though the review isn't blind, let's call this the academic journal model.

First uses of electronic technology did not change the workshop nor academic journal models. In workshops, students might work from laptops or shared files instead of hard copy. In the academic journal model, they might get the file via email to work on at home. Still, electronic tools were boons. In hard copy and oral-driven review technology, the work of peer review was no longer available to the reviewer once the review was given. With electronic review, both the writer and the reviewer would have a copy of the review work. That simple change allowed students, should instructors call for it, to reflect on their work as reviewers without relying on memory alone. They could call up the files and read through their comments.

I don't know of research that shows the prevalence of workshop peer review compared to academic journal peer review. The point here is that prior to the new technologies explored below, in both the workshop and academic journal models, the draft remains at the center. Comments reside in the draft margins.

In these kinds of technologies, where an instructor wants to coach students on giving and using feedback, the work becomes prodigious. A single writer may have to work with two copies of his or her draft, but the instructor with a class of 24 students, would need to look through 48 copies of drafts.

An instructor can choose to try to gather all those drafts and all the comments and then to coach the reviewers and writers on how to give better comments and make better use of the feedback. But that takes time most instructors do not have. And very often because it is hard to teach these two aspects of peer review, both students and instructors become disenchanted with the value of peer review. Writers don't find the feedback useful. Reviewers don't believe they can give feedback writers will find useful.

The criticism of peer review is well known. Before offering strategies for addressing them, Linda Nilson (2009) summarizes the complaints her research uncovered about the quality of student peer review work:

> too lenient or uncritical; focused on whether the evaluator
> likes or agrees with a work rather than its quality; overly
> critical and harsh; inaccurate; superficial; focused on trivial
> problems and mechanical errors; focused too much on con-
> tent alone; unrelated to the assignment's requirements; and
> not referenced to specific instances in the work. (2)

Confirming Nilson's analysis, other studies show peer review can be effective when well designed and well taught (Cho and MacArthur; Cho, Schunn, and Charney; Min; Zundert, Sluijsmans, and Merriënboer; Strasma; Cahill; Brammer and Rees; and Shih).

Students giving poor feedback is not a technology problem; it is a learning challenge. No technology on its own will make peer review more effective. However, for those committed to making peer review work, new technologies can help in powerful ways that were unavailable before. As I discuss below, new technologies provide methods for making peer review central and teachable, but instructors must be willing and able to reimagine their pedagogy in order to do this.

MULTIPLE REVIEWERS IN ONE DOCUMENT

Some of the work of seeing peer review in context has been simplified. It is possible for a class of 24 students do peer review in groups of three (two reviewers per document) and for instructors to see the comments from reviewers in just 24 documents instead of 48. The most prominent example of this is Google Docs, a platform that allows multiple students to make marginal or in-text comments which are viewable by writers, reviewers, and the instructors.

But even with this, coaching peer review remains a challenge. For faculty to get a sense of what is happening in peer review, they can collect the Google Doc URLs and visit each Doc one at a time and look at the comments. However, that is still 24 URLs to collect and visit.

Discerning trends in the review work, finding and sharing good comments to serve as models, coaching a writer on which advice to follow, can still take a long time. The only step saved has been in reducing the number of documents to open from 48 to 24.

Too often, peer review falters because it is only after the review cycle has been completed, after new drafts have been submitted, that instructors discover peer review comments have not been used by writers. By then, asking reviewers to improve their comments or writers to rethink their choices about using comments is too late.

THE POWER OF AGGREGATION

New peer review software aggregates comments. Instead of an instructor going from draft to draft to read comments, the software collects the comments. The new software also allows for comment types that use Likert Scales, writing criteria or feature identification, and other approaches that create data. The new software also allows writers to rate the usefulness of review comments, creating another form of data.

This aggregation of comments and data provides both qualitative and quantitative insights. Patterns can be revealed more quickly. Writer's judgments about the useful of reviews can be summarized and probed while the revision cycle in process. Instructors can better intervene in the review process to address the quality of the review work before the review cycle is complete.

Being able to see more fully the peer review dynamic as it occurs opens the door to making peer review more teachable. Aggregating comments from across drafts creates a corpus of writing that can be given the time and attention it needs to be reviewed and revised. Figure 11.1 represents a student document, "Student work under review," surrounded by feedback. The feedback is in the document.

SOFTWARE THAT AGGREGATES PEER REVIEW COMMENTS

In 2002, when I was working for Bedford/St. Martin's, a college textbook company that is now an imprint of Macmillan Learning, I worked with a professor and first year writing teacher from the University of Hawai'i named Walter Creed. Creed had written his own code to collect drafts and encourage peer review, and Bedford/St. Martin's helped bring it to market. We called the product *Comment*. It was the first software I saw that used aggregation (see Figure 11.2) to elevate the peer review comment from the margins of essays under review to a collection of work that could be read on its own.

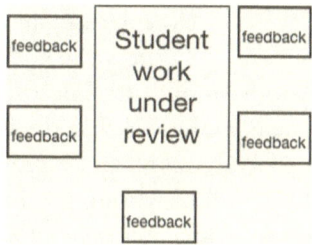

Figure 11.1. The essay at the center, review comments on the margin.

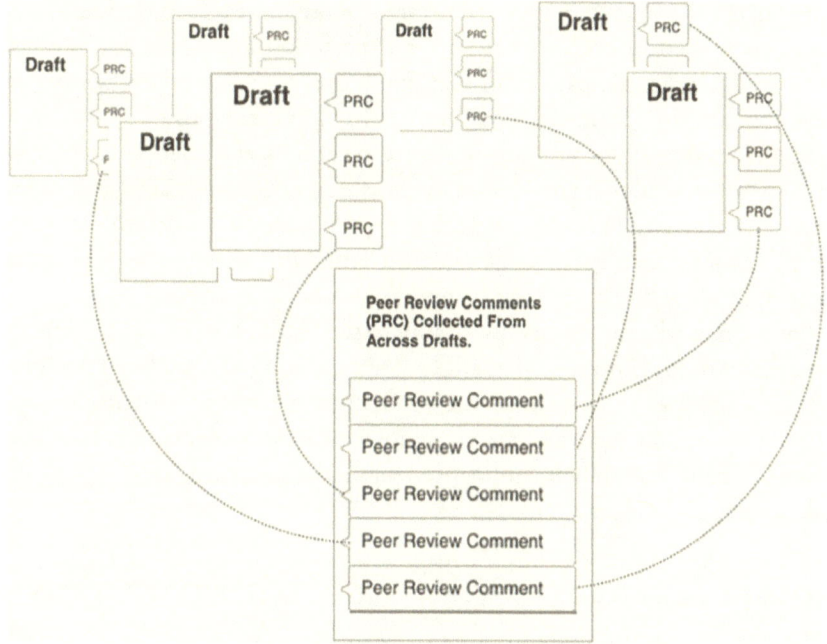

Figure 11.2. Feedback aggregated.

233

With feedback aggregated, writers, reviewers, and the instructor can make feedback their focus. Instead of using the writing under review to find and read the feedback, one can explore and read the feedback directly, referencing back to the work under review as needed. In formal academic peer review, very often an editor writes a cover letter or prepares a review collation as a way to aggregate review feedback for the writer. By doing this kind of aggregation automatically, it is easier to see patterns in feedback, to compare differing advice from among reviewers.

Comment had a feature that collected all the comments a student had written for classmates from all the different drafts upon which those comments were made. By aggregating a student's comments, it made it easier to make commenting more central to the economy and ecology of the course. Students could easily collect and see all the comments they wrote, either by assignment or across assignments.

This made reflecting on their ability to write comments easier to assign in the course. And this ability to have students reflect from an already assembled collection of their comments, helped me elevate the importance of peer review in the course. As I used the feature more, and increased student focus on the comments they wrote and the skill of writing good comments, I came to see that I was treating the feedback comment as a genre worthy of a writing course.

My evocation of genre is fairly informal. But what clicked for me then and now was a phrase from Carolyn Miller's "Genre as Social Action" where she writes "that a rhetorically sound definition of genre must be centered not on the substance or the form of discourse but on the action it is used to accomplish" (151). And for me, the path from that quote to seeing peer review writing as a genre was this: the comments have "action[s] . . . to accomplish."

Peer review comments have an audience, a context, and a purpose. The intellectual work of writing a good comment is as rich as the work of writing a good essay. We collect student essays and drafts for assessment of student growth as writers. *Comment* made it possible to do the same with student peer review writing: it collected it and made it more visible.

For me as a writing teacher, the ability to see a student's collected comments was a new window into how that student was evolving as a reader of writing, a thinker of writing, and—because the comments *are written*—a writer on writing. The same collection became a window for each student into those same processes and abilities. Their comments persisted as a *collected* body of work they could review and reflect upon.

FROM *COMMENT* TO TODAY: AGGREGATING VALID DATA

Despite being a wonderful little bit of software, *Comment* never found a foothold in the college composition classroom, and Bedford/St. Martin's stopped offering it about twelve years ago. Since then, a new wave of tools has emerged that foregrounds peer review. These new programs go beyond what *Comment* attempted. In addition to aggregating review comments, these newest programs have been designed to use quantitative and qualitative data to help instructors and students see patterns in the reading, thinking, and writing of both the work *under* review and the work *of* review.

The data comes not just from counting—such as the number of comments received in a document as you might find in Google Docs, or the number of edits made in a document as you might find on a Wiki page—but also from capturing judgments and choices. But for now, the thing to keep in mind is that newer software looks for and reports patterns. And in a writing course, that's a powerful thing.

The programs mentioned earlier—Eli Review, Peerceptiv, My Reviewer, and Calibrated Peer Review—emphasize student-to-student feedback and offer tools for helping teachers and students see the work of review.

INSIGHTS ON WRITING DERIVED FROM WORK OF REVIEW

Figure 11.2 shows the concept of aggregating review comments. What these four programs do that breaks new ground is not only aggregating comments, but they also aggregate data—qualitative and quantitative data—generated both from peer review comments themselves and, in three of the programs, from writers rating the usefulness of the feedback they received. What I hope to show in the following pages is why that ability to gather data and to express insights—patterns in the data about both the writing under review and the writing of reviews—via analytics offers such potential.

But first a reminder: we should not be put off by the term "data." Writing teachers have always relied on data. By data I mean simply information and knowledge of student performance collected and stored for the purposes of analysis. The result of the analysis become analytics—reports, patterns, insights—that lead to teaching and learning decisions.

Gradebooks, for example, contain data on student performance. Many programs require faculty to calculate mid-semester grades. Faculty must notify the administration about students whose grades are low so that academic advisors can reach out to the students and offer support. Or consider another example. Instructors might require assignment page counts or word counts; they may return work that is too short, keeping track of how many students need to resubmit their work. From an analysis of that data, they may create an analytic in the form of a list of students who consistently struggle to meet assignment requirements. Instructors might then meet with those students to find out why they struggle.

While data and analytics in writing courses are not new, what is new, in the context of this article, is how peer review software uses data and analytics to offer new insights into student drafting and revising processes. The value of data, thus insights from its analytics, will depend on good writing and peer review assignment design.

Let's look at an example from Eli Review. Eli offers a review question type called "Trait Identification." That tool simply asks a reviewer to check a radio button if a trait occurs. The instructor using Eli can define what a trait is and can create the directions and selections as required by their course, their assignment, and their teaching.

The traits in Figure 11.3 are tied to a writing assignment where students analyze a data set and make recommendations. To draft the assignment, students have to reference themes found in the data (first trait), explain how the themes are related (second trait), explain the implication of the relationship (third trait), and suggest a response or outcome or action (fourth trait).

For students to be able to draft writing that has these traits, and to review writing for these traits, the instructor will have had to taught students about these traits and their importance. This screenshot also signals that students, then, are learning about these traits in at least three ways: first, from the teaching about these traits prior to writing; second, from drafting writing that seeks to fulfill the traits; and third, from reviewing writing to see if the traits have been accomplished.

With that pedagogy and practice as context, what you see in this example is that the instructor knows where students are struggling. The report in Figure 11.3 shows fewer than half of the students reviewed have "a passage that suggests an appropriate outcome, response, or action to be taken." That's a significant insight. Normally to gain such an insight, an instructor would collect the drafts and take several days to read through them.

Trait Identification

Check the box to indicate whether the following are present:

Traits	Class Average
statements that reference two or more themes present in the data set	90%
an explanation of how the two themes or topics are related in specific terms	78%
a passage that explains implications of these relationships	74%
a passage that suggests an appropriate outcome, response, or action to be taken	46%

Figure 11.3. Trait identification.

But with the tool shown in Figure 11.3, the instructor learns about the struggle of students to meet the final trait in one peer review session. If this is the first question asked and is done during class, the instructor will learn this in 15 minutes. Imagine that. In 15 minutes instead of week an instructor knows that an element of the assignment causes half the class to struggle. So now the instructor can address the struggle and investigate with the class why a key trait is missing in half the drafts under review.

The key to making review data and reports valuable comes in crafting good questions to guide peer reviewers (Liu and Carless). That is, as the example above illustrates, one should only ask students to look for things they've been taught. The software brings the work of good instruction and of student writing and reviewing into view. It makes the learning from peer review visible in ways that were not before possible.

REVIEWING THE REVIEWERS—MAKING PEER REVIEW WORK ASSESSABLE

All the software under discussion also takes to heart, far more than software that came before it, is the value of writers giving feedback (Lundstrum and Baker). Eli, Peerceptiv, and CPR, in their user guides for students, explicitly discuss the benefits of giving reviews has for students who are learning to write.

For example, in advice to reviewers, Peerceptiv reminds students as they review to think of "aspects of your own work you want to improve" by asking "What can you take away from each review [you give] that allows you to become a better writer?"

Calibrated Peer Review points out that "students not only learn their discipline by writing, they also learn and practice critical thinking by evaluating . . . submissions from their peers" (n.p.).

Writing for Eli Review, Melissa Graham Meeks explains:

> . . . students' mastery of giving helpful comments depends on their inclusion of signals related to "describe-evaluate-suggest" pattern. The absence of these three moves results in bad feedback, which writers can't use to revise. But, bad feedback has a larger consequence: it doesn't lead to givers' gain. Givers' gain is the benefit reviewers get when they apply to their own work what they see other writers doing or not doing. (np).

A key feature of Eli, Peerceptiv and My Reviewers is for writers to rate the usefulness of reviews received. Each program provides each reviewer a helpfulness rating, and in each there is some comparison of a reviewer's helpfulness—whether on a particular review or overall—to class helpfulness averages. We'll use Peerceptiv screen shots to explore the value of this feature.

Peerceptiv's "Back Evaluate" allows a writer to give feedback on reviews received. Notice from the blue box labeled "Summary," that in Peerceptiv instructors can create prompts and guidelines for how review comments should be rated. The feedback asks (see notations 2 and 3) students to provide both quantitative and qualitative feedback on reviews.

Figure 11.5 shows the peer reviewers their "Back-Evaluation" helpfulness ratings, the comments the ratings address, and the qualitative feedback. Figures 11.4 and 11.5 are from peerceptiv.zendesk.com.

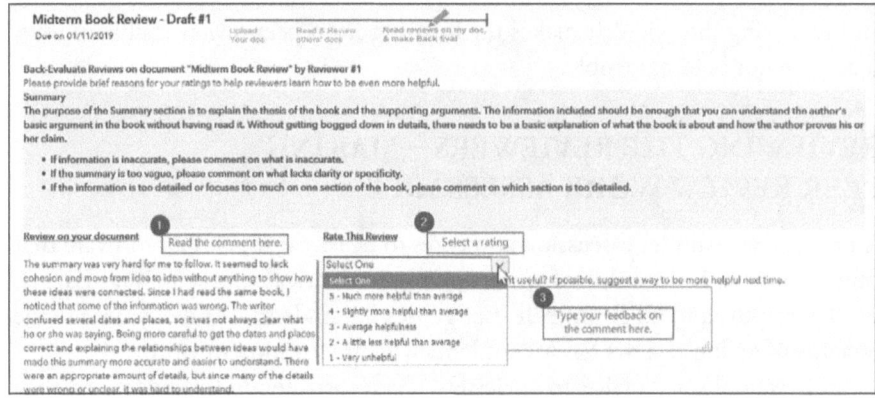

Figure 11.4. Peerceptiv's "back-evaluate".

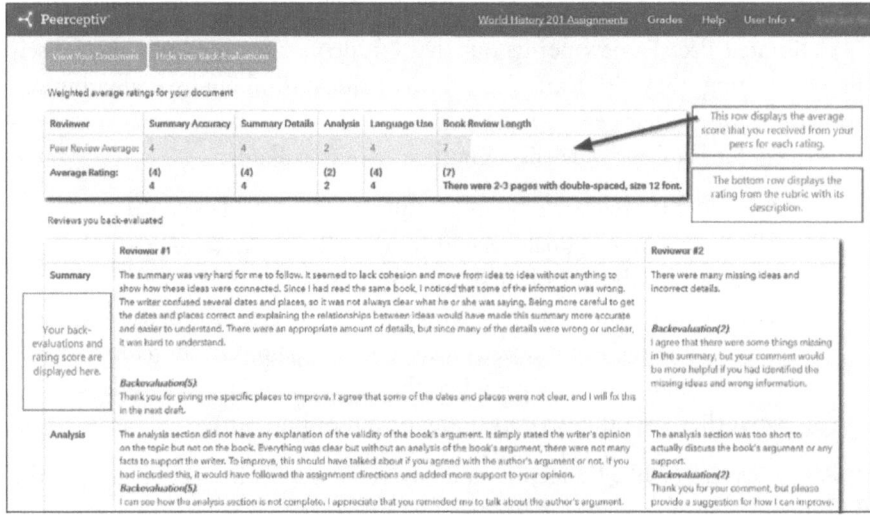

Figure 11.5. Helpfulness ratings.

How each program uses helpfulness measures varies, but their insights can be important to learning and learning motivation.

First, learning to write a good review takes practice. It's a close reading and writing skill students can and should get better at. Writing a good review helps not only the writer but also the reviewer because it gives reviewer more practice thinking carefully about writing.

Second, one of the reasons peer review often fails as a pedagogy is because reviewers don't know how or whether a writer uses the advice given. When reviewers get feedback from writers on how their reviews are being considered and might be applied, then those reviewers come to see that their review work isn't just busy work. In other words, it's hard to care about peer review if you think the writer or instructor aren't going to care about the quality of the feedback.

Now, one of the concerns I have heard from instructors about having students rate the feedback received from classmates is that they may just give all feedback good ratings. But that concern, really, is no different than that of instructors who avoid doing peer review at all because they don't believe students can or will give constructive feedback on writing.

However, we know that students can learn to give feedback on writing. And so it follows that students can also learn to rate and comment well on the feedback they received. Teaching students to give good feedback, as we see above in the brief look at the trait identification example from Eli Review, is matter of making good use of the software to create peer review guidelines and assignments that match what students are being taught. Similarly, in our look at Peerceptiv's "back-evaluation" tool, we see an example of guidelines being used to help students give meaningful feedback on comments received from reviewers.

Both examples show evidence of pedagogical thought and planning. The software builds on an instructor's pedagogical designs by aggregating feedback and revealing trends or allowing an instructor to focus on a particular student's performance. Thus the software makes it more possible to help teach students how to be better reviewers. Which helps them also to be become better writers if only because they are getting more practice working with writing through the reviewing writing, considering feedback received, and evaluating that feedback.

Christian D. Schunn, one of the creators of Peerceptiv, has been doing research on peer review for close to 20 years. Many of the tools and features from Peerceptiv grew out of that research. As Peerceptiv has evolved, his research on it and how it shapes peer review in classrooms has continued. A 2017 study co-authored with Melissa M. Patchan and Russell J. Clark found that students who believed their grade for doing peer review would be influenced by "back-evaluation" ratings of their feedback's helpfulness gave more feedback using comments on the texts and with a greater focus on critiques and solutions for writers to try.

These same students also did a better job at using the back-evaluation tool more consistently and richly.

That is, when students believe the work of review and rating reviews is important enough in the course, they do the work of rating reviews well. One of the benefits of this new crop of tools for teaching peer review as central to drafting and revising is this: their ability to collect and analyze student work, and their ability to build in evaluation by writers on reviews received, makes it aspects of the writing process more visible than ever before. And because this work can be created and seen, it can contribute to a course's assessment and grading practices.

A side note is in order here, Patchan, Schunn, and Clark's study focused on student *perceptions* that their helpfulness scores would be a factor in grading. Eli Review recommends against basing review grades on helpfulness ratings because that could lead students to inflate ratings. The goal is to teach students to give honest and constructive ratings in the same way they are being taught to give honest and constructive feedback. So while helpfulness ratings can have a place in the course grade, that place should be found through practices such as reflecting on what makes an effective comment, or being able to describe how writers used feedback given, and on how to rate feedback in ways that are honest and that will help classmates become better at giving feedback.

To further help assure that helpfulness ratings aren't inflated, both Eli and My Reviewers tie the ranking of feedback directly to revision planning. For example, at the University of South Florida where My Reviewers was developed, a common revision plan assignment requires students to "Summarize this feedback, analyze which comments you find most helpful, and then determine how you will revise your draft."

By tying analysis of a comments to how they will be used in revision, My Reviewers sets up a pedagogy that asks students to focus on the revisions they will make and to analyze and assess reviews with those needs in mind. In this way, revision planning influences how writers will rate peer feedback, increasing the likelihood that ratings will reflect analysis.

In Eli, there's a "Revision Plan" tool. If teachers assign revision plans, students follow three steps after a review.

In step 1, writers see all their feedback. Writers can rate the helpfulness of written comments using a five-star scale, with five being most helpful.

In step 2, writers create revision plans moving comments received into the revision plan. In Eli, the software records which comments go into a revision plan. For a reviewer, having a comment added to a classmate's revision plan becomes another factor in that reviewer's helpfulness rating.

In step 3, writers annotate the comments they've added to their revision plans, outlining why the comment is included and how the writer will work with it.

The Potential of Peer Review Software

These revision plans are then available for the instructor to review. The revision plans show the kinds of decisions writers make about how they will use the feedback received. They are both a metacognitive document and a practical revision tool that gives a writing instructor documented insight into how writers are using feedback.

Figure 11.6 shows an instructor view of a student's revision plan. In this plan, the writer, Katherine, has chosen a comment from a classmate that will guide her revision. Katherine added that comment to her revision plan. She also made a note about the comment and has indicated by a star ranking how helpful it is to her. Her revision plan concludes, in "Revision Notes," with her broader thinking about her next draft. The instructor has a box for giving the writer feedback on her plan.

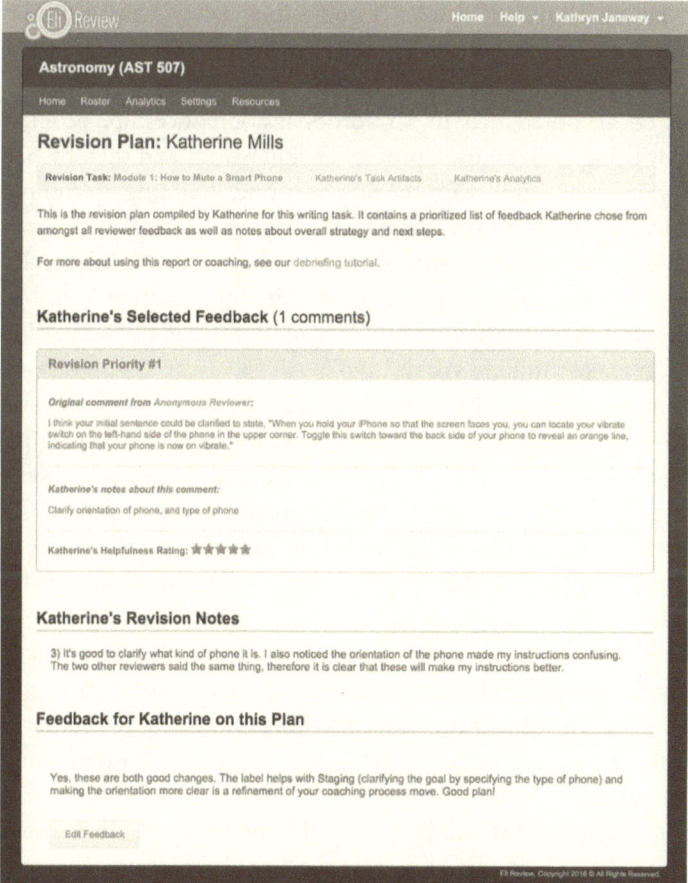

Figure 11.6. Revision plan. Image from https://elireview.com/support/guides/instructor/tasks/revision/.

If revision plans are shared with the reviewers whose comments make up the plan, those reviewers can also see the impact their feedback has in helping a writer revise. Reviewers learn not only what a writer feels about a comment based on the number of stars it may earn, but also whether the feedback is actually going to help a writer revise.

FINAL THOUGHTS

The more I explore and think about this new peer review software, the more I see it, in so many ways, as an ideal tool for enacting writing and the teaching of writing a form of cognitive apprenticeship, a term introduced in a 1991 essay by Allan Collins, John Seely Brown, and Ann Holum titled, "Cognitive Apprenticeship: Making Thinking Visible." I quote their article title in full because so much of what the newest peer review software does is exactly that: it attempts to make thinking visible.

Collins et. al. noted that in a traditional apprenticeship, people learn by observing or being shown how a process or skill works, and then by being given more and more responsibility for the task over time, building up complexity and nuance as the apprenticeship advances.

The authors write, "Apprenticeship involves learning a physical, tangible activity. . . . In schooling, the processes of thinking are often invisible to both the students and the teacher. Cognitive apprenticeship is a model of instruction that works to make thinking visible" (38).

In writing—as Donald Murray most famously noted—writing evolves and writers grow not just from receiving feedback, but also from giving it. It's why we have workshop pedagogies. In professional contexts—including academic contexts especially—peer review is a professional activity and skill. One grows as an academic thinker and writer by being both able to write and to review. The same holds for most of the careers students will go into—they will be called upon to write and to review

What I like about these new tools for peer review is that they make very visible the cognitive work students are doing as writers, as reviewers, and as emerging thinkers. Peer comments are visible thinking on writing. Writer ratings are of visible thinking on comments. Revision plans are visible thinking on decisions writers are making.

Most importantly this thinking is visible to students. They can see their review comments as a corpus of writing worthy of reflection. They can see the choices as on which comments to use. They can see as reviewers the kinds of comments writers use to guide revision.

In the end, the more we accurately see, the better we can teach, and the more students can learn. Used well, these new tools for peer review let us see more than we ever could before.

WORKS CITED

Brammer, Charlotte, and Mary Rees. "Peer Review from the Students' Perspective: Invaluable or Invalid?" *Composition Studies*, vol. 35, no. 2, 2007, pp. 71–85. JSTOR, https://www.jstor.org/stable/435501704.

Bruffee, Kenneth A. "Collaborative Learning and the 'Conversation of Mankind.'" *College English* 46.7 (1984): 635–52.

Cahill, Lisa. "Reflections on Peer Review Practices." *Strategies for Teaching First-Year Composition*, edited by Duane H. Roen et al., NCTE, 2002, pp. 301–07.

Calibrated Peer Review. "Overview." *Calibrated Peer Review Website*. http://cpr.molsci.ucla.edu/Overview. Accessed 15 Sept. 2017.

Cho, Kwangsu, and Charles MacArthur. "Student Revision with Peer and Expert Reviewing." *Learning and Instruction*, vol. 20, no. 4, 2010, pp. 328–38.

Cho, Kwangsu, et al. "Commenting on Writing: Typology and Perceived Helpfulness of Comments from Novice Peer Reviewers and Subject Matter Experts." *Written Communication*, vol. 23, no. 3, 2006, pp. 260–94.

Collins, Allan, et al. "Cognitive Apprenticeship: Making Thinking Visible." *American Educator*, vol. 6, no. 11, 1991, pp. 38–46.

Ede, Lisa, and Andrea Lunsford. "The Pedagogy of Collaboration." *Singular Texts, Plural Authors: Perspectives on Collaborative Writing*. Southern Illinois UP, 1990. Rpt. in *The Allyn and Bacon Sourcebook for College Writing Teachers*, edited by James C. McDonald. Allyn and Bacon, 1996. pp. 107–126.

Elbow, Peter, and Pat Belanoff. *Sharing and Responding*. McGraw-Hill, 1995.

Gere, Anne Ruggles. *Writing Groups: History, Theory, and Implications*. Southern Illinois UP, 1987.

Liu, Ngar-Fun, and David Carless. "Peer Feedback: The Learning Element of Peer Assessment." *Teaching in Higher Education*, vol.11, no. 3, 2006, pp. 279–90.

Lundstrom, Kristi, and Wendy Baker. "To Give is Better Than to Receive: The Benefits of Peer Review to the Reviewer's Own Writing." *Journal of Second Language Writing*, vol. 18, no. 1, 2009, pp. 30–43, https://doi.org/10.1016/j.jslw.2008.06.002.

Meeks, Melissa. "The Secret Sauce of Producing Better Writers." *Eli Review Blog*, https://elireview.com/2016/12/15/secret-sauce/. 15 Dec. 2016.

Meeks, Graham Melissa. "SFSU's Insights about Peer Learning Pedagogy." *Eli Review Blog*, https://elireview.com/2017/06/20/sfsus-insights-pedagogy/. 20 June 2017.

Min, Hui-Tzu. "The Effects of Trained Peer Review on EFL Students' Revision Types and Writing Quality." *Journal of Second Language Writing*, vol 15, no. 2, 2006, pp.118–41.

Murray, Donald. *The Essential Don Murray: Lessons from America's Greatest Writing Teacher*, edited by Lisa Miller and Thomas Newkirk. Heinemann, 2009.

Nilson, Linda B. "Helping Students Help Each Other: Making Peer Feedback More Valuable." *Essays on Teaching Excellence: Toward the Best in the Academy*, vol.14, no. 50, 2002–03, https://podnetwork.org/content/uploads/V14-N5-Nilson.pdf.

Patchan, Melissa, et al. "Accountability in Peer Assessment: Examining the Effects of Reviewing Grades on Peer Ratings and Peer Feedback." *Studies in Higher Education*, pp. 1–17, 2017, https://doi.org/10.1080/03075079.2017.1320374 .

Shih, Ru-Chu. "Can Web 2.0 Technology Assist College Students in Learning English Writing? Integrating Facebook and Peer Assessment with Blended Learning." *Australasian Journal of Educational Technology*, vol. 27, no. 5, 2011, pp. 829–45.

Strasma, Kip. "'Spotlighting': Peer-Response in Digitally Supported First-Year Writing Courses." *Teaching English in the Two-Year College*, vol. 37, no. 2, 2009, p.153.

Van Zundert, Marjo, et al. "Effective Peer Assessment Processes: Research Findings and Future Directions." *Learning and Instruction*, vol. 20, no. 4, 2010, pp. 270–79.

AFTERWORD.
ACCEPTING, SHARING, AND SURRENDERING CONTROL: COMBINING THE BEST OF OLD AND NEW IN PEER REVIEW AND RESPONSE

Steven J. Corbett
Texas A&M University, Kingsville

Student peer review and response is a microcosm of writing studies theory and practice. It incorporates collaborative learning, process, writing-to-learn, reader-response, performance, and motivation theories and practices. It asks us to question and seek to map the boundaries of our authority and control as teachers of writing. It raises questions about student diversity and identity, and concerns about technology and digital innovations and constraints. And it is advocated for by WPAs and WAC/WID leaders in workshops and in print nationally and internationally. Yet, strikingly, over the past few decades, there have been relatively few book-length treatments of peer review and response, the last being Steven Corbett, Teagan Decker, and Michelle LaFrance's collection *Peer Pressure, Peer Power: Theory and Practice in Peer Review and Response for the Writing Classroom* in 2014. It is high time for the next substantial work on this extremely important subject—and the editors and contributors to *Rethinking Peer Review* have delivered just that.

In their Introduction, editors Phoebe Jackson and Christopher Weaver lay out the narrative and drama of peer review, emphasizing the shifts and reassessment of important concepts from individual to collaborative, from autonomy to authority. The editors describe how—despite long-standing issues like student apathy or even resentment, and teacher concerns about the quality of feedback students can give each other—peer review and response remains widely utilized in writing courses.

The contributors to Part One elaborate on the challenges involved in peer review. Ian Anson, Chris Anson, and Kendra Andrews, in Chapter 1, analyze an enormous amount of data, situated within the context of feedback to student

DOI: https://doi.org/10.37514/PER-B.2023.1961.3.3

writing in general. The authors posit ways to make peer review and response more successful, including offering students clear guidelines and asking for meta-commentaries of sessions, and striving to advocate for and support it at the departmental and institutional levels. The authors also offer valuable suggestions for how their study could be replicated for different purposes. In Chapter 2, Bob Mayberry explores learning theory vs literary theory as an explanation for why creative writing workshops seem more in-line with process pedagogies, and why writing studies as a field began to drift away from the "big dreams" of the 1960s and '70s process movement. Along the way, Mayberry stylistically makes several compelling points including (echoing a long-held writing center sentiment) why grades have no place in a workshop classroom and why portfolios are a boon to composition in general and the practice of peer review specifically. And in Chapter 3, Christopher Weaver, who dances an attitude toward peer review and response as a problem they have tried hard to work out, ends up suggesting a move more toward a workshop-style class described by Mayberry in Chapter 2. Weaver also offers an interesting point of view on how they are coming to terms with authority issues by differentiating between two feedback-spaces in their class: their own instructional expectations and values space, and the students' peer review group-space that is relatively free of teacherly prescriptions.

The chapters in Part Two continue offering case studies and theoretical musings that balance rhetorically-situated issues of authority and control. Kay Halasek, in Chapter 4, takes an ecological and dialogic look at why and how to make peer response a practice connected intimately with the content and other writing tasks of the course. Like Chapter 1, this chapter also covers a huge amount of research data in very succinct and smart ways and offers readers paths for future research. Halasek makes a nice connection to the previous chapter (and a few others in this collection) in terms of the problem of students as teacher "proxy." In answer to this problem, Halasek offers Five Critical Questions that could be used as a heuristic of sorts for making peer response integrated, rhetorical, situated, reflective, and cumulative—in short, as the prime pedagogical mover of a writing course. Courtney Stanton, in Chapter 5, while meditating on Burkean identification in relation to peer review and response, also offers practical strategies that can work toward mindful use of terminology that can be shared by instructors and students during response. Nora McCook, in Chapter 6, examines peer review and response in relation to the important topic of transfer. The author makes a good point about how peer response is used in high school and first-year writing classes, but then not used as much in upper-division college courses. McCook makes an important point about the transferability of soft skills for the workplace. They provide compelling workplace examples of peer review in relation to forward-reaching transfer, reflection, and working toward student buy-in with peer review. McCook makes it clear why peer review is especially important and timely now as we get back to pre-COVID instructional forms (and current practices that may be informed by what we learned during COVID).

Contributors to Part Three illustrate ways peer review and response can be designed to cultivate inclusiveness and meet the needs of ELL students. Ellen Turner, in Chapter 7, offers a thoughtful qualitative study that relies heavily on substantial reflective quotes from students' experience with peer response. The author's findings on student anxiety and emotions in giving and receiving feedback from their peers and its implications, gives us much to think about in terms of scaffolding and reflective journaling in the service of helping students cope with response anxiety. Beth Kramer, in Chapter 8, sets up the exigence for and the problem of peer response for ELL. The author expresses the important idea of multiple models and choices in peer response methods and strategies, which is often (curiously) overlooked in the peer response scholarship. The two strategies of frequent low-stakes peer review and podcasts combines older methods with a more innovative approach that brings together the best of old and new.

Finally, the chapters in Part Four bring the promise of peer review and response fully into our digital age. Vicki Pallo, in Chapter 9, raises the issue of how sufficient time (which can be realized in online environments) is important for *all* students and points to the importance of an entire writing curriculum sensitive to this fact. To make the most of time and space in online environments for ELL students, the author offers useful recommendations involving starting perhaps in the classroom with training and then moving response online and, for completely-online courses, utilizing asynchronous methods of peer response. In Chapter 10, Phoebe Jackson echoes several other chapters on students acting as proxy for the instructor in peer review, the value of reflection and, especially, the idea of engaging students in the process and not necessarily the improvement of the written product. Jackson goes the extra step of how these concepts apply to the shift to an online environment, including scaffolding and reflection with illustrative examples from student writing. And Nick Carbone, in Chapter 11, rounds out Part Four with concrete examples and choices for ways to design and implement very nuanced and—due to the comprehensive, sophisticated online platforms he reports on—very *visible and accessible* peer review as the most useful teaching and learning activity in a writing class.

As contributors to this collection demonstrate, when designed thoughtfully and executed strategically, peer response pedagogies can push student agency, authority, and ownership of a course to its fullest potential. Yet, as with anything complex and multifaceted, peer response can throw off the most well-intentioned of practitioners. We've all heard the concerns, complaints, and cautionary tales from colleagues who have tried various peer response activities and either given up on peer review pedagogy or downplayed its role in their curriculums. The chapters in this collection offer all teachers of writing fresh perspectives on the importance of how and why—*if* as teachers and scholars we stay open, curious, persistent, and response-able—we might embrace and embark on further synergistic inquiry and experimentation into peer review and response.

For my part, I'd like to briefly touch on two often-overlooked yet highly relevant topics. First, I'll take us back to the ancient rhetorical tradition of peer critique, especially as described and evaluated by Quintilian, and some strategies influenced by that ancient rhetorical tradition I've developed for contemporary practice. Second, I'll discuss peer tutoring research and practice, to emphasize the increasing value of writing center and peer tutoring theory and practice for peer review and response.

THE MORE THINGS CHANGE . . . PEER-TO-PEER COMPETITION VERSUS COOPERATION FROM QUINTILIAN TO THE PRESENT

> It is a good thing therefore that a boy should have companions whom he will desire first to imitate and then to surpass: thus he will be led to aspire to higher achievement.
>
> – Quintilian, ca. 95

In the Introduction, the editors write that "the time is ripe for a collection of essays that assesses where peer review stands a half century after its emergence and that challenges us to rethink and reframe the practice going forward." But the uptake of peer review a half a century ago was really a pedagogical *re*emergence of an ancient practice. Quintilian's quote above hints at the long-understood notion of imitation in the service of learning. Further, for Quintilian and the Romans, the power of peer pressure was something to be utilized to its full potential. James Murphy explains that the systematic efforts to instill in Roman (male) students the habits of mind fostering effective expression were strengthened by instructors' use of peer critique: "What today would be called peer criticism is an integral part of the scheme; in the Roman interactive classroom the student-critic shapes his own critical judgment by assessing publicly what he hears and reads" (55). In working toward becoming habitually rhetorical in mind and action, students were encouraged to scrutinize both strong and weaker models of invention, arrangement, style, memory, and delivery. Yet, in his essay, Murphy downplays an idea that Quintilian emphasizes implicitly and explicitly throughout the first two books of his *Institutio Oratoria*—peer-to-peer competition. Quintilian called for an interactive rhetoric classroom where students were explicitly called upon to showcase their communicative strengths while coming to terms with their weaknesses, both their own and their peers'. Quintilian strongly believed that in order to do justice in preparing his students for the ups and downs of an often brutally competitive world, he needed to socialize them accordingly. Quintilian presages Lev Vygotsky's zone of proximal development (ZPD) when he relates how both stronger and weaker students received more benefit from the following peer-to-peer activity than from their instructors or parents alone:

> Having distributed the boys in classes, they made the order in which they were to speak depend on their ability, so that the boy who had made most progress in his studies had the privilege of declaiming first. The performances on these occasions were criticised. To win commendation was a tremendous honour, but the prize most eagerly coveted was to be the leader of the class. Such a position was not permanent. Once a month the defeated competitors were given a fresh opportunity of competing for the prize. Consequently success did not lead the victor to relax his efforts, while the vexation caused by defeat served as an incentive to wipe out the disgrace. (I.1.23–25)

For Quintilian and his contemporaries, there was great benefit in putting students on the spot, in providing them with rigorous rhetorical practice giving and taking criticism in their speaking and writing performances. Quintilian goes one step further, to comment on the recursive benefits this sort of systematic training also has for the instructor who, in handing over responsibility to the students, learns as time goes on how to better negotiate sharing pedagogical authority and control. And lest we think Quintilian an overly harsh taskmaster, I should note that in several spots in his book he offers some sage advice for loosening up and letting the young be young, as it were (II.4.5–8, II.4.10–11, II.4.14–15).

We can reevaluate what appears to be the contemporary distaste for student competition in writing courses in ways that blend teaching with student texts (Harris et al.) with peer review and response. The following activity can awake students' passion for competitive play: First, while students work in their response groups ask the group for a referral essay, one that doesn't have to be perfect, just worthy of continued conversation. Then ask the referred student if it would be okay to share that paper with the rest of the class (via email or shared files) for possible further discussion later. It's important to try to get a good sense if the student is hesitant or eager to share. If they seem hesitant or reluctant, probably best not to coerce obligation. Next, share the agreed-upon referrals with the entire class (the number depending on how long the papers are) with instructions to read each one, taking notes on the strengths and weaknesses and ranking each one. Then in the next class meeting ask students to state their top choice, while you write them on the board. Rank the papers, and—depending on how much time you have—discuss the top-ranking papers in order. Since students themselves voted on the top choices and the authors agreed to act as models, they can be held responsible for leading the discussion, and all other students can be invited to join in as they see fit. The ancient art of peer criticism in the writing and rhetoric classroom, so highly valued by Quintilian, can take on a fresh, contemporary feel if conscientiously orchestrated.

While most peer review and response activities might more subtly percolate students' natural competitive instincts, there's nothing like a good old-fashioned debate to bring their energy and passion to full boil (see Corbett "Great"). In short, exemplary student papers from previous courses can be pitted against each other, avoiding the potential for student anxiety. (It's probably better not to use texts from students from the same course in this situation due to the fact that students can get pretty emotionally intense.) Students read and analyze the strengths and weaknesses of these two strong papers—crucially, models of the same assignments they are working hard to revise. In essence, the former students who wrote these exemplary papers are acting as virtual models, extending their peer response presence and influence for the benefit of current students. For each of their major papers, then, students come to class prepared with evidence and, as they strategize with their team, build a progressively stronger case for why their respective model paper has better-met the expectations of the assignment. As I illustrate in the webtext "Great Debating," students take to this activity enthusiastically, and with much engagement, focus, and passion in their efforts to perform and enact all they've learned about rhetorical analyses, peer review and response, and argumentation throughout the term. With the stark memory of these debates fresh in their minds, students can face revising their major papers at the height of their rhetorical powers. The role of the instructor becomes that of the coach, encouraging rhetorical acumen win or lose, as described by Quintilian: "if he speaks well, he has lived up to the ideals of his art, even if he is defeated" (II.17.23). All in all, students can dance an attitude, and we can enthusiastically coach this dance (gradually, thoughtfully, and strategically ceding authority and control), that moves them in thought and action closer to responsible, authoritative, and confident team co-teachers. Perhaps these memorable rhetorical performances might enable students to successfully internalize salutary habits of mind and writing strategies and moves that they can carry with them into other communicative situations. One of these situations could be interactions and involvement with writing centers and peer tutoring.

WRITING CENTER AND PEER TUTORING THEORY AND PRACTICE CONTINUES TO ADD MUCH TO THE CONVERSATION

> ... traditional teaching assumes and maintains a negative competitive relationship among students. They are officially anonymous to one another, and isolated. Classroom learning is an almost entirely individual process.
>
> — Kenneth Bruffee, 1999

As several contributors to this collection have described, teacher-scholars throughout the 1980s were building peer response theories and practices for writing classrooms—often first-year composition courses. Concurrently, others explored peer-to-peer learning across the disciplines in writing centers and other peer tutoring programs. Suppose we gaze awhile at writing center and peer tutoring theory and practice. In that case, we will come upon much research that can inform and complement our work in peer critique in the writing classroom, including replicable, aggregate, and data-driven (RAD) research—like the kind presented by Anson, Anson, and Andrews in Chapter 1 and Halasek, in Chapter 4 of this volume—that has only proliferated since the 1980s.

Some wonderfully useful work on peer-to-peer teaching and learning applicable to writing classrooms was well underway by the late 1970s and early 1980s. The early work of Kenneth Bruffee, described in the 1978 "Brooklyn Plan" and the 1980 "Two Related Issues in Peer Tutoring," provided (anti)foundational theoretical rationales for the value of peer-to-peer collaborative tutoring and learning. Like Peter Elbow, Bruffee (and soon after, writing center practitioners like Muriel Harris) believed there was substantial, game-changing value inherent in surrendering and sharing pedagogical authority with students. Soon the promising bridges between peer review and response and peer tutoring would also emerge, including detailed, empirical study. For example, the often-overlooked five-year study of developmental and multicultural writers and teachers by Marie Nelson in her 1991 *At the Point of Need* supported the claims of Bruffee, Elbow, Anne Ruggles Gere, and Karen Spear with multimethod empirical data. Nelson's study of over 300 response groups (90 receiving intense focus), meeting in the writing center and facilitated by a graduate instructor, found a pedagogical pattern. Nelson found an inverse relationship between teacher control and student agency. When group facilitators acted in more directive and controlling ways at first, but gradually ceded control and direction of the group over to the students themselves, the students responded by accepting the responsibility of reciprocal tutoring/teaching, which they then internalized into their own self-regulating writing performances and products. Students would continue to reciprocally externalize this peer-to-peer pedagogy within their group.

This quest for synergy between writing classrooms, writing groups, and writing centers enables us to move beyond while still staying true to the best ideals in "The Idea of a Writing Center" (North; Boquet and Lerner). Harris's essay on peer response groups versus writing center tutorials concluded by suggesting we should continue practicing both, but left readers with few explicit connections. In a reconsideration of that 1992 essay, in her 2014 essay "A Non-Coda: Including Writing Centered Student Perspectives for Peer Review," Harris offers some explicit connections. Like several other authors in the same volume, Harris draws on writing center theory and practice combined with classroom peer response practice to speculate on how we just might be making some strides in working toward viable writing-center-inspired strategies for successful peer-to-peer reciprocal teaching and learning in writing classrooms. Harris's thoughtful reconsiderations and suggestions join the retrospect chorus of those like Robert Brooke, Ruth Mirtz, and Rick Evans, the other contributors to *Peer Pressure, Peer Power*, as well as the contributors to this collection, in admonishing a huge amount of preparation, practice, and follow-up when trying to make peer response groups work well. Harris suggests, like others in the same volume (see, for example, Reid), that perhaps successful peer review and response is the most promising goal we can strive toward in the writing classroom. Harris realizes there are multiple ways of reaching this goal: "Whatever the path to getting students to recognize on their own that they are going to have the opportunity to become more skilled writers, the goal—to help students see the value of peer review before they begin and then to actively engage in it—is the same" (281). Harris makes it clear that she believes a true team effort is involved in this process of getting students to collaboratively internalize (and externalize) the value of peer response, an effort that must actively involve student writers, instructors, and—as often as possible—peer tutors.

The current trajectory of writing center work increasingly includes empirical, RAD research that holds the sorts of implications for peer review and response Harris alludes to. Multimethod empirical studies like the ones reported on and advocated for in the extant work of those like Rebecca Babcock, Terese Thonus, Dana Driscoll, Isabelle Thompson, and Jo Mackiewicz, among increasingly others, can help us inquire more deeply into questions of student motivation, authority negotiation, trust building, and balancing when and how to accept, share, and surrender control. Writing center research like the kind gathered in Janine Morris and Kelly Concannon's 2022 collection *Emotions and Affect in Writing Centers* can also inform the type of important affective concerns in peer response reported on by Ellen Turner in Chapter 7 of this volume.

Research and practice involving writing fellows and course-based tutors (peer tutors attached to writing courses) offers further insights into how peer tutors act when they are more or less expected to possess some sort of authority, some kind of hybrid teacher-student aptitude (Moss et al.; Spigelman and Grobman; Hall and Hughes; Zawacki; Corbett "Using," *Beyond*). An understanding of the strategies that can encourage students to negotiate when and how to do more talking, questioning, or listening can add the complimentary "soft" collaborative touch to the perhaps harsher competitive instincts we can utilize via debates—uniting in many ways the pedagogically old with the new. Corbett's case study work is especially applicable to peer response because in several of his studies, the peer tutors—including developmental writers—were students who just finished the same course in which they were subsequently placed as tutors. This closer alignment with students' ZPD offers a look into how diverse students a bit closer to true "peer" status negotiate feedback strategies.

And Bradley Hughes, Paula Gilliespie, and Harvey Kail's analyses of the reflections of 126 former tutors from three institutions suggests some promising soft skills and habits of mind students immersed in peer-to-peer learning can take with them from those experiences including stronger listening and analytical abilities; values, skills, and abilities vital to family and professional relationships; and increased confidence in their writing and communication abilities. What if we extended that type of realization of skills and values, those (often privileged) experiences of peer tutors, to as many students as possible? If students were to experience systematic, iterated peer response activities in all of their writing courses (or courses that included some writing) vertically in their curriculum from the time they were freshman to their senior year, and then on to those continuing in graduate and professional schools and programs, they could get their share of stronger communicative skills and values.

CODA

If as compositionists and teachers of writing we turn our sights inward a bit—toward what we continue to theorize, research, and practice in the classroom and in writing centers and peer tutoring programs—we can better stabilize our pedagogical bridges between the past and the present. Then we can share what we've learned with colleagues across the disciplines. How we teach (and learn) peer response, including our habits of mind and attitude toward it, likely go a long way in determining whether or not newer writing instructors adopt peer response activities with their own students, not to mention, sustain the interests and commitments of our more experienced colleagues to experiment with it in their classrooms. We can look back at the history of peer response for starting points, even as we look forward to new experiments. We can gaze closer within our own field, even as we stare across boundaries toward what other fields and disciplines have to offer. And we can look and listen to the transitional journeys of less-experienced students and teachers, even as we look and listen to the authority of landmark researchers. For students and teachers at all levels and abilities, whose memories of peer response may not be glowing, it becomes important that we proceed in facilitating some of the unlearning that might need to happen to overcome lingering ambivalence. Peer response activities can certainly activate and encourage student writers' sense of community, and help students learn to trust more than just the teacher's point of view—but only if instructors can successfully nudge them toward understanding and appreciating the value so many of us see in this collaborative practice. This lofty goal will probably hinge on instructors' willingness to learn to let go of some of our pedagogical control, to gently surrender (and thereby share) some of our teacherly authority.

The study of peer review and response can help us answer age-old and contemporary questions in writing studies like habits of mind, knowledge transfer, and access and equity. How can what we know about peer tutoring enhance our abilities to coach students toward becoming better coaches of each other? How can students help their peers learn information and the necessary procedures to be able to do something with that knowledge that travels well beyond the classroom? I believe many possible answers to these questions are already right there in the pages of our many publications—including *Rethinking Peer Review*—and I am curious, inspired and excited by the prospect of future inquiries to come.

WORKS CITED

Boquet, Elizabeth H., and Neal Lerner. "Reconsiderations: After 'The Idea of a Writing Center.'" *College English*, vol. 71, no. 2, 2008, pp. 170–89.

Brooke, Robert, et al. *Small Groups in Writing Workshops: Invitations to a Writer's Life.* NCTE, 1994.

Bruffee, Kenneth A. "The Brooklyn Plan: Attaining Intellectual Growth through Peer-Group Tutoring." *Liberal Education,* vol. 64, no. 4, 1978, pp. 447–68.

———. *Collaborative Learning: Higher Education, Interdependence, and the Authority of Knowledge* 2nd ed. The John Hopkins UP, 1999.

———. "Two Related Issues in Peer Tutoring: Program Structure and Tutor Training." *College Composition and Communication*, vol. 31, no. 1, 1980, pp.76–80.

Corbett, Steven J. *Beyond Dichotomy: Synergizing Writing Center and Classroom Pedagogies*. The WAC Clearinghouse and Parlor Press, 2015, https://doi.org/10.37514/PER-B.2015.0599.

———. "Great Debating: Combining Ancient and Contemporary Methods of Peer Critique." *Kairos: A Journal of Rhetoric, Technology, and Pedagogy*, vol. 19, no. 2, 2015, http://kairos.technorhetoric.net/19.2/.

———. Using Case Study Multi-Methods to Investigate Close(r) Collaboration: Course-Based Tutoring and the Directive/Nondirective Instructional Continuum." *The Writing Center Journal*, vol. 31, no. 1, 2011, pp. 55–81.

Corbett, Steven J., et al., editors. *Peer Pressure, Peer Power: Theory and Practice in Peer Review and Response for the Writing Classroom*. Fountainhead Press, 2014.

Elbow, Peter. *Writing Without Teachers*. Oxford UP, 1973.

Gere, Anne Ruggles. *Writing Groups: History, Theory, and Implications*. Southern Illinois UP, 1987.

Harris, Joseph, et al., editors. *Teaching with Student Texts: Essays toward an Informed Practice*. Utah State UP, 2010.

Harris, Muriel. "Writing Center Tutorials vs. Peer-Response Groups." *College Composition and Communication*, vol. 43, no. 3, 1992, pp. 369–383.

Hughes, Bradley, et al. "What They Take with Them: Findings from the Peer Tutor Alumni Research Project." *The Writing Center Journal*, vol. 30, no. 2, 2010, pp. 12–46.

Morris, Janine and Kelly A. Concannon, editors *Emotions and Affect in Writing Centers*. Parlor Press, 2022.

Moss Beverly J., et al., editors. *Writing Groups Inside and Outside the Classroom*. Lawrence Erlbaum Associates, 2004.

Murphy, James J. "The Key Role of Habit in Roman Writing Instruction." *A Short History of Writing Instruction: From Ancient Greece to Modern America* 2nd ed., edited by James J. Murphy. Hermagoras, 2001, pp. 35–78.

Nelson, Marie Wilson. *At the Point of Need: Teaching Basic and ESL Writers*. Boynton/Cook, 1991.

North, Stephen M. "The Idea of a Writing Center." *College English*, vol. 46, no. 5, 1984, pp. 433–46.

Quintilian, Marcus Fabius. *The Institutio Oratoria*. Trans. H.E. Butler. G.P. Putnam's Sons, 1921 (Orig. pub. ca. 95).

Reid, E. Shelley. "Peer Review for Peer Review's Sake: Resituating Peer Review Pedagogy." *Peer Pressure, Peer Power: Theory and Practice in Peer Review and Response for the Writing Classroom*, edited by Steven J. Corbett et al., Fountainhead Press, 2014, pp. 217–31.

Spear, Karen. *Sharing Writing: Peer Response Groups in English Classes*. Boynton/Cook, 1988.

Spigelman, Candace, and Laurie Grobman, editors. *On Location: Theory and Practice in Classroom-Based Writing Tutoring.* Utah State UP, 2005.

Vygotsky, Lev S. *Mind in Society: The Development of Higher Psychological Processes.* Harvard UP, 1978.

Zawacki, Terry Myers. "Writing Fellows as WAC Change Agents: Changing What? Changing Whom? Changing How?" *Across the Disciplines,* vol. 5, 2008, https://doi.org/10.37514/ATD-J.2008.5.2.05.

CONTRIBUTORS

Kendra L. Andrews is Assistant Teaching Professor at Wake Forest University, where she teaches in the writing program with a focus on writing in the 21st century and writing across the curriculum. Her work has appeared in *Kairos* as well as several edited collections on teaching writing at the university level.

Chris M. Anson is Distinguished University Professor and Director of the Campus Writing and Speaking Program at North Carolina State University. He has published 19 books and 140 articles and book chapters on writing and has spoken across the U.S. and in 33 other countries. He is Past Chair of the Conference on College Composition and Communication and Past President of the Council of Writing Program Administrators and is currently Vice Chair of the International Society for the Advancement of Writing Research.

Ian G. Anson is Associate Professor in the Department of Political Science at UMBC in Baltimore, Maryland. Dr. Anson completed a Ph.D. in political science and a M.S. in applied statistics at Indiana University—Bloomington in 2015. Dr. Anson's primary scholarly interests lie at the intersection of the fields of public opinion, political communication, and political behavior. His work often focuses on partisan biases, motivated reasoning, and factual misperceptions in American public opinion. Dr. Anson also contributes to the scholarship of teaching and learning (SoTL), and studies research methodologies such as automated text analysis and the design of experiments.

Nick Carbone began teaching writing with computers in 1989 by sneaking his class into the secretarial sciences (he is not making that name up) classroom so that his students could learn WordStar. Since then, he's directed a college writing program, WAC program, and writing center, was a Director for Digital Teaching and Learning for a college textbook publisher, and was an instructional designer and e-learning content developmental editor of online learning companies. He writes about technology and teaching, and wonders what will come next about writing and the teaching of writing online.

Steven J. Corbett is Director of the University Writing Center and Associate Professor of English at Texas A&M University, Kingsville. He is the author of *Beyond Dichotomy: Synergizing Writing Center and Classroom Pedagogies* (2015) and co-editor of *Peer Pressure, Peer Power: Theory and Practice in Peer Review and Response for the Writing Classroom* (2014), *Student Peer Review and Response: A Critical Sourcebook* (2018), *Writing In and About the Performing and Visual Arts: Creating, Performing, and Teaching* (2019), and *Writing Centers and Learning Commons: Staying Centered While Sharing Common Ground* (forthcoming). His articles on writing pedagogy have appeared in a variety of journals, periodicals, and collections.

Kay Halasek is Professor of English and Director of the Michael V. Drake Institute for Teaching and Learning at Ohio State University. Her research spans a range of topics, including feminist historiography, writing program administration, and composition theory and pedagogy. She is the author of A Pedagogy of Possibility: Bakhtinian Perspectives on Composition Studies, which received the CCCC Outstanding Book award. As director of the institute, she leads enterprise research and policy initiatives related to teaching and learning.

Phoebe Jackson is Professor Emerita of English and former chair of the English Department at William Paterson University. Her research and publications include work in modern and contemporary American women writers and in composition studies. Along with Christopher Weaver, she is the co-editor of *Writing in Online Courses: How the Online Environment Shapes Writing Practices* and with Emily Issacs, co-editor of *Public Works: Student Writing as Public Text*.

Beth Kramer is Senior Lecturer in the Rhetoric Department of Boston University's College of General Studies. She has over a decade of experience teaching composition and research skills as part of a global, interdisciplinary program. She is currently studying new ways to integrate multimodal learning into composition courses, and has recently presented her work at MLA, NeMLA, and AGLS. In 2017, she co-edited an issue of Impact interdisciplinary journal devoted to podcasting in the classroom.

Bob Mayberry is a retired Professor of Composition, Creative Writing, and Drama who continues to write short stories, plays, and a detective novel. Director of Composition at TCU, UNLV, GVSU and CSUCI, he's run out of acronyms to work for. Fired from UNLV for trying to institute portfolio grading, student-teacher conferences, and process pedagogy, he remains committed to the workshop approach he experienced earning his MFA in playwriting at Iowa.

Nora McCook is a writing and literacy studies scholar whose research and teaching focuses on social and historical contexts of writing/literacy instruction. Her work addresses a range of learning contexts including school and community literacy initiatives, writing program professional development, college writing classrooms, and an early twentieth-century training school for nurses. She currently teaches first-year, digital, and professional writing and language diversity courses at Bloomfield College in New Jersey.

Vicki A. Pallo is Professor at Virginia Commonwealth University, where she primarily teaches writing and research courses. After spending several years as an Editor & Project Manager for a Seattle consulting firm, she earned her M.A. and Ph.D. in English Literature from Binghamton University, SUNY, with an emphasis on 18th- and 19th-century British Literature. Today, her research centers on the scholarship of teaching and learning, especially the way in which technology impacts these practices.

Courtney Stanton is Assistant Teaching Professor in the Writing Program at Rutgers University-Newark, where she teaches first-year writing and advanced courses in rhetoric and social change. Her primary research focus is the intersection of first-year-writing theory and pedagogy with critical disability theory; other interests include writing-about-writing pedagogy and disability representation. Her work has appeared in journals including *Composition Studies*, *Double Helix*, *The Journal of Pedagogical Development*, and *CEA Forum*, as well as numerous volumes on disability within media and culture.

Ellen Turner is Senior Lecturer in English Literature at Lund University, Sweden. She has published articles on modernist literature, detective fiction, and physical cultures, as well as E. M. Hull and the desert romance genre. In addition to her literary interests, she has taught extensively on undergraduate and postgraduate academic writing courses, and has co-developed a MOOC in academic writing, specifically aimed at second-language learners of English.

Christopher Weaver is Director of the Program in Writing and Rhetoric at William Paterson University, where he teaches courses in writing, literature, and composition theory and practice at all levels, from freshmen to graduate students. He writes about composition theory and pedagogy and is the co-editor with Phoebe Jackson of *Writing in Online Courses* and the co-editor with Fran Zak of *The Theory and Practice of Grading Writing*.

INDEX

A

actionable feedback 70, 128, 138
Addison, Joanne 126
Adler-Kassner, Linda 107, 108
agency 9, 19, 60, 61, 63, 64, 67, 69, 71
Amores, Maria 151
Andrade, Maureen Snow 190
anxiety 166, 170, 173, 174, 175, 178, 188, 190, 195, 198
assessment 77, 81, 82, 90, 120, 155, 173, 179, 234
audience 8, 28, 29, 35, 48, 68, 70, 77, 78, 90, 92, 114, 124, 127, 128, 136, 192, 197, 200, 207, 210, 211, 215, 217, 222, 223, 234
authority 7, 19, 48, 51, 52, 54, 60, 62, 63, 64, 67, 71, 72, 80, 107, 114, 125, 151, 157, 165, 169, 188, 193

B

Baker, Wendy 85, 192, 211
Barnett, Ronald 148
Bean, John 76, 87
Belcher, Diane D. 195, 197
Berkenkotter, Carol 207
Bishop, Wendy 49
Bizzaro, Patrick 49
Blair, Elizabeth 136
Boase-Jelinek, Daniel 152
Boud, David 149, 153
Braine, George 17, 189, 190
Brammer, Charlotte 19, 62, 102, 171, 208
Brannon, Lil 60
Breslin, Caroline 150, 212
Brown, John Seely 242
Bruffee, Kenneth 6, 45, 61, 64, 69, 76, 79, 123, 206, 207, 230
Burke, Kenneth 100, 105, 106, 108, 109

C

Carless, David 169, 170, 172, 176, 177, 210
Carson, Joan G. 191
Chang, Carrie Yea-huey 149
Chen, Yingling 175
Cherry, Roger 104
Chi, Michelene T.H. 85
Ching, Kory Lawson 7, 8, 63, 67, 68, 125
Cho, Kwangsu 211
Cho, Young Hoan 211
Clark, Elizabeth 193
Clark, Russell J. 239, 240
Cole, Mikel 176, 177
collaboration 9, 18, 36, 45, 61, 65, 70, 76, 82, 123, 125, 127, 128, 136, 137, 148, 150, 169, 170, 173, 174, 177, 179, 182, 188, 190, 193, 194, 197, 200, 206, 208, 210, 214, 222, 224, 225
Collins, Allan 242
computer-mediated feedback 7, 152, 201, 209, 243
Cooley, Nicole 48
Cooper, Marilyn 83
Corbett, Jenny 83
Corbett, Steven J. 8, 9, 82, 84, 85
Coulson, Debra 153

D

Dass, Rozita 172
Decker, Teagan E. 8
Demasio, Antonio 50
Devaele, Jean-Marc 148, 165
DeWitt, Scott Lloyd 86
Diffendal, Lee Ann 101
DiGiovanni, Lee Ann 196, 199

Index

DiPardo, Anne 82
discourse community 5, 6, 70, 214
discussion boards 91, 139, 143, 196, 219, 225
Dixon, Helen R. 109
Dixson, Dante 177
Downs, Doug 37
Driscoll, Dana Lynn 83

E

Ede, Lisa 81, 105, 230
Edwards, Patricia A. 173
Elbow, Peter 5, 42, 45, 61, 70, 206, 230
English language learners 75, 78, 166, 183, 201, 209, 210
Evans, Norman W. 190
expressivism 10, 45, 61, 122

F

Finley, Ashley 127
first-year composition 37, 61, 83, 120, 121, 131, 132, 135, 142, 190, 205, 207, 208, 214
First-year composition 120
Flower, Linda 123
Flynn, Elizabeth 7, 75, 209
Freedman, Sarah Warshauer 82

G

Gaillet, Gaillet, Lynée Lewis 124
Gao, Helen 175, 176
Gere, Anne Ruggles 6, 7, 77, 125, 207, 230
grading 4, 6, 42, 44, 53, 54, 55, 65, 70, 72, 77, 79, 81, 84, 102, 104, 172
Green, Gareth P. 179
Griffith, Kevin 80, 82

H

Haake, Katharine 44
Hall, Mark 61, 63, 68
Hansen, Jette G. 153
Hardaway, Francine 80

Harris, Muriel 123, 206
Harvey, Marina 153
Hawe, Eleanor M. 108
Heron, Gavin 172
Herrington, Jan 152
Holum, Ann 242
Howard, Rebecca Moore 123
Hyland, Fiona 194
Hyland, Ken 189

I

improvement imperative 209, 210, 225

J

Jack, Jordynn 81
Jardine, George 124
Jesnek, Lindsey M. 19, 169, 172, 208

K

Keogh, Rosemary 153
Kessler, Gregg 194, 195, 197
Kim, Soo Hyon 188
Knoblauch, C.H. 60

L

LaFrance, Michelle 8, 87
Lardner, Ted 49
Leahy, Anna 47
learning theory 51
learning-writing-by-reviewing-process hypothesis 212
Leki, Illona 191
Light, Greg 159
Li, Guogang 173
Liu, Jun 152, 153, 195
Liu, Ngar-Fun 169, 170, 172, 176, 177, 210
lower-level classes 125, 140, 171, 172
low stakes assignments 214, 215
low-stakes assignments 135, 155, 156, 170, 177, 179, 182, 217, 218, 219, 222
Lundstrom, Kristi 85, 192, 211

M

MacArthur, Charles 211
MacIntyre, Peter 148, 165
Mamiseishvili, Ketevan 174, 182
Matsuda, Paul Kei 188, 189
McGee, Sharon James 126
McNair, Tia Finley 127
Meeks, Melissa Graham 66, 70, 210, 237
metacognition 83, 120, 133, 134, 222, 241
Miller, Carolyn 234
Morrow, Donna 210
Moxley, Joseph Michael 46
Mulder, Raoul 151
Murau, Andrea 151, 153
Murphy, John M. 150
Murray, Donald 45, 48, 60, 230, 242

N

Nagaswami, Girija 196, 199
Nelson, Gayle L. 150
Nicol, David 150, 152
Nielsen, Kristen J. 75, 80
Nilson, Linda 231
Nystrand, Martin 84

O

Ochsner, Robert 50
Oleksiak, Peter 209, 210
online peer review 183, 201, 206, 214
Ostrom, Hans 43, 49

P

Parfitt, Elizabeth 68, 69
Parker, Jenni 152
Patchan, Melissa M. 239, 240
peer review
  asynchronous vs synchronous 187, 196, 200
  descriptive vs. evaluative 61, 87
  frequency of 177, 179, 229
  genre of 9, 59, 68, 69, 82, 91, 119, 120, 122, 130, 131, 132, 234
  goals of 10, 44, 47, 72, 80, 93, 140, 175, 179, 225
  higher vs. lower order 3, 19, 28, 78, 110, 144, 178, 181, 188, 191, 207, 211, 220
  instruction in 9, 67, 70, 71, 113, 122, 140, 159, 165, 182, 200, 225, 243
  perceptions of 37, 62, 65, 78, 102, 121, 135, 153, 165
Perkins, David 121
Perkins, David A. 134
Perl, Sondra 133
Popta, Esther van 212
portfolio 119
portfolios 54, 122, 130
Pritchard, Jane Ruie 210
process pedagogy 3, 5, 7, 18, 42, 55, 59, 61, 63, 64, 65, 99, 119, 125, 132, 133, 138, 188, 205, 207
Pryal, Katie Rose Guest 81
Pyle, Daniel 175

R

Raimes, Ann 191
Rees, Mary 19, 62, 102, 171, 208
reflection 71, 83, 91, 122, 130, 138, 140, 166, 170, 176, 182, 191, 213, 215, 222, 225, 231, 234, 240
revision 4, 17, 18, 19, 20, 29, 35, 36, 42, 71, 79, 85, 87, 89, 93, 99, 101, 114, 119, 134, 144, 192, 194, 196, 197, 198, 199, 205, 207, 208, 209, 211, 213, 229, 230, 232, 240, 241
rhetoric 3, 9, 18, 19, 29, 35, 37, 67, 68, 69, 78, 82, 84, 88, 91, 93, 114, 120, 122, 124, 127, 128, 130, 136
Robertson, Liane 37
role or reviewer 125
roles of reviewers 5, 78, 79, 81
roles of teachers 11, 46, 68, 69, 100, 114

Rollinson, Paul 85, 196, 197, 198, 199
rubric 46, 53, 63, 64, 84, 88, 92, 207

S

Sadler, Randall W. 152, 199
Saloman, Gavrial 121
Salomon, Gavrial 134
Sauro, Shannon 195, 199
scaffolding 83, 84, 138, 153, 154, 155, 159, 161, 165, 166, 178, 214, 225
Shepherd, Ryan 130, 134
Show, Mei Lin 189, 191
Silva, Pedro 178
Silva, Tony 188, 189
Smith, Cheryl C. 190, 193
Smith, Cheryl Hogue 158
social constructivism 3, 6, 61, 77, 122, 169
social interaction (connectedness) 148, 151, 170, 176
Sommers, Nancy 20
Sousa, David 194
Spear, Karen 7, 207
student-centered pedagogy 45, 50, 62, 64, 124, 147
Sukumaran, Kavitha 172

T

Taczak, Kara 133, 223
teaching for transfer (TFT) 3, 37, 113, 120, 122, 140
Thomson, Avril 150
Topping, Keith 128, 129, 166
Tuck, Jackie 20
Tuzi, Frank 198, 199

U

upper-level writing courses 3, 120, 126, 171, 205, 208

V

Van den Berg, Ineke 129
Värlander, Sara 149
voice 5, 45, 51, 79, 104, 154, 181, 188, 197

W

Walker, David 153
Walsh, Kate Padgett 84
Wardle, Elizabeth 107, 108
Warschauer, Mark 194, 197, 198
WEx, The Writers Exchange 76
Wilson, Frank 50
Winer, Lise 150, 153
Winkelmes, Mary-Ann 132
workload for teachers 18, 20, 80, 121, 125
workplace skills 64, 119
workshop pedagogies 3, 41, 60, 61, 125, 229, 231, 242
Worrell, Frank 177
writing about writing 3, 139, 209
writing across the curriculum (WAC) 80, 162, 230

X

Xu 180

Y

Yancey, Kathleen Blake 193, 223
Yastıba, Gülşah Çınar 149
Yastıbaş, Ahmet Erdost 149

Z

Zeidner, Moshe 147

www.ingramcontent.com/pod-product-compliance
Lightning Source LLC
Chambersburg PA
CBHW060554080526
44585CB00013B/564